Advance Praise for

COGNITIVE INFILTRATION

"David Ray Griffin has written a devastating critique of Cass Sunstein's major effort to situate all critics of the official 9/11 story in the garbage pail of 'conspiracy theory.' Bringing to bear his formidable philosophical and theological skills, Griffin brilliantly illuminates this cognitive/political concern, demonstrating that the American people will never find out what really happened on that fateful day until we as citizens insist on considering all available evidence with a fresh and open mind."
—**RICHARD FALK, professor emeritus, Princeton University**

"There should be a book entitled the 'Courage of David Ray Griffin.' His continuing efforts to speak truth to power regarding issues of 9/11/2001 are most admirable. Griffin's *Cognitive Infiltration* addresses the central denial of key government officials in both parties who, when faced with overwhelming factual evidence of serious problems with the 9/11 Commission's report, lash out at the very people seeking truth and justice. Cass Sunstein is one of those Harvard 'insiders' who not only denies open democratic questioning of 9/11, but overtly advocates the disruption and cognitive infiltration of such groups."
—**PETER PHILLIPS, Professor of Sociology, Sonoma State University, and President of Media Freedom Foundation/Project Censored**

"Unrestrained and unchallenged combination of top level political power and academic intellectual arrogance can be a dangerous prelude to governmental censorship and potential criminalization of individuals who dare to challenge 'official' versions of various catastrophes and major events of a highly controversial nature. Dr. David Ray Griffin exposes and analyses this grave concern in an objective, scholarly dissection of a sociopolitical proposal set forth by Cass Sunstein in 2008. Readers of *Cognitive Infiltration* will be both shocked and enlightened by this well documented and brilliantly written book."
—**CYRIL H. WECHT, M.D., J.D., past president, American Academy of Forensic Sciences, and past president, American College of Legal Medicine**

"In 2009, President Obama appointed a Harvard Law School professor, Cass Sunstein, to be head of the White House's Office of Information and Regulatory Affairs. This was after Sunstein had made a controversial proposal, which would later inflame the internet, for 'cognitive infiltration' of the 9/11 Truth Movement, with the aim of 'breaking up the hard core of extremists who supply conspiracy theories.' Professor Griffin has responded to Sunstein's dangerous argument with a patient, point-by-point and much needed refutation. He relentlessly shows how Sunstein himself is guilty of the very mentality he warns against: closed-mindedness and refusal to debate. Those who seek to prevent 2010 from becoming 1984 will want to arm themselves with this valuable book."
—**PETER DALE SCOTT, professor emeritus of English, University of California, Berkeley, and author of *Drugs, Oil, and War***

"David Ray Griffin is the preeminent expert on the events of September 11, 2001; his research is consistently careful, thorough, and objective. His previous books are necessary reading for all Americans, and there is no doubt that thousands of Americans in government circles have read them, studied them, and, in some cases, worried about them. In *Cognitive Infiltration*, Griffin impartially dissects Harvard Constitutional Law Professor Cass Sunstein's controversial essay, co-written by conservative law professor Adrian Vermeule, entitled 'Conspiracy Theories: Causes and Cures.' Surprisingly, given the sensitivity and potential divisiveness of the topic, Griffin has produced a fair, generously fact-filled, often funny, assessment. Additional interest is provided by the suggestion that Sunstein—far from being an enemy of both the Constitution and the 9/11 Truth Movement—may in fact be a secret supporter and a potential bridge-builder from the current government fictions regarding 9/11 to an improved national consensus about what really happened."
—**KAREN KWIATKOWSKI, Ph.D., USAF Lt Colonel (retired), member of Veterans for 9/11 Truth**

COGNITIVEINFILTRATION

AN OBAMA APPOINTEE'S PLAN TO
UNDERMINE THE 9/11 CONSPIRACY THEORY

David Ray Griffin

OLIVE
BRANCH
PRESS

An imprint of Interlink Publishing Group, Inc.
www.interlinkbooks.com

First published in 2011 by

OLIVE BRANCH PRESS
An imprint of Interlink Publishing Group, Inc.
46 Crosby Street
Northampton, Massachusetts 01060
www.interlinkbooks.com

Library of Congress Cataloging-in-Publication Data

Griffin, David Ray, 1939–
Cognitive infiltration : an Obama appointee's plan to undermine the 9/11 conspiracy theory / by David Ray Griffin.
p. cm.
Includes bibliographical references and index.
ISBN 978-1-56656-821-0 (paperback)
1. September 11 Terrorist Attacks, 2001--Causes. 2. Conspiracies--United States--History--21st century. 3. Sunstein, Cass R.--Political and social views. I. Title.
HV6432.7.G7465 2010
973.931--dc22
2010026003

Printed and bound in the United States of America

Cover image of the World Trade Center © Gary Hurtz/Dreamstime.com

Book design by Juliana Spear

CONTENTS

CASS SUNSTEIN'S "CONSPIRACY THEORIES"

Cass R. Sunstein graduated from Harvard Law School in 1978 and then, after clerking for Supreme Court Justice Thurgood Marshall, taught at the University of Chicago Law School from 1981 until 2008, at which time he became the Felix Frankfurter Professor of Law at Harvard Law School. After Barack Obama—who had become a friend of Sunstein's while teaching at Chicago's Law School from 1992 until 2004—entered the White House, he made Sunstein the administrator of his Office of Information and Regulatory Affairs.[1]

It should not be assumed, however, that Sunstein received this appointment simply because he and Obama were friends. He had become a highly respected law professor. In fact, the White House, in nominating him for the appointment, called him "the most cited law professor on any faculty in the United States."[2] In 2008, Elena Kagan, then the dean of Harvard Law School (whom Obama later made the US solicitor general, after which he elevated her to the Supreme Court), called Sunstein "the pre-eminent legal scholar of our time—the most wide-ranging, the most prolific, the most cited, and the most influential."[3]

More recently, however, Sunstein's reputation has been damaged by the discovery of an essay he co-authored with Adrian Vermeule, a younger professor at Harvard Law School. A draft version of this essay, entitled "Conspiracy Theories" and dated January 15, 2008, was posted online.[4] A shortened and otherwise significantly revised version, entitled "Conspiracy Theories: Causes and Cures," was posted online in August 2008,[5] then published in the *Journal of Political Philosophy* in June 2009.[6]

Previous Critiques
The online discussion of this essay has involved some rather harsh criticisms. For example, the slant of an article by Marc Estrin, which initiated the online discussion, was summed up in the headline put on it: "Got Fascism?"[7]

Another caustic judgment was leveled by Cyril H. Wecht (M.D., J.D), past president of the American Academy of Forensic Sciences. Wecht called the paper's proposal that the government employ agents to infiltrate and disrupt groups promoting anti-government conspiracy theories an "egregious and dangerously frightening proposition."[8]

In a Fox Business blog entitled "Stealth Propaganda," former ABC correspondent John Stossel used humor to criticize Sunstein's proposal, writing: "This reads like an *Onion* article: Powerful government official proposes to combat paranoid conspiracy groups that believe the government is out to get them . . . by proving that they really are out to get them."[9]

Writing a critique entitled "An Attack from Harvard Law on the Escalating 9/11 Truth Movement," Bill Willers, emeritus professor of Biology at the University of Wisconsin-Oshkosh, charged that Sunstein and his Harvard co-author have "carefully avoided any relevant material from within the mountain of easily available credible information that would dash their thesis. For academics ostensibly wedded to truth this is shameful."[10]

According to Mark Crispin Miller, professor of culture and communication at New York University, Sunstein's essay shows that he does not "[give] a hoot about the truth" or about "protecting [democracy]."[11]

Glenn Greenwald, characterizing the essay as "spine-chilling" and "truly pernicious," focused on its recommendation that the infiltrating agents employ covert propaganda. This would be illegal, Greenwald pointed out, because of "long-standing statutes prohibiting government 'propaganda' within the U.S." (by which he meant US government propaganda directed at its own citizens). Finally, noting a passage in which Sunstein and Vermeule referred to "imaginable conditions" under which the government "might ban conspiracy theorizing" or "impose some kind of tax, financial or otherwise, on those who disseminate such theories," Greenwald wrote:

> I'd love to know the "conditions" under which the government-enforced banning of conspiracy theories or the imposition of taxes on those who advocate them will "have a place." That would require, at a bare minimum, a repeal of the First Amendment.

"Anyone who believes this," Greenwald concluded, should "be barred from any meaningful government position."[12]

If these judgments become widely shared, then his essay on conspiracy theories will have resulted in a terrible reversal of Sunstein's reputation—from "the pre-eminent legal scholar of our time" to a person with such an unconstitutional and even fascist mindset that he should be permanently barred from public office.

This Book's Approach

Such a drastic reversal of opinion raises the question: Is it possible that the initial critiques of the Sunstein–Vermeule essay have misunderstood it? A more thorough examination of this essay seems in order.

The critiques by Estrin, Wecht, Stossel, Willers, Miller, and Greenwald all abstracted from a central feature of the essay: the fact that the "conspiracy theories" with which it is primarily concerned are those related to the attacks of 9/11. This fact was expressed most clearly in the draft version of the essay, in which Sunstein and his co-author said:

> Our main though far from exclusive focus—our running example—involves conspiracy theories relating to terrorism, especially theories that arise from and post-date the 9/11 attacks.[13]

In the essay as printed in the journal, the phrase "main . . . focus" was deleted from this sentence, so that it now reads:

> Our running example involves conspiracy theories relating to terrorism, especially theories that arise from and post-date the 9/11 attacks.[14]

This and other alterations in the journal version, however, do not change the fact that 9/11 conspiracy theories, which continue to provide the essay's "running example," constitute the essay's main focus.

Critiques that abstract from this fact are entirely proper, because the legal and constitutional issues are the same irrespective of what one may think about the merits of various 9/11 conspiracy theories.

In my own response to the essay by Sunstein and Vermeule, however, I focus on their treatment of people they call "9/11 conspiracy theorists," especially "the hard core of conspiracy theorists"— those "who supply conspiracy theories."[15]

The present critique treats this essay as if it had been written by Sunstein alone, both because he was its senior author and also because he now occupies an office in which he might be able to get its proposals carried out.

Also, employing the type of two-level analysis fruitfully applied to Leo Strauss's writings by Shadia Drury,[16] this critique suggests that Sunstein's essay may have an esoteric as well as an exoteric level of meaning.

According to Drury, Strauss believed that political philosophy needed to contain two levels: an esoteric core, in which the truth is stated in a way that will be grasped only by the wise few, and an exoteric coating, consisting of "noble illusions" required by the masses.[17] As Strauss himself put it, socially responsible philosophers will write in such a way as to:

> [R]eveal what they regard as the truth to the few, without endangering the unqualified commitment of the many to the opinions on which society rests. They will distinguish between the true teaching as the esoteric teaching and the socially useful teaching as the exoteric teaching.[18]

In an analogous way, I will suggest, we can perhaps distinguish between two levels of meaning in Sunstein's essay. On the one hand, there would be an esoteric level, in which Sunstein cryptically expressed his true beliefs about 9/11 conspiracy theories and what to do about them. If expressed openly at the time the essay appeared, these ideas might have ruined his chances of obtaining a position in which he could influence government policy. Understood in terms of its surface or exoteric meaning, on the other hand, the essay expressed Sunstein's views in a way that would not make him appear unsafe in the eyes of people with influence.

If this analysis has merit, the negative reactions to the essay by liberals and libertarians have been based on reading it only in terms of its exoteric level. If they see it as also having the esoteric level that I suggest, liberals and libertarians, while perhaps not being fully happy with some of its proposals, should look on it more kindly because of its good intentions.

Sunstein's Argument: Ten Theses

Sunstein's argument, which is quite complex, can be summarized in terms of the following ten theses:

1) A conspiracy theory is best defined as "an effort to explain some event or practice by reference to the machinations of powerful people, who attempt to conceal their role (at least until their aims are accomplished)."[19]

2) Although conspiracy theories can be both justified and true, and although the US government has sometimes spread false conspiracy theories, anti-government conspiracy theories in the United States are usually both unjustified and false.

3) According to the 9/11 conspiracy theory, "U.S. officials knowingly allowed 9/11 to happen or even brought it about,"[20] and "U.S. government officials destroyed the World Trade Center and then covered their tracks."[21]

4) People typically accept the 9/11 conspiracy theory "not as a result of a mental illness . . . or of simple irrationality, but as a result of a 'crippled epistemology,' in the form of a sharply limited number of (relevant) informational sources."[22] The main cause of belief in the 9/11 conspiracy theory, in short, is "informational isolation."[23]

5) The 9/11 conspiracy theory is "demonstrably false"; it is also unjustified, being based on evidence that is "weak or even nonexistent"; and it has led to a "degenerating research program."[24]

6) 9/11 conspiracy theorists, being extremists, are likely to become violent, "with terrifying consequences." Even if not, the 9/11 conspiracy theory "can still have pernicious effects from the government's point of view, . . . by inducing unjustifiably widespread public skepticism about the government's assertions, or by dampening public mobilization and participation in government-led efforts," or by "undermin[ing] democratic debate."[25]

7) "Conspiracy theories turn out to be unusually hard to undermine," but "[i]f government can dispel [false and harmful] conspiracy theories," such as the 9/11 conspiracy theory, "it should do so."[26]

8) In seeking to undermine the 9/11 conspiracy theory, the government should take a twofold approach: besides dealing with the theory's demand side, by seeking to inoculate the public against it, the government should also address its supply side, by seeking to "debias or disable its purveyors."[27]

9) Although one might think that the government could use credible public information to cure the 9/11 conspiracy theory's purveyors of their false beliefs, this approach will not work, because this theory has "a self-sealing quality," which makes its purveyors "resistant to correction," especially by "contrary evidence offered by the government."[28]

10) Accordingly, because the government of an open society cannot (normally) "ban 'conspiracy theories'" or "tax . . . those who disseminate such theories," the best approach is for the government to "engage in *cognitive infiltration of the groups that produce conspiracy theories*."[29]

In the following chapters, I examine these ten theses in order. In each case, I begin with the exoteric meaning. After providing a critique of it, I then explore the possibility of a deeper, esoteric meaning—one with radically different implications.

A Note about the "Esoteric Interpretation"

As readers begin to see the nature of the "esoteric interpretation" of Sunstein's essay suggested in this book, they may reasonably wonder whether it is to be taken seriously. A short answer can be indicated with an allusion to the dictum of Reinhold Niebuhr—reportedly Barack Obama's favorite theologian[30]—who said, speaking of certain biblical symbols, that they should be taken "seriously but not literally."[31] A longer answer is provided in the Conclusion.

CHAPTER I
CONSPIRACY THEORIES DEFINED

The first thesis of Sunstein's argument states:

A conspiracy theory is best defined as "an effort to explain some event or practice by reference to the machinations of powerful people, who attempt to conceal their role (at least until their aims are accomplished)."[32]

Is this really the best definition?

1. One-Sided Definition

Discussions of the term "conspiracy theory" are often tendentious. Many commentators, wanting to discredit some particular conspiracy theory, define the term itself in a one-sided way, according to which conspiracy theories as such are irrational. Given such a definition, people who accept some particular conspiracy theory can be dismissed as mentally ill, or at least irrational. New Zealand philosopher Charles Pigden, to whose writings on conspiracy theories Sunstein refers,[33] has pointed out that, given the conventional wisdom, which accepts this one-sided definition:

> [T]o call someone "a conspiracy theorist" is to suggest that he is irrational, paranoid or perverse. Often the suggestion seems to be that conspiracy theories are not just suspect, but utterly unbelievable, too silly to deserve the effort of a serious refutation. It is a common ploy on the part of politicians to dismiss critical allegations by describing them as conspiracy theories.[34]

Sunstein is not guilty of this ploy. He does not suggest that conspiracy theories as such are irrational, and he specifically denies that "conspiracy theories are a sign of mental illness, such as paranoia."[35]

His proffered definition is, nevertheless, one-sided. Like those who equate conspiracy theories as such with *irrational* conspiracy theories, he has committed the common genus/species fallacy. That is, rather than providing a generic definition, which would cover conspiracy theories of every type, he has equated the genus (conspiracy theories) with one of its species: conspiracy theories about powerful people.

Sunstein himself, interestingly, pointed out that his definition did not cover all or even most conspiracy theories: "[M]any conspiracy theories involve people who are not especially powerful (friends, neighborhoods, fellow employees, family members, and so forth)."[36]

Why, then, did Sunstein employ his admittedly inadequate definition, according to which a conspiracy theory is "an effort to explain some event or practice by reference to the machinations of powerful people"? He offered a two-part justification. The first part consists of his suggestion that a generic definition is not possible:

> [V]arious views that people label "conspiracy theories" may well relate to each other through a family-resemblance structure, such that necessary and sufficient conditions cannot be given even in principle.[37]

But that is patently untrue: A suitable generic definition can be derived from any good dictionary. In a 2007 book, for example, I wrote:

> A *conspiracy*, according to my dictionary,[38] is "an agreement to perform together an illegal, treacherous, or evil act." To hold a conspiracy theory about some event is, therefore, simply to believe that this event resulted from, or involved, such an agreement. This, we can say, is the generic meaning of the term.[39]

Contrary to Sunstein's claim that it is probably impossible to give a definition specifying necessary and sufficient conditions for a belief to be called a conspiracy theory, this definition does exactly that (at least if it is understood that the "agreement" is one that was made in secret).

Sunstein's suggestion that a generic definition may be impossible is especially puzzling in light of the fact that the above-quoted article by Charles Pigden, to which Sunstein referred his readers, contained such a definition: "[A] conspiracy theory is simply a theory that posits a conspiracy—a secret plan on the part of some group to influence events by partly secret means."[40]

2. The Purpose Served by Sunstein's One-Sided Definition

Given the fact that Sunstein was evidently aware that a generic definition of conspiracy theories was readily available, why, we must wonder, did he suggest otherwise and provide a definition that admittedly applied to only a narrow range of such theories? For a clue, we need to look at the second part of his two-part justification, in which he wrote:

> [T]his account is the most useful for our particular purposes, and it seems to capture the essence of the most prominent and influential conspiracy theories about public affairs.[41]

As suggested earlier, when a one-sided definition is given, it is likely for the purpose of scoring a polemical point. Pigden, for example, noted that a pejorative definition, according to which conspiracy theories as such are unworthy of credence, allows dishonest people to dismiss some allegation by calling it a "conspiracy theory," thereby implying that there is no need to examine the purported evidence for it.

What are the "particular purposes" served by Sunstein's one-sided definition, according to which a conspiracy theory is "an effort to explain some event or practice by reference to the machinations of powerful people, who attempt to conceal their role"? As we will see in the next chapter, it allows Sunstein to make a move similar to the one criticized by Pigden: It allows him to claim that, although conspiracy theories as such are not inherently unbelievable, *most conspiracy theories in the United States can be presumed to be unjustified and false,* because we have an open society with a free press, so that powerful people would seldom, if ever, be able to conceal their machinations for very long.

Then, on the basis of that presumption, Sunstein simply dismisses the theory that the attacks of September 2001 were the result of secret "machinations by powerful people" in the Bush–Cheney administration, calling this theory false and unjustified without examining any of the evidence presented by those who espouse this theory.

3. Sunstein's Possible Esoteric Meaning

That, at least, is what we would properly conclude about Sunstein's strategy if we take his essay at face value. But what if this essay, like the writings of Leo Strauss, contains a deeper, esoteric meaning, intended only for the few, as well as a surface meaning, intended for the many?

The suspicion that Sunstein's essay has a deeper meaning, different from that conveyed by a literal reading of the text, is suggested by the very fact that his definition of "conspiracy theory" is so obviously problematic, as pointed out by Sunstein himself.

As we saw, after giving his very non-inclusive definition, according to which conspiracy theories are about the machinations of the powerful, he immediately alerted the reader to this definition's inadequacy, pointing out that "many conspiracy theories involve people who are not especially powerful (friends, neighborhoods, fellow employees, family members, and so forth)."

Next, after suggesting that no adequate generic definition of conspiracy theories could be given, he pointed astute readers—those he would have wanted to grasp his deeper intention—to an essay by philosopher Charles Pigden, which provides such a definition. This definition, moreover, clearly indicates that conspiracy theories are not exclusively about powerful people, such as government officials, because a conspiracy is simply "a secret plan on the part of some group to influence events by partly secret means." Should we not take this as a hint that Sunstein was telling us not to take his explicit definition seriously if we want to understand his true intentions?

It seems possible, furthermore, that another point is implicit in Sunstein's reference to Pigden's essay, which is entitled "Conspiracy Theories and the Conventional Wisdom." According to the conventional wisdom, Pigden pointed out, conspiracy theories are accepted only by certain types of persons—those who are "irrational, paranoid or perverse." However, Pigden countered:

> [I]f a conspiracy theory is simply a theory that posits a conspiracy, then every politically and historically literate person is a big-time conspiracy theorist, since every such person subscribes to a vast range of conspiracy theories. That is, historically literate people believe organized bodies of propositions that explain alleged facts by positing conspiracies. For there are many facts that admit of no

non-conspiratorial explanation and many conspiracy theories that are sufficiently well-established to qualify as knowledge. It is difficult, if not impossible, to mount a coup without conspiring, a point that is evident to all. Hence anyone who believes there are such things as coups must subscribe to a set of conspiracy theories however vague. Although some assassinations are due to "lone gunmen" many are group efforts, and the efforts of those groups are usually planned in secret. . . . Thus anyone who knows anything about the Ides of March or the assassinations of Archduke Franz Ferdinand or the Tsar Alexander II is bound to subscribe to a conspiracy theory, and hence to be a conspiracy theorist. But coups and assassinations are not even the half of it. Disappearances are usually conspiratorial affairs, since if you want to disappear someone, you had better not let them know when you are coming. . . . And if you are organizing a campaign of disappearances, it is well to keep your activities secret. . . . [M]ass killings generally are often planned and partly executed in secret, the Holocaust being the supreme example, though one might also cite Stalin's purges.[42]

Assuming that Sunstein intended his careful readers to see this passage, was he not telling them that he, like every other sensible person, accepts the truth of a large number of conspiracy theories, so we should not take seriously the statements in his essay suggesting that conspiracy theories are almost always false?

Even at the surface level, to be sure, Sunstein's essay indicates that not all conspiracy theories are false. He wrote, for example: "Of course some conspiracy theories have turned out to be true, and under our definition, they do not cease to be conspiracy theories for that reason."[43] This passage, however, suggests that a true conspiracy theory is a very rare thing. Indeed, he even sometimes suggests that there are *no* true conspiracy theories, writing in one place, for example, that "conspiracy theories are a subset of the larger category of false beliefs."[44]

But as if to signal his careful readers—those who read footnotes—that this is not his view, he has a note saying:

For the point that some conspiracy theories turn out to be true, and several attempts to explore the philosophical implications of that fact, see Charles Pigden, "Conspiracy theories and the conventional wisdom."[45]

And when readers do turn to Pigden's essay, they find his observation that true conspiracy theories are not rare at all, which was quoted above, and also his rebuttal of "the simple assumption that conspiracy theories as such are unlikely to be true." It is indeed the case, Pigden acknowledges, that conspiracy theories are more likely to be false than true. But this is a fact about theories in general, not a fact unique to conspiracy theories:

> The space of possible theories is large; the space of true theories, small. . . . The fact that theories in general are more likely to be false than true does not mean that we should give up theorizing or enquiring into theories. By the same token, the fact that conspiracy theories are more likely to be false than true does not mean that we should give up conspiracy theorizing or enquiring into conspiracy theories.[46]

Because Sunstein referred the reader to Pigden's discussion of the "philosophical implications" of the fact that some conspiracy theories are true, can we not reasonably presume that Sunstein agrees with this philosopher on the point at hand: that "conspiracy theories as such are no less worthy of belief than theories of other kinds"?[47] If so, Sunstein would be hinting that conspiracy theories are no more inherently suspect than physical, biological, economic, social, or psychological theories. In Pigden's words:

> Some conspiracy theories are sensible and some are silly, but if they are silly this is not because they are conspiracy theories but because they suffer from some specific defect—for instance, that the conspiracies they postulate are impossible or far-fetched. But conspiracy theories as such are not epistemologically unclean.[48]

We could thereby see Sunstein's reference to Pigden's work as offering an implicit criticism of the title of his own essay, "Conspiracy Theories: Causes and Cures." If conspiracy theories are often true—and are, in fact, no more likely to be false than other types of theories—then his subtitle should not suggest that they are diseases of the mind for which we need "cures." Also, there would be no need to have a special discussion about the "causes" of conspiracy theories: They would be regarded, like other theories, simply as attempts to explain various phenomena.

Sunstein's reference to Pigden's article could, therefore, be seen as a clever way to let his astute readers know that his whole essay, including its title, is misguided.

If this esoteric reading of Sunstein's definition of conspiracy theories has merit, then we could anticipate that his argument as a whole will, when subjected to this reading, have implications radically different from those entailed by a purely exoteric reading of his essay.

Chapter 2

Conspiracy Theories in America as Usually False

The second thesis of Sunstein's argument says (in my paraphrase):

Although conspiracy theories can be both justified and true, and although the US government has sometimes spread false conspiracy theories, anti-government conspiracy theories in the United States are usually both unjustified and false.

Sunstein's concern, he indicates, is solely with conspiracy theories that are "false, harmful, and unjustified."[49] Of those three adjectives, two—"false" and "unjustified"—are involved in the present thesis. We begin, of course, with the surface (exoteric) reading of this thesis.

1. Truth and Justification

It might be thought that "true" and "justified" are synonymous: that for a theory to be true is for it to be justified, and vice versa, which would mean that "true theory" and "justified theory" could be used interchangeably. For a theory to be false, therefore, would be for it to be unjustified, and vice versa. But this is not necessarily the case. As Sunstein points out:

> Justification and truth are different issues. . . . A true belief may be unjustified, and a justified belief may be untrue.[50]

To explain: Truth is simply a matter of correspondence, so that a belief is true if, and only if, the proposition—the meaning—that it affirms corresponds to reality.[51] But justification, as Sunstein is using it (correctly) in this passage, is a matter of whether particular people have good reasons for believing the propositions they affirm. Their beliefs are justified to the extent that these people hold them *rationally*, in light of the information available to them.

Given this meaning of "justified," a theory's being true and its being justified (held rationally) are different matters. On the one hand, as Sunstein puts it, people who believe preposterous theories about some issue "may well be responding quite rationally to the informational signals that they receive," so that "those beliefs may well be justified from the standpoint of the individuals who hold them."[52] Their beliefs would, therefore, be justified but false. On the other hand, other individuals may happen to hold true beliefs about the issue, even though they hold these beliefs for bad reasons, and hence irrationally. Their beliefs would be unjustified but true.

We can speak of "knowledge," I would add, only when both elements are present, hence the traditional—and proper—definition of knowledge: "justified true belief."[53]

In any case, the distinction between truth, on the one hand, and rationality and justification, on the other, enables Sunstein to say that, although most conspiracy theories are false, the people who hold these false theories "typically do so not as a result of a mental illness . . . or of simple irrationality."[54] This distinction, therefore, allows Sunstein to avoid making the outrageous claim that most people who accept conspiracy theories are irrational or mentally ill, while also allowing him to claim, nevertheless, that most conspiracy theories—meaning, of course, most conspiracy theories about the machinations of powerful people—are false.

2. Conspiracy Theories in Open Societies

Sunstein, however, does not quite make that claim. Rather, he claims only that most conspiracy theories are false when they are about powerful people *in open societies*, such as the United States. One reason for this qualification is that, in such societies, there is a free press, which makes it hard for any secret machinations of the powerful to remain secret for very long—a fact that is not true in closed societies:

> In a closed society, secrets are far easier to keep, and distrust of official accounts makes a great deal of sense. In such societies, conspiracy theories are . . . more likely to be true . . . . But when the press is free, and when checks and balances are in force, it is harder for government to keep nefarious conspiracies hidden for long. . . . [I]nstitutional checks make it less likely, in such societies, that powerful groups can keep dark secrets for extended periods, at least if those secrets involve illegal or nefarious conduct.

Then, stating that the United States, France, and the United Kingdom are examples of open societies, Sunstein says that theories about illegal or nefarious conspiracies by the government "are less likely to be either true or justified in such societies."[55]

It should be noted that, in making this point, Sunstein has used "justified" in a second way: Previously, the question of whether a theory is justified was said to be a matter of *the information available to the person in question*, who might belong to an informationally deprived sub-society. As long as the person was rational in holding the theory, given the information available to him or her, Sunstein had said, the theory would be justified, regardless of whether it was true or false. In the just-quoted statement, however, Sunstein employed a new definition: a theory is justified only if it is *justified in the light of the information available in the larger society*.

Given this new definition, the distinction between true and justified theories is virtually obliterated: To consider a theory justified in light of the information available in the "larger society," which today is effectively the world as a whole, is operationally the same as considering it true.[56]

Sunstein's statement that he is concerned only with conspiracy theories that are unjustified (as well as false and harmful), which was quoted above, was based on this second meaning, as shown by the fuller statement, in which he says:

> [W]e are concerned only with (the many) conspiracy theories that are false, harmful, and unjustified (not in the sense of being irrationally held by those individuals who hold them, but from the standpoint of the information available in the society as a whole).[57]

It is in this sense, he claims, that conspiracy theories about governments in open societies—"including the United States, the United Kingdom, and France"—are unjustified. Accordingly, Sunstein writes:

> This is not . . . a general claim that conspiracy theories are unjustified or unwarranted in all imaginable situations or societies. Much depends on the background state of knowledge-producing institutions. If those institutions are generally trustworthy, in part because they are embedded in an open society with a well-functioning marketplace of ideas and free flow of information, and if it is difficult to dupe many diverse institutions simultaneously (as the 9/11 conspiracy theories require), then conspiracy theories will usually be unjustified.[58]

Given this second way of using the term unjustified," which is Sunstein's dominant usage, to consider a theory unjustified is effectively the same as considering it false, and vice versa. There is no need, therefore, to continue referring to the conspiracy theories with which Sunstein is concerned as "unjustified"—as illustrated by the fact that Sunstein often speaks of conspiracy theories as simply "false and harmful" (without adding "unjustified").[59]

In any case, the Sunstein claim at hand, according to which anti-government conspiracy theories in the United States are usually unjustified in light of all the information available—which means that they can be considered false—is also based on a second premise, namely, that we Americans can "assume a well-motivated government."[60] Sunstein admits, to be sure, that this assumption is not always true:

> [R]eal-world governments can themselves be purveyors of conspiracy theories, as when the Bush administration suggested that Saddam Hussein had conspired with Al Qaeda to support the 9/11 attacks.[61]

Sunstein also admits that our leaders have proposed, and in some cases actually engaged in, illegal and nefarious conspiracies:

> The Watergate hotel room used by Democratic National Committee was, in fact, bugged by Republican officials, operating at the

behest of the White House. In the 1950s, the Central Intelligence Agency did, in fact, administer LSD and related drugs under Project MKULTRA, in an effort to investigate the possibility of "mind control." Operation Northwoods, a rumored plan by the Department of Defense to simulate acts of terrorism and to blame them on Cuba, really was proposed by high-level officials.[62]

Sunstein states, nevertheless, that the existence of "a well-motivated government" is "a standard assumption in policy analysis." This statement might be taken, unkindly, to mean that policy analysts routinely use this assumption, even though it is false. Sunstein's actual meaning, however, seems to be that we American citizens can assume that our government has *in general* been well-motivated, so that the above-mentioned nefarious conspiracies can be regarded as aberrations.

Sunstein's second thesis, in sum, is that any particular anti-government conspiracy theory in the United States will probably be false, for two reasons: (1) Our government is in general well-motivated, so it will engage in illegal or nefarious conspiracies only rarely, if at all. (2) Even if our government were occasionally to do this, the conspiracy would be quickly exposed, because we have an open society with a free press, which makes it very hard "for government to keep nefarious conspiracies hidden for long." The following two sections will be devoted to these claims.

3. Government Conspiracies: Not Rare Occurrences

As we have seen, Sunstein admitted that the US government has engaged in some illegal and nefarious conspiracies. But by mentioning only four such conspiracies (Northwoods, MKULTRA, Watergate, and the allegation that Saddam Hussein had aided the 9/11 attacks), while claiming that our government has in general been well motivated, Sunstein implied that these four examples were exceptions. But they were not. Here is a very selective list of illegal and/or nefarious operations by the US government—some of which were directed against the American people, some not—that it tried to keep secret:

Operation Mockingbird (1948–?): This was (is?) a CIA program to control, or at least influence, both foreign and domestic media by developing "assets" in them. An article about this operation said that, in the 1950s, "some 3,000 salaried and contract CIA employees were eventually engaged in propaganda efforts."[63] In 1976, a report by the Church Committee (of the US Senate) on the government's intelligence activities said: "The CIA currently maintains a network of several hundred foreign individuals around the world who provide intelligence for the CIA and at times attempt to influence opinion through the use of covert propaganda."[64] The following year, former *Washington Post* reporter Carl Bernstein (of Watergate fame) published an article stating that these assets included some of America's most influential journalists, whom he named, and that the Church Committee covered up the full truth of the media's cooperation with the CIA.[65]

NATO–CIA Clandestine Operations in Europe (1950–1985): In efforts to prevent the election of leftist governments in countries such as Italy (where the effort was known as Operation Gladio), France, and Belgium, deadly attacks—including the 1980 bombing of the train station in Bologna that killed 80 people—were organized by NATO and the CIA, which then had evidence planted to implicate leftists.[66]

Regime Change in Iran (1953): The Eisenhower administration's CIA, working with the British government and a former Nazi collaborator, organized a coup that toppled Iran's democratically-elected government of Mohammad Mosaddeq, who had nationalized Iran's oil. As a result, British and American oil companies made greater profits, but the Iranian people were subjected to the authoritarian rule of Mohammad Reza Shah Pahlavi—"the Shah of Iran"—who became increasingly autocratic and brutal until he was overthrown in the Iranian revolution of 1979.[67]

Regime Change in Guatemala (1954): The Eisenhower administration overthrew the democratically-elected government of Jacobo Arbenz, who had introduced agrarian reform, through which land was returned to the native peoples for the first time since the Spanish conquest.[68]

COINTELPRO (1956–1971): This acronym stands for the FBI's Counter Intelligence Program, which targeted various organizations that the director (J. Edgar Hoover) considered subversive, including not only communist, socialist, and militant black nationalist organizations, but also (nonviolent) civil rights organizations—such as the NAACP and the Southern Christian Leadership Conference (including Martin Luther King himself)—the women's rights movement, and the anti-Vietnam war movement. Instructing FBI agents to "expose, disrupt, misdirect, discredit, or otherwise neutralize" these organizations, Hoover added: "Under no circumstances should the existence of the program be made known outside the bureau."[69] Congress and the courts eventually declared this program unconstitutional by virtue of violating the rights of free speech and free association.

Civil War in Indonesia (1957): In an effort to get control of its oil, the United States provoked, then took part in, a civil war in Indonesia that resulted in some 40,000 deaths. This illegal war, the results of which provided the preconditions for the mass slaughter of 1965 (see below), was kept secret from the American people until a book about it appeared in 1995.[70]

Gulf of Tonkin "Incident" (1964): In order to get Congressional authorization to "take all necessary measures" against North Vietnam, the Johnson administration falsely claimed that US ships in the Gulf of Tonkin had been attacked by North Vietnamese boats. By now, everyone admits that this attack never occurred.[71]

Regime Change and Mass Slaughter in Indonesia (1965): An intentionally unsuccessful coup was fabricated by the Johnson administration's CIA and Pentagon, so that army strongman General Suharto could, after blaming the "attempted coup" on Indonesia's Communist Party, use it as a pretext to begin a general slaughter. Employing arms and "shooting lists" provided by the Johnson administration, Suharto killed hundreds of thousands—perhaps as many as a million— people.[72]

A Coup in the Birthplace of Democracy (1967): In 1964, the Johnson administration tried to persuade Greece's prime minister, George

Papandreou, to accept its solution to a dispute involving Cyprus, but Papandreou refused, explaining that it would be unacceptable to Greece's parliament and contrary to its constitution. Johnson reportedly replied: "Fuck your Parliament and your Constitution." The next year, the CIA bribed enough members of Papandreou's party to topple his government. Then in 1967, when he was about to be returned to power by the voters, a military junta, led by the CIA's man in Greece, George Papadopoulos, staged a coup, as a result of which Papadopoulos became known as "the first CIA agent to become Premier of a European country."[73]

Assassination of Chile's President Allende (1973): After failing to prevent the victory of Marxist Salvador Allende in Chile's 1970 presidential election, in 1973 President Richard Nixon carried out his earlier threat to "smash...that son of a bitch Allende." Along with Secretary of State Henry Kissinger and Chilean General Augusto Pinochet, he planned a September 11 coup in which the presidential palace was specifically targeted and Allende was killed. His government, which had adhered to Chile's constitution, was replaced by the brutal rule of Pinochet, which lasted for seventeen years, during which he authorized kidnapping, torture, mass murder, drug trafficking, and various other crimes.[74]

October Surprise (1980): Republican presidential nominee Ronald Reagan made a secret deal with the Iranian government not to release American hostages in order to ruin President Jimmy Carter's reelection chances.[75]

CIA–Contra "Dark Alliance" (1980s): With the CIA's approval and sometimes assistance, Nicaraguan Contras smuggled cocaine into Los Angeles and the San Francisco Bay Area to support their war against the democratically elected Sandinista government. This operation was exposed by Gary Webb in a book called *Dark Alliance*.[76]

Iran–Contra Affair (1985): During the Reagan administration, senior US figures agreed to facilitate the sale of arms to Iran through Israel, in spite of an arms embargo, in order to secure the release of hostages from Iran and to provide secret funding for the Nicaraguan Contras—even though any US funding had been made illegal by

Congress. The exposure of this conspiracy in 1986 led to criminal convictions for many administration figures.[77]

Regime Change in Panama (1989): After a several-month campaign to demonize Panamanian strongman General Manuel Noriega, the US military—using tanks, helicopters, rockets, and its new F-117A stealth fighters—launched an attack on his country that killed several thousand civilians. (The Central American Human Rights Commission report was entitled "Panama: More than an Invasion, . . . a Massacre."[78]) Calling it "Operation Just Cause," the administration of George H. W. Bush provided several pretexts, but its real reason for this attack, evidently, was its desire to have a more pliable puppet in place by the time the Panama Canal passed back into Panamanian hands on January 1, 2000, combined with other motives, including its desire to show off some of the military's new weapons for marketing purposes.[79]

Phony Testimony to Support Iraq Invasion (1991): After getting a green light from the Bush administration, Saddam Hussein invaded Kuwait (in response to that country's OPEC violations and other policies that were preventing Iraq's economic recovery after its long war with Iran). But then President Bush expressed outrage and began making the case to go to war. In doing so, he repeatedly cited the testimony of a fifteen-year-old Kuwaiti girl, who told a US Congressional caucus that, while working as a volunteer in the al-Adnan hospital in Kuwait City, she saw Iraqi troops ripping premature babies from incubators and leaving them "on the cold floor to die." This girl was really Nayirah al-Sabah, the daughter of the Kuwaiti ambassador to the United States. She and six other "witnesses" had been coached by the Hill & Knowlton public relations firm, which had been given a $2 million contract by the Kuwaiti government to sell the war to the American people.[80]

Deadly Lie at Ground Zero (2001): A week after 9/11, the EPA issued a statement assuring the people of New York City that the "air is safe to breathe." It specifically said that the air did *not* contain "excessive levels of asbestos"[81]—even though a *Boston Globe* story a few days earlier had reported "levels of asbestos up to four times the safe level, placing unprotected emergency workers at risk of disease."[82] It was later learned that, although the EPA had intended to issue a warning, the Bush–Cheney White House forced it to remove all cautionary statements, so that it deleted the warnings about the potentially harmful effects of airborne dust containing asbestos, lead, glass fibers, and concrete.[83] As a result, 60 to 70 percent of the 40,000 rescue and clean-up workers suffer from various debilitating illnesses, including cancer, and some have already died.[84]

Regime change in Haiti (1991, 2004): In 1990, Jean-Bertrand Aristide, who articulated the aspirations of Haiti's poor, was elected to the presidency by a large margin. In 1991, the Bush administration supported a coup engineered by Haiti's elite.[85] In 1994, the Clinton administration returned Aristide to power, after he agreed to business-friendly economic policies. But after he won 92 percent of the vote in 2000 and continued to work on behalf of the poor, the administration of the younger George Bush effected a coup in 2004, albeit "in a manner that wasn't widely criticized or even recognized as a coup at all," because Aristide was put in a position in which he had no choice but to "resign." He was then put on a plane by the US military and flown to the Central African Republic, where he still remains as this is being written.[86]

Although this list is significant, it constitutes only a small portion of the US government conspiracies since World War II. The four conspiracies mentioned by Sunstein are, therefore, by no means aberrations. Given this history, we cannot presuppose a "well-motivated government."

Support for this conclusion is provided, interestingly, by the fact that in Sunstein's essay, in which he contends that most claims about government-sponsored conspiracies are false, he rather casually proposed a new governmental conspiracy: As his tenth thesis indicates, Sunstein's proposal for dealing with the 9/11 Truth Movement involves using anonymous government agents and secretly hired experts to infiltrate it. Sunstein even admitted that he was proposing a conspiracy, speaking of "the sort of conspiratorial tactic we have suggested."[87] Sunstein, to be sure, would say that this is not a *nefarious* conspiracy, but a benign one, because its "aim is to undermine false and harmful conspiratorial theorizing." That, however, would be a very contentious matter of opinion, and the kind of conspiratorial tactic he proposed would, in any case, almost certainly be illegal, as we will see in Chapter 10. Sunstein's essay, therefore, undercuts its own claim that the US government, being well-motivated, would rarely if ever sponsor nefarious or illegal conspiracies.

4. America's Free Press: Always Anxious to Expose Government Conspiracies?

I turn now to Sunstein's second claim, according to which we in America have a "free press," which makes it hard for the government "to keep nefarious conspiracies hidden for long."

The most obvious problem with this claim, given the preceding discussion of illegal and/or nefarious conspiracies, is that only a few of these events were reported quickly by the US press. Many were *never* reported, and most of the others were reported only long after it would have been possible to do anything about them.

Another problem with Sunstein's claim is that these events, discussed above, constitute only a small portion of the nefarious and/or illegal government activities that have gone almost entirely unreported. Here are some more:

Evidence for a Stolen Election (2004): One recent example involves evidence that the presidential election of 2004 was stolen by the Republicans. The following year, New York University professor Mark Crispin Miller presented abundant evidence for this conclusion in *Harper's* magazine, usually considered a reputable publication.[88] However, although television news shows are supposed to like explosive stories, they did not pick up this one, so it did not become part of the national conversation. Miller then presented this evidence more extensively in a book entitled *Fooled Again*,[89] but as far as the mainstream media was concerned, this book might as well not have been published.

The Downing Street Memo (2005): On May 1, London's *Sunday Times* published a memo containing the official minutes from a briefing given by Richard Dearlove, then head of MI-6 (Britain's equivalent of the CIA), to Prime Minister Tony Blair and other members of his cabinet. This briefing had been given on July 23, 2002, about eight months before the attack on Iraq. Having just returned from a meeting with members of the Bush administration, Dearlove reported that it had decided to bring about regime change in Iraq by launching a war, which was to be "justified by the conjunction of terrorism and WMD." As to how the Bush administration could be certain that intelligence reports would support Iraq's possession of weapons of mass destruction, Dearlove said that "the intelligence and facts were being fixed around the policy."[90] The next day, a *New York Times* article mentioned the *Times'* story, but the memo's explosive statement that the facts and the intelligence would be "fixed" was buried in the fifteenth paragraph and not further discussed. Six weeks later, the "paper of record" published another story on the memo, portraying it as insignificant.[91] The rest of the US press followed suit, with the result that most of the American people, having never heard of the memo, believe that the Bush administration went to war on the basis of "bad intelligence." The US press thus helped conceal the conspiracy.

Explosive Testimony by Sibel Edmonds (2008): Three years after its Downing Street Memo story, the *Sunday Times* published another explosive front-page story. This time it was based on an interview with former FBI translator Sibel Edmonds (who in 2006 had been given the First Amendment Award by the PEN American Center and Newman's Own).[92] In 2007, she had announced that, in spite of a gag order slapped on her by a federal court, she would tell everything she knew about US government misconduct to any TV network that would promise to air the entire interview. Not a single network accepted her offer, and no major US newspaper or magazine interviewed her. But London's *Sunday Times* interviewed her and published a story reporting her allegations that senior US officials, "including household names," had had improper relationships with agents of other countries, even helping them plant "moles" in academic and military institutions and acquire nuclear secrets.[93] Journalist Chris Floyd called it "one of the most important stories of the last quarter-century,"[94] and Dave Lindorff said that "there is enough in just this one *London Times* story to keep an army of investigative reporters busy for years."[95] But America's mainstream press completely ignored the story.

Having provided descriptions of three stories censored by the US press, I will now simply give the headlines of some stories discussed by Project Censored, which for the past three decades has issued annual reports describing "The News That Didn't Make the News":

"CIA and the Death Squads: 20 Years of Immorality, 10 Years of Illegality" (1984).[96]

"U.S. Troops Exposed To Depleted Uranium during Gulf War" (1997).[97]

"U. S. Weapons Mass Destruction Linked to the Deaths of a Half-Million Children" (1999).[98]

"The U.S. and NATO Deliberately Started the War with Yugoslavia" (2000).[99]

"Evidence Indicates No Pre-War Genocide in Kosovo and Possible U.S./KLA Plot to Create Disinformation" (2000).[100]

"Planned Weapons in Space Violate International Treaty" (2000).[101]

"International Report Blames U.S. and Others for Genocide in Rwanda" (2001).[102]

"U.S. Intentionally Destroyed Iraq's Water System" (2003).[103]

"Bush Administration Behind Failed Military Coup in Venezuela" (2004).[104]

"US/British Forces Continue Use of Depleted Uranium Weapons Despite Negative Health Effects" (2004).[105]

"Another Year of Distorted Election Coverage" (2006).[106]

"Over One Million Iraqi Deaths Caused by US Occupation" (2009).[107]

"The Mysterious Death of Mike Connell—Karl Rove's Election Thief" (2010).[108]

As these censored stories illustrate, Sunstein's picture of the United States—as "an open society with a well-functioning marketplace of ideas and free flow of information," in which it is difficult "for government to keep nefarious conspiracies hidden for long"—is a false idealization. The falsity of this premise undermines Sunstein's conclusion that "conspiracy theories will usually be unjustified."[109]

5. A Possible Esoteric Reading

Taken at face value, therefore, Sunstein's second thesis is wholly without merit. But is it not possible that Sunstein, by virtue of the obviousness of this fact, was thereby signaling astute readers that he was trying to convey a different meaning—perhaps one that would have been too dangerous, if he wanted to keep his reputation with people and institutions of influence, to state openly at the time? Several features of Sunstein's defense of his second thesis could be taken as clues that this, indeed, was his intention.

One such feature is provided by the above-discussed fact that, having suggested that we Americans can assume a "well-motivated government," Sunstein immediately gave four examples to the contrary: Northwoods, MKULTRA, Watergate, and the claim about Saddam–Osama cooperation. Although one could read this very brief list of examples, as I did above, as an attempt to imply that there had been only a few government conspiracies, would not Sunstein have realized that readers knowing anything about US political history would immediately think—as I did—of many more examples? Is it not likely that he was thereby reminding us that, although the assumption of a well-motivated government is presupposed in policy analysis, it is obviously false?

Also, did Sunstein not indicate that he was sending a double message by the fact that, in the very essay in which he was suggesting that most claims about government-sponsored conspiracies were false, he was himself proposing such a conspiracy? Did he not make this even more obvious by pointing it out, referring to "the sort of conspiratorial tactic we have suggested"?

There may be, likewise, a hidden level of meaning in his discussion of the United States as having a free press that would quickly expose any illegal and/or nefarious actions the government would be trying to keep secret. Would not Sunstein have realized that many readers would quickly think of all sorts of events of this nature that the press did not reveal quickly, if ever? Was Sunstein not thereby hinting that, just because America's mainstream press has not identified 9/11 as a conspiracy planned by the Bush–Cheney administration, we cannot safely assume that it was not? Did Sunstein not provide an additional hint by including, among his very short list of true conspiracy theories, that administration's fabrication of the Saddam–Osama connection? In the case of the Bush–Cheney administration, Sunstein appeared to be saying, we could *not* assume a government so well-motivated that its orchestration of 9/11 would be unthinkable.

In the above discussion of Sunstein's first thesis, moreover, we saw that, by sending us to the writings of Charles Pigden, he may have been alerting careful readers to the fact that he believes neither that all conspiracy theories are false nor even that conspiracy theories are more likely to be false than theories of other types. And now, in supporting his second thesis, he says that those who accept conspiracy theories are not necessarily irrational—that belief in various conspiracy theories can be rationally justified, given the information available to the person in question.

He does state, to be sure, that an anti-government conspiracy theory that is rationally justified from the perspective of the individual holding it is likely to be unjustified—perhaps even preposterous—"in light of the information available in the wider society."[110] He does not say, however, that this is always the case, only that it *usually* is, which leaves open the possibility that some particular anti-government conspiracy theories might be true.

Also, in speaking of open societies, he says only that they make it *"harder* for government to keep nefarious conspiracies hidden for long,"[111] not that they make it *impossible*. He thereby leaves open the possibility that a conspiracy could have remained secret from September 2001 to the present day.

Furthermore, two crucial statements about open societies are formulated in conditional, rather than categorical, language. One of these says:

> [W]hen the press is free, and *when* checks and balances are in force, it is harder for government to keep nefarious conspiracies hidden for long.[112]

The other one says:

> [C]onspiracy theories are [not necessarily] unjustified or unwarranted in all imaginable situations or societies. Much depends on the background state of knowledge-producing institutions. *If* those institutions are generally trustworthy, in part because they are embedded in an open society with a well-functioning marketplace of ideas and free flow of information, and if it is difficult to dupe many diverse institutions simultaneously (as the 9/11 conspiracy theories require), then conspiracy theories will usually be unjustified.[113]

So, given the fact that these conditions do not obtain in the United States at the present time—a fact of which Sunstein would surely be aware—he has not provided a good reason to believe that anti-government conspiracy theories will usually be unjustified.

Sunstein can be read, finally, as providing a concrete example of yet another anti-government conspiracy theory that has been shown to be true, even though the US press has largely concealed this fact. In giving examples of conspiracy theories that exemplify his (exoteric) definition, according to which they refer to the machinations of powerful people, he includes the view "that Martin Luther King, Jr. was killed by federal agents."[114] The average reader is clearly supposed to understand Sunstein as indicating that this theory, along with the others in the list, is false.

In the footnote to this passage, however, Sunstein refers readers to a book on this subject by attorney William F. Pepper, *An Act of State: The Execution of Martin Luther King*.[115] Serious readers—those who read footnotes and look up their references—will find in this book that Pepper, having conducted a 30-year investigation into King's assassination, arranged for a civil action suit on behalf of King's family, which did not believe the government's claim that King had been killed by James Earl Ray. Employing 70 witnesses, Pepper presented evidence that King was the victim of a conspiracy involving organized crime, Memphis police, the US military, the CIA, and the FBI. The evidence was so convincing, readers of the book learn, that it took the jury only an hour to render the verdict. But the country's "free press" has for the most part concealed this fact from the American public.

Has Sunstein not thereby indicated to discerning readers—in a way that would not endanger his position in polite society—that the conspiracy theory about the King assassination—probably along with some of the other theories in his list (such as "the view that the Central Intelligence Agency was responsible for the assassination of President

John F. Kennedy")—is actually true,[116] in spite of the fact that the mainstream press and everyone in public office must maintain otherwise?

This esoteric reading of Sunstein's second thesis is, of course, only a possible reading. To see whether this way of interpreting his essay holds up, we will need to examine his other theses.

CHAPTER 3
THE 9/11 CONSPIRACY THEORY DEFINED

Sunstein's third thesis, which is a definition, states:

According to the 9/11 conspiracy theory, "U.S. officials knowingly allowed 9/11 to happen or even brought it about,"[117] *and "U.S. government officials destroyed the World Trade Center and then covered their tracks."*[118]

1. The Definition Understood Exoterically

Given this definition, the import of Sunstein's second thesis, which says that "anti-government conspiracy theories in the United States are likely to be both unjustified and false," would be that one can safely presume that the 9/11 conspiracy theory is false and—in light of the information available to US citizens in general—unjustified.

However, is the definition given above the best way to define "the 9/11 conspiracy theory"? This definition fits, of course, with Sunstein's explicit (exoteric) conception of a conspiracy theory in general, according to which it is "an effort to explain some event or practice by reference to the machinations of powerful people."[119]

As we saw earlier, however, Sunstein pointed out that this is not really a generic definition, applying to all conspiracy theories of every type, because "many conspiracy theories involve people who are not especially powerful (friends, neighborhoods, fellow employees, family members, and so forth)."[120]

This acknowledgment opens the way to suspect that, even though Sunstein's definition of "the 9/11 conspiracy theory" seems straightforward enough, a deeper definition might be hidden in his discussion.

2. The Definition Understood Esoterically

At the outset of his essay, as we saw earlier, Sunstein states that, although it is about conspiracy theories in general, his "running example involves conspiracy theories relating to terrorism, especially theories that arose from and post-date the 9/11 attacks."[121] By speaking of post-9/11 "theories" (in the plural), he could be suggesting that there is more than one "9/11 conspiracy theory."

Next, recall Sunstein's acknowledgment that "many conspiracy theories involve people who are not especially powerful (friends, neighborhoods, fellow employees, family members, and so forth)." That final phrase—"and so forth"—opens the way to any number of possibilities. A 9/11 conspiracy theory could claim, for example, that the 9/11 attacks, instead of being engineered by powerful people in charge of states, resulted from a conspiracy between Osama bin Laden—a stateless individual—and a bunch of young Muslim men, a few of whom had taken some piloting lessons.

Sunstein, in fact, says just this. Most respectable public figures avoid speaking of this official account of 9/11 as a "conspiracy theory," evidently preferring to use this term, thanks to its negative connotations, only for the view that 9/11 was, at least partly, an inside job. But not Sunstein: "The theory that Al-Qaeda was responsible for 9/11 is," he forthrightly declares," a "conspiracy theory."[122]

The more complete statement, to be sure, says: "The theory that Al-Qaeda was responsible for 9/11 is thus a justified and true conspiracy theory." Sunstein thereby explicitly contrasts this 9/11 conspiracy theory with the alternative version—according to which members of the Bush–Cheney administration were responsible—as true and false conspiracy theories, respectively. The point at hand, however, is that the Bush–Cheney administration's theory, according to which bin Laden and several of his al-Qaeda followers were responsible for the 9/11 attacks, is a conspiracy theory every bit as much as is the alternative theory. Sunstein even reinforces this point by saying: "[S]ome conspiracy theories have turned out to be true, and under our definition, they do not cease to be conspiracy theories for that reason."[123]

By seeing Sunstein's essay as having such a hidden meaning, therefore, one can see it as moving, ever so cautiously, in the direction of implying that its real target—the 9/11 conspiracy theory that is "false, harmful, and unjustified"—is the official conspiracy theory, according to which these amazing attacks were carried out by an unlikely crew (amateur pilots and "muscle hijackers" armed only with knives and box-cutters), on the basis of plans formulated in an unlikely location (Afghanistan).

CHAPTER 4
9/11 CONSPIRACY THEORISTS AS EPISTEMOLOGICAL CRIPPLES

According to Sunstein's fourth thesis:

People typically accept the 9/11 conspiracy theory "not as a result of a mental illness . . . or of simple irrationality, but as a result of a 'crippled epistemology,' in the form of a sharply limited number of (relevant) informational sources."[124] *The main cause of belief in the 9/11 conspiracy theory, in short, is "informational isolation."*[125]

Besides saying that people who hold this theory are epistemological cripples, Sunstein offers a sociological explanation for their condition. It comes about, he suggests, because they are "embedded in isolated groups or small, self-enclosed networks," in which they are "exposed only to skewed information."[126]

Sunstein also gives an alternative definition of his key concept, saying:

> In some domains, people suffer from a "crippled epistemology," in the sense that they know very few things, and what they know is wrong.[127]

This definition is problematic. Given the traditional definition of "knowledge," according to which it is *justified true belief*, one cannot "know" something that is false. People may strongly *believe* false propositions; they may *think* they know them to be true. But the belief in a false proposition cannot be called *knowledge*. Sunstein cannot meaningfully say, therefore, that "what they know is wrong."

Fixing this alternative definition would be, however, a fairly simple matter. Sunstein would only need to say: *In some domains, people suffer from a "crippled epistemology," in the sense that they do not know many things, and what little they think they know is wrong.* In any case, Sunstein's account of crippled epistemologies in terms of information deprivation is his main account. The alternative account simply refers to the ignorance that results from such deprivation.

A Note about "Crippled Epistemology"

"Crippled epistemology," I wish to add, is a confused and confusing term for a *distorted process of belief formation*, meaning one that is likely to result in a system of false beliefs, and hence ignorance. Although I use this term throughout this critique, because it is far too central to Sunstein's essay to ignore or change, I hope my book will not encourage any further use of this misnomer. (I have a long note devoted to explaining why this term is a misnomer.[128])

1. Sunstein's Primary Claim

Sunstein's fourth thesis—that those who hold the 9/11 conspiracy theory do so because of a "crippled epistemology"—is, he says, his "primary claim." It requires, therefore, careful scrutiny.

This thesis has been regarded as offensive, with Glenn Greenwald calling it a "condescending, self-loving belief."[129] This charge is not unjust, because Sunstein is saying (at the exoteric level) that people who regard 9/11 as an inside job do so because they are informationally deprived—compared, of course, with people such as Sunstein, who accept the "true conspiracy theory," according to which "Al-Qaeda was responsible for 9/11."[130] Sunstein's claim leaves no room for the possibility that some people who disagree with him on this point might be as well informed as he, or even *better* informed.

Sunstein's "primary claim," moreover, seems to be held on a purely *a priori* basis, with no appeal to empirical evidence to support it. Sunstein is aware that the people he calls "9/11 conspiracy theorists" typically "call themselves the '9/11 Truth Movement.'" He has even referred to this movement's oldest well-known website, 911Truth.org, saying "see (www.911truth.org)."[131] He knows, therefore, that this is an organized movement with a presence on the internet, and he knows of the existence of at least one website from which he could have acquired information about this movement. And yet his essay shows no signs of his having engaged in any empirical examination of representative members of the 9/11 Truth Movement, in order to see if "informational isolation" seems a plausible way to account for their beliefs.

Surely, however, the truth of such an important and belittling claim—which in essence says: "You disagree with me because you're ignorant"—cannot simply be presupposed. To evaluate the plausibility of Sunstein's thesis, one would need to look at representative members of the 9/11 Truth Movement.

2. My Own Intellectual History

Because I have probably published more about the 9/11 attacks than anyone else in the movement and have come to be regarded as one of its leading spokespersons, I would have to be considered part of what Sunstein calls the "hard core of [9/11] conspiracy theorists."[132] His description of why people come to accept what he considers the false 9/11 conspiracy theory should, therefore, apply preeminently to me. For this reason, and also because I am (of course) most familiar with my own intellectual history, I will begin by providing some reasons for thinking that Sunstein's explanation does not seem a plausible way to account for my 9/11 beliefs.

I will begin with one thing I have in common with Sunstein: a connection to Harvard. In my case, this is not because I studied or taught there, but because my philosophical worldview has been shaped primarily by Alfred North Whitehead, who taught in Harvard's philosophy department in the second quarter of the twentieth century. Before coming to Harvard, Whitehead had taught mathematics at Cambridge University, had collaborated with his former student Bertrand Russell on *Principia Mathematica*, and had then written some books in scientific philosophy, including an alternative to Einstein's formulation of relativity theory.[133] While at Harvard, he wrote several still-influential books, including *Science and the Modern World* (1925), *Religion in the Making* (1926), *The Function of Reason* (1929), and his major work, *Process and Reality: An Essay in Cosmology* (1929)—on the basis of which his way of thinking came to be called "process philosophy."[134]

I also have in common with Sunstein a connection to Chicago: Charles Hartshorne, who had served two years as a post-doctoral assistant to Whitehead at Harvard and later became the second most important process philosopher, taught for most of his career in the

University of Chicago's philosophy department and also in its divinity school.[135] One of his students there was John B. Cobb Jr., who later became the leading "process theologian" and my own professor at Claremont School of Theology and Claremont Graduate School, where I studied from 1963 to 1968. Upon my return to Claremont to teach in 1973, Cobb and I established the Center for Process Studies, which is devoted to exploring the fruitfulness of Whiteheadian-Hartshornean thought in various fields.

I have published several books in which I have discussed process philosophy and applied it to many issues, including the problem of evil,[136] religious pluralism,[137] the relation between science and religion,[138] the mind-body problem,[139] evolutionary theory,[140] and the philosophy of physics.[141] Running through all of these discussions is a treatment of that branch of philosophy to which Sunstein refers, namely, epistemology: the issue of what we know and how we know it.[142] I was also the co-editor of the corrected edition of Whitehead's *Process and Reality*, which deals with cosmology and metaphysics (the two main branches of which are ontology and epistemology).[143]

Some of my edited volumes arose out of conferences I had organized on behalf of the Center for Process Studies and/or the Center for a Postmodern World, a sister organization that I established in Santa Barbara. Through these conferences, I had extended interactions with some of the leading thinkers of the past 70 years, including physicist David Bohm, chemist Ilya Prigogine, psychologist James Hillman, architect Charles Jencks, philosopher Charles Hartshorne, international law professor Richard Falk, systems theorist Erwin Laszlo, economist Herman Daly, and several of the leading evolutionary biologists, including Theodosius Dobzhansky, William Thorpe, Sewall Wright, and C.H. Waddington.

From 1987 to 2004, I edited a series for the State University of New York Press called "SUNY Series in Constructive Postmodern Thought," which published 31 volumes.

Since starting to work on 9/11, I have written nine books on this subject. These books include a critique of *The 9/11 Commission Report*;[144] a critique of *Popular Mechanics*' defense of the official account of 9/11;[145] a critique of the 2006 "inside story of the 9/11 Commission" by its co-chairs, Thomas Kean and Lee Hamilton;[146] a critique of the official report on the destruction of the Twin Towers put out by NIST (the National Institute of Standards and Technology);[147] and a critique of NIST's report on the collapse of World Trade Center 7.[148] Also, far from using only material produced by fellow members of the 9/11 Truth Movement (as suggested by Sunstein's comment about "self-enclosed networks"), my books' endnotes—which in the most recent four books average 60 pages—show that I cite reports written by a large number of "informational sources" from around the world.

As to the quality of my 9/11 work, my first two books earned me the Helios Foundation Award for 2006; my 2007 book, *Debunking 9/11 Debunking*,[149] received a Bronze Medal in the 2008 Independent Publisher Book Awards; and my 2008 book, *The New Pearl Harbor Revisited*,[150] was a *Publishers Weekly* "Pick of the Week"—an honor bestowed on only 51 books a year. The editors there evidently did not consider my sources of information excessively restricted. They said, in fact: "Citing hundreds, if not thousands, of sources, Griffin's detailed analysis is far from reactionary or delusional."[151]

I do not believe, in sum, that anyone looking at my books and curriculum vitae would conclude that I have suffered from "informational isolation" in general or "a sharply limited number of (relevant) informational sources" in relation to 9/11 in particular.

3. Other Members of the 9/11 Truth Movement

Sunstein's suggested explanation as to why people accept conspiracy theories is equally absurd when applied to other members of the 9/11 Truth Movement. The idea that they are "informationally isolated" individuals does not fit the fact, for example, that many of them are academics. The website Patriots Question 9/11, which lists people who have publicly questioned the official story of 9/11, includes over 400 professors, some of whom have taught at institutions in the same league as Sunstein's own.[152] Could Sunstein with a straight face tell these professors that the reason they disagree with him about 9/11 is because they have been "informationally isolated"?

Sunstein might say, however, that what is needed to make a rational judgment about 9/11 is not simply information in general, such as might be possessed by professors in the humanities, but *relevant* information. A high percentage of the members of the 9/11 Truth Movement, however, have education and professional training in relevant fields, a fact that has become more visible in recent years through the formation of numerous 9/11 professional organizations, including Architects and Engineers for 9/11 Truth,[153] Firefighters for 9/11 Truth,[154] Intelligence Officers for 9/11 Truth,[155] Journalists and Other Media Professionals for 9/11 Truth,[156] Lawyers for 9/11 Truth,[157] Medical Professionals for 9/11 Truth,[158] Pilots for 9/11 Truth,[159] Political Leaders for 9/11 Truth,[160] Religious Leaders for 9/11 Truth,[161] and Veterans for 9/11 Truth.[162] I will next show the completely unempirical nature of Sunstein's characterization of the 9/11 Truth Movement by giving brief descriptions of a few of the members of these organizations.

Architects for 9/11 Truth

A knowledge of architecture is relevant, of course, to the question of whether the Twin Towers could have come down, and in the way they did, because of the airliner impacts plus the ensuing fires, and whether WTC 7 could have come down, and in the way it did, because of fires on a few of its 47 floors. Here are some of the architects who have joined Architects and Engineers for 9/11 Truth:

—Daniel B. Barnum, an award-winning Fellow of the American Institute of Architects; founder of the Houston AIA Residential Architecture Committee.

—David A. Johnson, an internationally known architect and city planner, who has chaired the planning departments at Syracuse and Ball State universities and also served as president of the Fulbright Association of the United States.

—Kevin A. Kelly, a fellow of the American Institute of Architects, who wrote *Problem Seeking: An Architectural Programming Primer*, which has become a standard textbook.

—Dr. David Leifer, Coordinator of the Graduate Program in Facilities Management at the University of Sydney, and former professor at Mackintosh School of Architecture.[163]

—Paul Stevenson Oles, a Fellow of the American Institute of Architects, which in 1989 called him "the dean of architectural illustrators in America"; co-founder of the American Society of Architectural Perspectivists.

Engineers for 9/11 Truth

An understanding of engineering principles is also obviously relevant to evaluating the official story, according to which al-Qaeda pilots brought down the three WTC buildings by flying airplanes into two of them. Here are some engineers who belong to Architects and Engineers for 9/11 Truth:

—Dr. John Edward Anderson, Professor Emeritus of Mechanical Engineering at the University of Minnesota, and former Professor of Aerospace and Mechanical Engineering at Boston University.

—Dr. Robert Bowman, former head of the Department of Aeronautical Engineering at the US Air Force Institute of Technology, and the Director of Advanced Space Programs Development ("Star Wars") under Presidents Ford and Carter.

—Dwain Deets, former Director for Research Engineering and Aerospace Projects at NASA Dryden Flight Research Center, where his work earned him the NASA Exceptional Service Award and inclusion in "Who's Who in Science and Engineering."

—Dr. Joel Hirschhorn, former Professor of Metallurgical Engineering at the University of Wisconsin, Madison, and a former member of the Congressional Office of Technology Assessment's staff.

—Dr. Jack Keller, Professor Emeritus of Engineering at Utah State University, who was named by *Scientific American* in 2004 as one the world's 50 leading contributors to science and technology benefiting society.

—Dr. Heikki Kurttila, Safety Engineer and Accident Analyst for Finland's National Safety Technology Authority.

—Edward Munyak, a Mechanical and Fire Protection Engineer, who has served as Fire Protection Engineer for the State of California and the US Departments of Energy and Defense.[164]

Intelligence Officers for 9/11 Truth

Surely if any professionals would have the training and experience to tell the difference between true and false conspiracy theories, it would be intelligence officers. Presently employed intelligence officers cannot, of course, publicly dispute the government's conspiracy theory if they want to keep their jobs, but here are some of the *former* intelligence officers who have expressed skepticism about the government's 9/11 conspiracy theory.

—Terrell E. Arnold, who served as an analyst in the US State Department's Office of Intelligence and Research, then became the Principal Deputy Director of the State Department's Office of Counterterrorism.

—William Christison, who had a 28-year career with the CIA, during which he became the National Intelligence Officer for South Asia, Southeast Asia, and Africa, and, finally, the Director of the CIA's Office of Regional and Political Analysis, supervising over 200 experts doing political analysis for every region in the world.[165]

—Senator Mike Gravel, who in the 1950s served in the Communications Intelligence Service in Germany and in the Counter- Intelligence Corps in France. Representing Alaska for two terms in the US Senate, he became famous in 1971 for entering over 4,000 pages of the (until then still-secret) Pentagon Papers into the US Senate record, thereby increasing the support for ending the Vietnam war.

—Annie Machon, former Intelligence Officer for MI5 (the British equivalent of the FBI), where she served in the Counter-Subversion department, the Irish counter-terrorism section, and, finally, international counter-terrorism; author of a book (after her 1996 resignation) blowing the whistle on illegal activities within both MI5 and MI6 (the British equivalent of the CIA).[166]

—Ray McGovern, 30-year Army Intelligence officer and CIA analyst, who prepared the *President's Daily Brief* for three presidents (Nixon, Ford, and Reagan) and also conducted morning briefings for

Vice President Bush and other senior advisers to President Reagan.[167]

Can anyone read these brief bios without laughing at Sunstein's claim that these people must all be informationally deprived?

Journalists for 9/11 Truth

Although mainstream journalism has thus far tended to ridicule the 9/11 Truth Movement, some members of the profession have publicly expressed agreement with this movement's argument that a new investigation into the 9/11 attacks is needed. These journalists include:

—Giulietto Chiesa, an Italian journalist who served for nineteen years as a correspondent in Moscow, after which he became a member of the European Parliament and produced *Zero*, a documentary film about 9/11.

—Fiammetta Cucurnia, a journalist for one of Italy's leading newspapers, *La Repubblica*, who previously served for nine years as a correspondent in Moscow.

—Bruno Larebière, the Bordeaux-based editor-in-chief of the French weekly *Minute*.

—Jean-Marie Molitor, the Paris-based director of three French magazines: *Minute*, *Monde & Vie*, and *Le Choc du mois*.

—Isabel Pisano, a Madrid-based journalist for RAI and a member of Ordine Nazionale di Giornalisti Italiani.

—Barrie Zwicker, formerly a reporter for the *Detroit News*, the *Toronto Star*, and the *Globe and Mail*, he became a commentator for Vision TV in Toronto and a journalism lecturer at Ryerson University. In 2006, Zwicker published *Towers of Deception: The Media Cover-up of 9/11*.[168]

Would Sunstein be able to maintain, with plausibility, that these journalists' beliefs about 9/11 can be explained by the poverty of their limited contact with sources of information?

Lawyers for 9/11 Truth

People with training and experience in the law, Sunstein surely believes, have some of the intellectual tools needed to decide between the competing 9/11 conspiracy theories. Some of the members of Lawyers for 9/11 Truth are:

—Roy Andes, former assistant attorney general of Montana.

—Dennis Cunningham, who has been involved in several high-profile cases, such as those arising from the Attica Prison rebellion and the 2002 prosecution of FBI agents and Oakland police officers who had framed Earth First! activists in 1990.

—Ferdinando Imposimato, honorary president of Italy's Supreme Court, who was formerly the senior investigative judge presiding over the trials dealing with the assassination of President Aldo Moro and the attempted assassination of Pope John Paul II.

—Dr. Christopher Pollman, Professor of Law at Université Paul Verlaine–Metz (France), who in 2001-02 was a Visiting Fellow at Harvard Law School.

—Dr. Burns Weston, professor emeritus of law at the University of Iowa, and honorary editor of the *American Journal of International Law*.[169]

Medical Professionals for 9/11 Truth

People in the medical professions have been attracted in large numbers to the 9/11 Truth Movement, perhaps in part because their profession, by its very nature, combines a scientific perspective with a concern for human welfare. In any case, these medical professionals would in no way recognize themselves in Sunstein's description of typical members of the 9/11 Truth Movement. Here are some examples:

—Dr. Mary Ellen Bradshaw (M.D.), former chief of the bureau of school health services in the US Department of Public Health, and former president of the American Association of Public Health Physicians.

—Dr. Steven Jonas (M.D., M.P.H.), professor at Stony Brook University's School of Medicine; fellow of the American Public Health Association; fellow of the New York Academy of Medicine; fellow of the Royal Society of Medicine; founding editor of Springer's Series on Medical Education; and author/editor of over 30 books.

—Dr. Michael D. Knox (Ph.D.), Professor of Medicine and Distinguished Professor of Mental Health Law at the University of South Florida; chairman and CEO of the US Peace Memorial Foundation; and 2007 recipient of the Psychology of Peace and Social Justice prize given by Psychologists for Social Responsibility.

—Dr. Jonathan B. Weisbuch (M.D., M.P.H.), formerly Chief Health Officer, Maricopa County, AZ; Medical Director, LA County Dept. of Health Services; Director, Department of Health and Social Services, Wyoming; President of the American Association of Public Health Physicians (AAPHP); editorial consultant, American Journal of Public Health. Author of more than 40 academic articles.

—Dr. Richard D. Welser (Ph.D.), clinical neuropsychologist and forensic psychologist; formerly the Chief Psychologist in the General Psychiatry Division, Broughton Hospital, Morganton, North Carolina.[170]

Pilots for 9/11 Truth
Experienced pilots obviously have a relevant type of expertise, because they are in position to judge the plausibility of the official account of the four 9/11 airliners, including the alleged flight paths and the Air Force's explanations for its failures to intercept the airliners. Pilots for 9/11 Truth, which challenges the plausibility of the official account, has attracted many experienced pilots, including those described below:

—Captain Ross "Rusty" Aimer, retired from a 40-year career as a pilot for six airlines, including United Airlines, for which he flew the two airplanes involved on 9/11: Boeing 757s and 767s; served on the board of directors for the Airline Pilots Association; currently CEO for an aviation consulting company.

—Rob Balsamo, former commercial pilot; co-founder of Pilots for 9/11 Truth.

—Major Jon I. Fox, a former Marine Corps fighter pilot, with special training to do interceptions; now retired following a 35-year commercial aviation career.

—Ralph W. Omholt, retired commercial airline pilot, who during his long career flew the Boeing 727, 737, 747, 757, and 767.

—Joel M. Skousen, former US Marine Corps fighter pilot and commercial pilot; member of the Experimental Aircraft Association and the Aircraft Owners and Pilots Association; former Chairman of the Conservative National Committee in Washington DC and Executive Editor of *Conservative Digest*.[171]

Political Leaders for 9/11 Truth

Being in a position of political leadership, especially at the national level, surely provides a type of experience useful in evaluating the conspiracy theories about 9/11. The following list is a selection from people who have joined Political Leaders for 9/11 Truth, thereby publicly stating their skepticism about what Sunstein calls "the true [9/11] conspiracy theory."

—Dr. Andreas von Bülow (Ph.D.), former state secretary in the Federal Ministry of Defense, West Germany; former minister of research and technology; former member of the German Parliament.

—Yukihisa Fujita, member of the House of Councilors in the National Diet of Japan, representing the Democratic Party (which became the ruling party in 2009); former member of the House of Representatives; co-chair of Political Leaders for 9/11 Truth.

—Dr. Sergey Ivanovic Kolesnikov (M.D., Ph.D.), member of the State Duma, where he is vice president of the Committee for Eco Defense; former Deputy Director of the Russian Academy of Medical Sciences; Co-President of International Physicians for the Prevention of Nuclear War; recipient of the Government Prize for Science and Technology and the designation Distinguished Scientist of Russia.

—Jesse Ventura, former Governor of Minnesota, having earlier been a member of the US Navy Underwater Demolition Team and the US Navy Seals.[172]

Interlude

Is it not obvious that there is no similarity between the real-world members of the 9/11 Truth Movement and Sunstein's portrayal, according to which it is composed of people "embedded in isolated groups or small, self-enclosed networks," in which they are "exposed only to skewed information"?[173] This complete disjunction between portrayal and reality will become even more apparent as we look at three more organizations.

Religious Leaders for 9/11 Truth

Religious leaders, most people probably assume, do not have any kind of expertise for judging between competing conspiracy theories. Be that as it may, leading members of Religious Leaders for 9/11 Truth bear no relationship to the isolated individuals with "crippled epistemologies" described—or rather imagined—by Sunstein. Here are some examples:

—Dr. John B. Cobb, Jr., professor emeritus of Theology at Claremont School of Theology (California) and founding director of the Center for Process Studies, which has employed Whiteheadian philosophy in a variety of areas; author of influential books on many topics, including religious pluralism, economic theory (with ecological economist Herman Daly), and evolutionary theory; co-editor of a volume of Christian, Jewish, and Muslim essays about 9/11.

—James Douglass, author of the highly acclaimed book about the Kennedy assassination, *JFK and the Unspeakable*.

—Dr. Joseph C. Hough, Jr., former Dean of the Claremont School of Theology; former Dean of Vanderbilt Divinity School; President and Professor of Social Ethics Emeritus at Union Theological Seminary in New York; Interim President at Claremont Graduate University; and author of books on black power, theological education, and theology in the university.

—Dr. Sandra Lubarsky, professor of religious studies at Northern Arizona University; author of works on religious pluralism from a Jewish perspective; co-editor of a volume on the relation of Jewish theology and process philosophy; and co-editor of a volume of Christian, Jewish, and Muslim essays about 9/11.

—Dr. Gene Reeves, who has taught at Rikkyo University (in Tokyo) and served as a consultant for Rissho Kosei-kai; author of a new translation of the Lotus Sutra; formerly the head of the Meadville/ Lombard Theological School in Chicago, where he became acquainted with Barack Obama when they both worked on Harold Washington's mayoral campaign.

—Dr. Douglas Sturm, professor emeritus of religion and political science at Bucknell University; former chair of the editorial board for the *Journal of Law and Religion*; former president of the Society of Christian Ethics.[174]

Scientists for 9/11 Truth

If the examples already given have shown the falsity of Sunstein's claim that people accept the inside-job conspiracy theory about 9/11 only because they exist in isolated communities and networks in which they have no access to relevant information, a look at the membership of Scientists for 9/11 Truth will completely seal the case. Here is a sampling:

—Dr. David L. Griscom, former research physicist at the Naval Research Laboratory; principal author of 100 papers in scientific journals; fellow of the American Association for the Advancement of Science; and fellow of the American Physical Society.

—Dr. Niels Harrit, professor of chemistry at the University of Copenhagen, with a specialty in nanochemistry; first author of "Active Thermitic Material Observed in Dust from the 9/11 World Trade Center Catastrophe," published in the *Open Chemical Physics Journal* in 2009.

—Dr. Steven E. Jones, former Professor of Physics at Brigham Young University; initiator of the research that led to the publication of the co-authored paper, "Active Thermitic Material Observed in Dust from the 9/11 World Trade Center Catastrophe," in the *Open Chemical Physics Journal*.

—Dr. Lynn Margulis, professor at the University of Massachusetts-Amherst, where she is Distinguished University Professor as well as a professor in the Department of Geosciences; recipient of the National Medal of Science in 1999.

—Dr. John D. Wyndham, former research fellow at the California Institute of Technology, who had previously earned a Ph.D. in Physics at Cambridge University.[175]

Veterans for 9/11 Truth

If 9/11 was indeed an inside job, then it was in large part an operation of the US military, which would have had to fake the hijackings, prevent any fighter jets from intercepting the airliners, and make sure that the Twin Towers was struck and the Pentagon damaged. People with military experience would, therefore, be in a better position than most citizens to judge whether the official explanation made sense. By joining Veterans for 9/11 Truth, many military veterans, including those listed below, have expressed their skepticism about the official account.

—Commander Ralph Kolstad, retired from 20-year career in the US Navy, where he was a fighter pilot and also an air combat instructor at the US Navy Fighter Weapons School (Topgun).

—Lt. Col. and Dr. (Ph.D.) Karen U. Kwiatkowski, retired from a 20-year career in the US Air Force, where she was a political-military affairs officer in the Office of the Secretary of Defense; also a staff member for the director of the National Security Agency.

—Lt. Col. Shelton F. Lankford, retired from a 20-year career in the US Marine Corps, where he was a fighter pilot with over 300 combat missions flown; recipient of the Distinguished Flying Cross and 32 Air Medals.

—Lt. Col. Jeff Latas, retired from a 20-year US Air Force career, where he was a combat fighter pilot, with experience in Desert Storm and four tours of duty in the Northern and Southern Watch; also a Pentagon Weapons Requirement Officer and part of the Pentagon's Quadrennial Defense Review; recipient of the Distinguish Flying Cross for Heroism, four Air Medals, four Meritorious Service Medals, and nine Aerial Achievement Medals.

—Col. Ronald D. Ray, retired from a career in the US Marine Corps, during which he became a highly decorated Vietnam veteran (Bronze Star, Purple Heart, and two Silver Stars) and served as deputy assistant Secretary of Defense (during the Reagan Administration); later appointed by George H. W. Bush to the American Battle Monuments Commission; and finally served as military historian and deputy director of field operations for the US Marine Corps Historical Center.

—Lt. Col. Guy S. Razer, retired from a 20-year career in the US Air Force, during which he served as a command fighter pilot and also as an instructor at the Air Force Fighter Weapons School and in NATO's Tactical Leadership Program; also a weapons effects expert responsible for the choice of the most appropriate aircraft and munitions to destroy steel-and-concrete superstructures.[176]

4. Evaluation

As we have seen, Sunstein's "primary claim"— according to which people who view 9/11 as an inside job have "crippled epistemologies" with a "sharply limited number of (relevant) informational sources," because they exist in "self-enclosed networks" that leave them in "informational isolation"—is disproved by a concrete examination of the intellectual leadership of the 9/11 Truth Movement. The dozens of people mentioned above do not come close to fitting Sunstein's description.

The reason why the beliefs of these people cannot be explained through the concept of "crippled epistemology" becomes clear if we turn to the essay from which Sunstein derived this concept, "The Crippled Epistemology of Extremism," by political philosopher Russell Hardin. In a crucial passage, Hardin wrote:

> [Edward] Said's "simple accessibility to the entire world" . . . undercuts the possibility of sustaining the crippled epistemology of extremism. Sustaining such an epistemology requires exclusion of knowledge of, and therefore traffic with, most of the rest of the entire world.[177]

This "accessibility to the entire world," which can be had through travel, schools, libraries, bookstores, movies, television, and the internet, is something that all the members of the 9/11 Truth Movement listed above have. It is no surprise, therefore, that Hardin's concept of "crippled epistemologies" does not apply to them. Sunstein has tried to use it to explain the beliefs of people who have no relation to the kinds of people Hardin was discussing.

5. An Esoteric Reading of Sunstein's Fourth Thesis

The fact that the beliefs of the members of the 9/11 Truth Movement cannot be explained as a consequence of crippled epistemologies would be obvious to anyone who knows much about this movement. Surely Cass Sunstein, a Harvard-trained lawyer who has been deemed worthy to teach in the prestigious law schools of both Chicago and Harvard, would not seek to undermine a movement about which he knew next to nothing. So why would he have given an impression of the 9/11 Truth Movement's membership that is so obviously false? As before, an otherwise inexplicable feature of Sunstein's essay becomes intelligible if taken as a hint about the existence of a deeper meaning.

We can see this meaning as a twofold point. On the one hand, we can read Sunstein as providing hints that, in saying that 9/11 conspiracy theorists have crippled epistemologies, he is not referring to those who hold the Bush–Cheney administration and the Pentagon responsible for the attacks. One such hint would be provided by his acknowledgment, in a footnote, that the preferred designation of those who hold the inside-job conspiracy theory is "the 9/11 Truth Movement." Serious readers, who examine footnotes and look up the references, would quickly see that the leadership of this movement could in no way be called "informationally isolated." A second hint would be provided by his reference to Hardin's essay, which portrays people as developing crippled epistemologies when they are walled off from outside sources of information. People who read Hardin's essay will see even more clearly that no sensible person would try to explain the beliefs of the core members of the 9/11 Truth Movement as resulting from crippled epistemologies.

The other half of the twofold point would be, of course, the same point for which we have seen hints in the previous chapters, namely, that when Sunstein refers to the false 9/11 conspiracy theory, he is actually referring to the government's theory. If we apply this interpretation to Sunstein's fourth thesis, according to which people can accept the 9/11 conspiracy theory only if they have a "crippled epistemology" in the sense of "a sharply limited number of (relevant) informational sources," then it suddenly makes perfect sense: It fits what we know of the official reports about 9/11, such as *The 9/11 Commission Report* and NIST's reports on the Twin Towers and WTC 7.

The 9/11 Commission Report

With regard to the 9/11 Commission, Professor Bill Willers says: "[T]here has rarely been a 'theory' more resistant to opposing information—more absolutely and officially 'self-sealing'—than the mockery that is the official 9/11 Commission Report." Referring to restrictions on informational sources available to it, Willers points out that Philip Zelikow, who was appointed to the position of executive director, "became the primary instrument in the prevention of information flow to the Commission."[178]

The fact that Zelikow did this was revealed most fully in a 2008 book entitled *The Commission: The Uncensored History of the 9/11 Investigation*, by former *New York Times* reporter Philip Shenon, who had been assigned by the paper to cover the 9/11 Commission. Shenon revealed, for example, that even before his staff had begun its research, Zelikow had already written a detailed outline of what would become the Commission's final report, "complete with 'chapter headings, subheadings, and sub-subheadings,'" and that Zelikow then conspired with the Commission's co-chairs, Thomas Kean and Lee Hamilton, to keep the existence of this outline a secret from the staff, lest they think that Zelikow "had determined the report's outcome."[179] Shenon also revealed that Zelikow did everything he could to prevent direct contact between the researchers and the commissioners:

> Zelikow's micromanagement meant that the staff had little, if any, contact with the ten commissioners; all information was funneled through Zelikow, and he decided how it would be shared elsewhere.[180]

Zelikow even, Shenon revealed, "controlled what the final report would say."[181] Although the first draft of each chapter was written by one of the investigative teams, "Zelikow rewrote virtually everything that was handed to him—usually top to bottom."[182]

Shenon's book was published in 2008, the same year that the draft version of Sunstein's article was posted on the internet, so it is likely that he had not seen Shenon's book. But the ways in which Zelikow had controlled the Commission had leaked out. In my 2005 book on the 9/11 Commission, for example, I quoted a disgruntled member of the staff as saying: "Zelikow is calling the shots. He's skewing the investigation and running it his own way."[183] I also cited an author who had himself offered to testify to the Commission's staff and thereby gained "some first-hand experience with the way Zelikow exercised his control over the investigation," as he found that "most of the points he had made to [the staff person who interviewed him] were either omitted, distorted, or disputed in the final report."[184] I treated, moreover, the experience of the highly credible Sibel Edmonds (the former FBI translator whose later testimony to London's *Sunday Times* was mentioned above), who reported that, although she had been interviewed by the Commission for over three hours, during which she revealed many potentially explosive things, she found that the Commission's report mentioned not a single one of them.[185]

In 2005, moreover, Harvard historian Ernest May—who had earlier been Zelikow's professor and who had helped him write the advance outline for the Commission's final report—published "a memoir of the 9/11 Commission" in the *New Republic*, in which he revealed how the drafts of the chapters were written: Although various members of the Commission's staff wrote the first drafts, revised drafts were then produced by the "front office," which was headed by Zelikow.[186]

In any case, whatever be the full explanation for this result, *The 9/11 Commission Report* did, in fact, reflect a "crippled epistemology," in the sense of "a sharply limited number of (relevant) informational sources." The basis for the limitation can be stated simply: The Commission was open only to "informational sources" that would confirm the premise with which the Commission, under Zelikow's leadership, began its work: that the 9/11 attacks were planned and carried out entirely by al-Qaeda.

That the Commission began with this premise is not simply an inference: Kean and Hamilton themselves state it. In their 2006 book providing the "inside story" on the 9/11 Commission, they said that, unlike "conspiracy theorists," they did not start with a conclusion and then gather evidence to support it. Instead, they claimed:

> We were not setting out to advocate one theory or interpretation of 9/11 versus another. Our purpose was to fulfill our statutory mandate, gathering and presenting all of the available and relevant information.[187]

In that same book, however, they say that, having accepted Zelikow's view that the Commission would do its work by means of "a staff organized around subjects of inquiry,"[188] they "assigned the subject of 'al-Qaeda' to staff team 1," then told team 1A to "tell the story of al-Qaeda's most successful operation—the 9/11 attacks."[189] If that is not starting with a theory—indeed, with a *conclusion*—what would be?

In any case, the 9/11 Commission adhered rigorously to this theory, or conclusion, filtering out all information that did not fit. One can see this by comparing the Commission's report with my first 9/11 book, *The New Pearl Harbor*, which contained literally dozens of facts and reports that contradicted the official account of 9/11. This book appeared early in 2004, about five months before *The 9/11 Commission Report* was completed, and the Commission had multiple copies of it (as I learned from a number of sources). And yet the Commission's report simply ignored virtually all of these facts and reports, while distorting the remainder. This systematic exclusion of all information that contradicted the official story is reflected in the title of my critique, *The 9/11 Commission Report: Omissions and Distortions*.

In their book giving "the inside story of the 9/11 Commission," moreover, Kean and Hamilton pointed out the basis for this systematic exclusion. In writing their preface to *The 9/11 Commission Report* in 2004, they had said that their mandate was to investigate "facts and circumstances relating to the terrorist attacks of September 11, 2001," in order "to provide the fullest possible account of the events surrounding 9/11."[190] But in their 2006 "inside story" book, they provided a significantly modified account of the Commission's mandate. Saying that they had the task of "gathering and presenting all of the available and relevant information *within the areas specified by our mandate*,"[191] they described the mandate thus:

> The law creating the 9/11 Commission allowed for us "to ascertain,
> evaluate, and report on the evidence developed by all relevant
> governmental agencies regarding the facts and circumstances
> surrounding the attacks."[192]

So they were *not*, as they had suggested in the preface to *The 9/11 Commission Report*, to provide *all of the 9/11-related evidence* they might discover, in order "to provide the fullest possible account of the events surrounding 9/11." They were "allowed . . . to . . . report on [only] the evidence developed by . . . governmental agencies." And no governmental agency during the Bush–Cheney administration would have knowingly provided information contradicting that administration's conspiracy theory, according to which the 9/11 attacks were orchestrated by al-Qaeda.

Accordingly, if to have "a sharply limited number of (relevant) informational sources" is to have a "crippled epistemology," then the 9/11 Commission's epistemology was about as crippled as it could possibly have been. To summarize:

—The outline for the Commission's report, "complete with 'chapter headings, subheadings, and sub-subheadings,'" had been written in advance.

—The Commission could only use evidence that had been supplied by governmental agencies.

—The Commission was open only to evidence that was consistent with its unquestioned premise that the 9/11 attacks had been "al-Qaeda's most successful operation."

—If any evidence came to the Commission that did not fit this premise—such as testimony from former FBI translator Sibel Edmonds or evidence contained in my *New Pearl Harbor*—Philip Zelikow as executive director would make sure that it did not find its way into the final report.

—Most of this information was available in the public realm, even before the publication of Shenon's book. So whether or not Sunstein knew all the details, he would surely have known enough to be aware that the sources of information that were allowed to contribute to the 9/11 Commission's report had been severely restricted, so that the government's al-Qaeda conspiracy theory, insofar as it was purveyed by the 9/11 Commission, was based on an extremely crippled epistemology.

NIST

The epistemology of NIST (the National Institute of Standards and Technology), which put out the official reports on the destruction of the World Trade Center, was no less crippled. Besides surely knowing this himself, Sunstein could have presupposed that his well-informed readers would also know it.

For example, in the chapter on NIST's report on the Twin Towers in my 2007 book, *Debunking 9/11 Debunking*, I cited the case of William Rodriguez, the janitor who reported having experienced a huge explosion in the basement of the North Tower about 90 minutes before this building came down. Assuming at the time that NIST was a truth-seeking body, he was anxious to report his experience to its staff. However, he reported:

> I contacted NIST . . . four times without a response. Finally, [at a public hearing] I asked them before they came up with their conclusion . . . if they ever considered my statements or the statements of any of the other survivors who heard the explosions. They just stared at me with blank faces.[193]

Also, the long list of "other survivors who heard the explosions" included over 100 members of the Fire Department of New York. The testimonies of these men and women, which had been recorded shortly after 9/11, were made available to NIST (before they were made publicly available on a *New York Times* website in August 2005[194]), which made use of them.[195] But NIST made no mention of the numerous, often dramatic, reports of explosions contained in these testimonies. Nor did NIST invite any of the members of the FDNY to testify about explosions.

However, as I reported in my 2008 book, *The New Pearl Harbor Revisited*, two city officials did tell NIST about being trapped for 90 minutes or so by a huge explosion in WTC 7, which evidently occurred at about 9:30AM, long before either of the Twin Towers had collapsed. These officials were Michael Hess, New York City's corporation counsel, and Barry Jennings, Deputy Director of Emergency Services for the New York City Housing Authority. NIST handled their testimonies by changing the timeline to make it appear that the event they reported as a huge explosion was simply the impact of debris from the collapse of the North Tower (which occurred at 10:28).[196]

NIST was also not open to sources providing scientific evidence that incendiaries and explosives had been used to bring the buildings down. When some scientists asked whether the steel from the collapsed buildings had been "tested for explosives or thermite residues," NIST replied: "NIST did not test for the residue of [thermite or other explosives] in the steel."[197] In January 2008, reporter Jennifer Abel of the *Hartford Advocate* related a conversation she had had with Michael Newman, a NIST spokesman. Abel asked: "[W]hat about that letter where NIST said it didn't look for evidence of explosives?" Newman replied: "Right, because there was no evidence of that." Puzzled, Abel asked: "But how can you know there's no evidence if you don't look for it first?" Newman responded: "If you're looking for something that isn't there, you're wasting your time . . . and the taxpayers' money."[198]

Assuming that Sunstein's research for writing his paper made him aware of some of this information, he would have known that the epistemologies of NIST were about as crippled as possible. By being aware of some of the evidence that they had ignored, moreover, he would have known that they were able to endorse, and then become purveyors of, the false 9/11 conspiracy theory only by excluding an enormous amount of relevant informational sources.

In terms of the hidden meaning of Sunstein's essay suggested above, moreover, we could understand quite differently than we did above his explanation that people who accept false conspiracy theories "typically do so not as a result of a mental illness . . . or of simple irrationality," but as a result of a "crippled epistemology." Although when understood exoterically, this statement seemed condescending and even arrogant, it is quite realistic if we see Sunstein as explaining why people accept the false 9/11 theory, according to which the attacks were orchestrated by al-Qaeda.

Sunstein's sociological explanation, as we saw, is that when people have crippled epistemologies, this is typically because they exist in "self-enclosed networks" leaving them in "informational isolation."

Being aware that the mainstream press has supported the false 9/11 conspiracy theory, Sunstein's hidden meaning would be that the people who live in self-enclosed networks, thereby suffering from informational isolation, are those people—a good portion of the American population—who rely entirely on the mainstream press for their information. Not looking for alternative informational sources on the internet, they are entirely unaware of the enormous amount of evidence refuting this theory that has been provided by credible architects, engineers, firefighters, intelligence officers, lawyers, pilots, scientists, and veterans.

It is here that we can see the value of Sunstein's alternative description of epistemological cripples, saying (in my revised wording): *In some domains, people suffer from a "crippled epistemology," in the sense that they know very few things, and what little they think they know is wrong.* Reading this at the esoteric level, we can see it as a hint that we should apply this description to Sunstein's own statement in which he affirmed the conventional wisdom that "Al-Qaeda was responsible for 9/11." Understood in terms of the esoteric level of meaning suggested here, Sunstein would be saying: *Most people do not know much about 9/11, and what little they think they know— namely, that Al-Qaeda was responsible for 9/11—is wrong.*

That this may indeed be part of the hidden meaning of Sunstein's article will be supported by still more evidence in the latter part of the next chapter.

CHAPTER 5
THE 9/11 CONSPIRACY THEORY AS DEMONSTRABLY FALSE

In his fifth thesis, Sunstein makes the following threefold claim:

The 9/11 conspiracy theory is "demonstrably false"; it is also "unjustified," being based on evidence that is "weak or even nonexistent"; and it has led to a "degenerating research program."[199]

Actually, what is demonstrably false as well as unjustified is this thesis itself—when evaluated at the exoteric level, with which we begin.

1. Demonstrably False?

The first part of this thesis—that the position of the 9/11 Truth Movement is demonstrably false—can be dismissed quickly, for three reasons.

First, Sunstein gives absolutely no evidence for this claim. As a lawyer, he surely knows that he cannot expect people to accept his claims unless he gives some evidence for them. If the theory in question *has* been demonstrated, or at least *could* be demonstrated, to be false, one would assume that Sunstein would inform readers of some of the evidence that would provide this demonstration, or at least tell them where they can find it.

Second, if the theory in question were indeed demonstrably false, one would not expect it to be accepted by growing numbers of professional people—such as architects, engineers, firefighters, intelligence officers, journalists, medical professionals, pilots, political leaders, religious leaders, scientists, and veterans—but it is, as we saw in the previous chapter.

Third, if the 9/11 Truth Movement's theory were indeed demonstrably false, we would expect that, insofar as there are conversions from one 9/11 conspiracy theory to the other, the conversions would be primarily from the 9/11 Truth Movement's theory to the official theory. But the conversions go almost entirely in the opposite direction. These conversions, moreover, are almost always irreversible: Every year, we learn of more people who have been converted from the official to the alternative theory. But we seldom hear of people who, after having accepted the views of the 9/11 Truth Movement, have switched back to the official theory. (The only exceptions seem to be cases in which people came to see their expressions of support for the 9/11 Truth Movement as posing threats to their careers.[200])

2. Unjustified Because Devoid of Evidence?

The "theory" of the 9/11 Truth Movement, at the most fundamental level, is that the official story, according to which the attacks were planned and carried out by al-Qaeda terrorists, is false, and that the falsity of this story implies that 9/11 was, at least partly, an inside job. Contrary to Sunstein's claim that the evidence for this position is weak or nonexistent, it is extremely strong. It points, moreover, to the falsity of virtually every aspect of the official story.

Evidence Against the Al-Qaeda Conspiracy Theory
I begin with evidence against the idea that the attacks were carried out by members of al-Qaeda under the inspiration of Osama bin Laden.

No Hard Evidence for Bin Laden's Responsibility: At the foundation of the official account of 9/11 is the claim that Osama bin Laden ordered the attacks. As Edward Haas of the Muckraker Report learned, however, the FBI does not list 9/11 as one of the terrorist acts for which he is wanted.[201] The reason, Haas was told in 2006 by the FBI's head of investigative publicity, Rex Tomb, was that "the FBI has no hard evidence connecting Bin Laden to 9/11."[202]

When Todd Leventhal, head of the US State Department's "counter-misinformation" office, was asked about this fact, he tried to dismiss it as of no significance, saying:

> The FBI poster says he [Osama bin Laden] is wanted for the August 7, 1988 bombings of the U.S. embassies in Tanzania and

Kenya, for which he was formally indicted. But he has not yet been formally charged with the September 11 attacks in a U.S. court of law, so he is not wanted for this reason. This was explained by an FBI spokesman and others knowledgeable about such matters in an August 28, 2006 article in The Washington Post.[203]

The question, however, is *why* bin Laden "has not yet been formally charged with the September 11 attacks." This question was not answered, in spite of Leventhal's suggestion to the contrary, in the *Washington Post* article to which Leventhal referred, which was by Dan Eggen. After pointing out the absence of any reference to 9/11 among the terrorist acts for which the FBI wants bin Laden, Eggen wrote:

> The absence has . . . provided fodder for conspiracy theorists who think the U.S. government or another power was behind the Sept. 11 hijackings. From this point of view, the lack of a Sept. 11 reference suggests that the connection to al-Qaeda is uncertain. . . . FBI officials say the wanted poster merely reflects the government's long-standing practice of relying on actual criminal charges in the notices.[204]

Like Leventhal, hence, Eggen simply reported that "actual criminal charges" had not been filed; he did not explain why not.

Further seeking to justify the fact that the FBI's "most wanted" pages on bin Laden do not list him as wanted for 9/11, Eggen quoted David N. Kelley, a former US attorney in New York, as saying:

> It might seem a little strange from the outside, but it makes sense from a legal point of view. . . . If I were in government, I'd be troubled if I were asked to put up a wanted picture where no formal charges had been filed, no matter who it was.[205]

It is certainly true that the FBI could not list bin Laden as wanted for a crime if he has not been formally charged with that crime. The question at hand, however, is why "no formal charges had been filed." Eggen, Kelley, and Leventhal all dodged this question.

This question had been clearly answered, however, by Rex Tomb, who said in response to Haas's question:

Bin Laden has not been formally charged in connection to 9/11. . . .
The FBI gathers evidence. Once evidence is gathered, it is turned
over to the Department of Justice. The Department of Justice then
decides whether it has enough evidence to present to a federal
grand jury. In the case of the 1998 United States Embassies being
bombed, Bin Laden has been formally indicted and charged by a
grand jury. He has not been formally indicted and charged in
connection with 9/11 because the FBI has no hard evidence
connecting Bin Laden to 9/11.[206]

The answer could not be clearer: The Department of Justice did not
indict bin Laden for 9/11 because the FBI did not provide it with any
hard evidence of bin Laden's responsibility for the 9/11 attacks. If Todd
Leventhal were a truthful public servant, he would have pointed out
that it was Tomb, rather than Eggen, who had answered the question.
It would appear, however, that Leventhal is a propagandist.

This appearance is confirmed in an article by him entitled "Al
Qaida Confirms It Carried Out the September 11 Attacks." Beginning
with two standard claims of the Bush–Cheney conspiracy theory,
Leventhal wrote: "Both Osama bin Laden and Khalid Sheikh
Mohammed, the mastermind of the September 11 attacks, have
confirmed that al Qaida planned and carried out the September 11
attacks."

Leventhal sought to buttress the bin Laden part of this claim by
referring to several audio- and videotapes, in which bin Laden
supposedly confessed. In doing so, however, Leventhal simply
presupposed the truth of a disputed assumption, namely, that these
"Osama bin Laden confession tapes" are authentic. Leventhal, for
example, wrote:

> The first direct indication of al Qaida involvement came in a video-
> tape of bin Laden talking to a group of supporters in November
> 2001, which was obtained by U.S. forces in Afghanistan in late
> November and released on December 13, 2001. Independent schol-
> ars gave [sic] verified that the translation released by the U.S.
> government is accurate.[207]

Leventhal failed to mention the fact that many other independent
researchers have declared this video a fake (an issue that was raised
in the press at the time of the video's release[208]). For example, when

Professor Bruce Lawrence of Duke University, widely considered America's leading academic bin Laden expert,[209] was asked about this tape, he said, "It's bogus," adding that friends of his in the Department of Homeland Security "also know it's bogus."[210] There were at least five reasons why Lawrence and others made this judgment.

First, bin Laden had previously denied his involvement in the 9/11 attacks many times.[211] Second, although the US military claimed that it had found the tape in a house in Jalalabad, Afghanistan, it provided no evidence to support this claim.[212] Third, although this tape was supposedly made on November 9,[213] its bin Laden figure is obviously much healthier than bin Laden was when he made a tape on November 3 and also when he made one sometime between November 16 (the date of the US bombing of the mosque at Khost, which is mentioned by bin Laden in the video) and December 27 (the date on which the video was released by the US government)—at which time he had a white beard and a "gaunt, frail appearance," according to London's *Telegraph*, and seemed to be suffering from kidney disease and a stroke, according to Dr. Sanjay Gupta.[214] Fourth, some of the physical features of the man in the video are different from those of the Osama bin Laden of undoubtedly authentic videos.[215]

The fifth reason for considering this video a fake is that the man in the video said several things that the real bin Laden, even if he had planned the 9/11 attacks, would not have said. Talking about the fact that the Twin Towers collapsed totally, for example, the tape's bin Laden figure said that he was "thinking that the fire from the gas in the plane would melt the iron structure of the building and collapse the area where the plane hit and all the floors above it only."[216] Being an engineer, the real bin Laden would have known that iron (or steel) does not melt until it reaches about 2,800 degrees Fahrenheit, which is a thousand degrees higher than the fires—as diffuse, hydrocarbon fires—could have possibly reached.[217]

Another video in which bin Laden confessed to the 9/11 attacks, according to Leventhal, appeared on October 30, 2004.[218] But Leventhal simply ignored the fact that many features of this video suggest that it was a fake. Although he pointed out that it appeared on October 30, he failed to mention the significance of this date: that it was just a few days before the 2004 presidential election, in which voters would choose between George W. Bush and John Kerry. Other relevant but unmentioned points are that CIA officials said that the tape seemed intended to help Bush, and that both Bush and Kerry later said that it did, in fact, help Bush win.[219] Leventhal also did not mention that, whereas bin Laden's talks normally employed religious language heavily and portrayed historical events as divinely ordained, this one was very different, employing few religious terms and providing a purely secular analysis of historical developments.[220] Leventhal also failed to point out, finally, that although this talk was addressed to the American people, the person in this video spoke in Arabic—even though the real bin Laden could speak English impeccably.[221]

It is not only Bruce Lawrence and members of the 9/11 Truth Movement, moreover, who consider these tapes inauthentic. The same judgment has been made by former CIA operative Robert Baer,[222] and also by former Foreign Service officer Angelo Codevilla, who is now a professor of international relations at Boston University and a senior editor of the *American Spectator*.[223]

In any case, the remainder of Leventhal's article consists of excerpts from *The 9/11 Commission Report*, which, he claimed, "confirms that al Qaida planned and executed the attacks." The Commission's "reconstruction of events," Leventhal pointed out, was "based largely on information provided by [alleged] September 11 planners Khalid Sheikh Mohammed (KSM), Ramzi Binalshibh, and others."[224]

Leventhal did *not* point out, however, that this "information" was provided to the Commission by the CIA and that, because of the CIA's stance, Thomas Kean and Lee Hamilton—the chair and vice chair, respectively, of the 9/11 Commission—called it untrustworthy. On page 146 of *The 9/11 Commission Report*—the second page of Chapter 5—they inserted a box stating:

> Chapters 5 and 7 rely heavily on information obtained from captured al Qaeda members. . . . Assessing the truth of statements by these witnesses . . . is challenging. Our access to them has been limited to the review of intelligence reports based on communications from the locations where the actual interrogations take place. . . . [W]e [were not] allowed to talk to the interrogators so that we could better judge the credibility of the detainees and clarify the ambiguities in the reporting. We were told that our requests might disrupt the sensitive interrogation process.[225]

Having not reported this caveat, Leventhal certainly did not report Kean and Hamilton's even stronger statements in 2006 and 2008.

In their 2006 book *Without Precedent*, subtitled *The Inside Story of the 9/11 Commission*, Kean and Hamilton complained that, besides having no success in "obtaining access to star witnesses in custody . . . , most notably Khalid Sheikh Mohammed," they also were not permitted to observe his interrogation through one-way glass or even to talk to the interrogators.[226] Therefore, Kean and Hamilton wrote:

> "We . . . had no way of evaluating the credibility of detainee information. How could we tell if someone such as Khalid Sheikh Mohammed . . . was telling us the truth?"[227]

The obvious answer, of course, was that they could not.

In 2008, after it had been revealed that the CIA had destroyed videotapes of its interviews of al-Qaeda detainees—the very interviews about which the 9/11 Commission had sought to get information—Kean and Hamilton wrote a *New York Times* Op-Ed piece charging the CIA with obstruction. Besides reporting the CIA's refusal to allow them access to the al-Qaeda detainees, which led to their "caveats on page 146 in the commission report," they wrote: "The agency did not disclose that any interrogations had ever been recorded," even though the 9/11 Commission "did ask, repeatedly, for the kind of information that would have been contained in such videotapes. . . . We call that obstruction."[228]

So, in addition to saying in 2006 that they "had no way of evaluating the credibility of [the information reportedly supplied by al-Qaeda detainees] such as Khalid Sheikh Mohammed," Kean and Hamilton stated in 2008 that the CIA was guilty of obstruction for refusing to turn over, or even to acknowledge the existence of, videotapes of the interrogations—videotapes that gave the lie to the CIA's claim that for it to fulfill the 9/11 Commission's request to observe the interrogations "might disrupt the sensitive interrogation process."

As for the real reason for the CIA's refusal to allow these videotapes to be viewed by people outside the agency, there have been various speculations. One is that it was to conceal the fact that torture had been employed to obtain the information. But another suggested explanation is that it was to conceal the fact that these men did not really make all of the statements attributed to them, which would mean that the CIA had simply made up some of the claims that it attributed to al-Qaeda detainees such as Khalid Sheikh Mohammed. Given the information currently available, we cannot, of course, say that this was the real reason. But we also cannot say that it was not.

In any case, Kean and Hamilton have themselves made abundantly clear that the narrative about Osama bin Laden in *The 9/11 Commission Report* is not trustworthy. But Todd Leventhal, providing propaganda for the US State Department in 2009, wrote as if this issue had never been raised.

Alleged Hijackers Not Devout Muslims: The official story holds that the four airliners were hijacked by devout Muslims ready to die as martyrs to earn a heavenly reward. "Ringleader" Mohamed Atta, in particular, was said by the 9/11 Commission to have become very religious, even "fanatically so."[229] But numerous reports indicated otherwise. The *San Francisco Chronicle*, for example, reported that Atta and other hijackers had made "at least six trips" to Las Vegas, where they had "engaged in some decidedly un-Islamic sampling of prohibited pleasures."[230] Even in the days immediately before 9/11, when young Muslim men planning for martyrdom would presumably have been preparing themselves for their heavenly reward, Atta and others were reported to be drinking heavily, cavorting with lap dancers, and bringing call girls to their rooms.[231] This incongruous behavior was even noted in a *Wall Street Journal* editorial with an ironic title, "Terrorist Stag Parties."[232]

Alleged Hijackers Not on Passenger Manifests: Besides not being devout Muslims, the "hijackers" were evidently not even on the airliners. One basis for this conclusion is the set of passenger manifests for the four flights. A passenger manifest lists all the passengers on a flight, so if the alleged hijackers had purchased tickets and boarded the flights, as the official story has it, their names would have been on the manifests. But the four flight manifests released by the airlines after 9/11 have none of their names, not even any Middle Eastern names.[233]

No Arab Names on Flight 77 Autopsy List: Having noted that there were no Middle Eastern names on the flight manifests, Dr. Thomas Olmsted—a psychiatrist and former naval officer—sent a FOIA request to the Armed Forces Institute of Pathology to obtain the autopsy list for American Flight 77. Fourteen months later, he reported in June 2003, he finally received the list. What he discovered was indicated by the title of his report: "Still No Arabs on Flight 77."[234]

No Pilot Squawked the Hijack Code: Perhaps the strongest evidence against hijackers is provided by a feature of the reported events that contradicts the claim that hijackers broke into the pilots' cabins. If pilots suspect that an attempted hijacking is in progress, they are to enter the standard hijack code (7500) into their transponders, thereby alerting FAA flight controllers on the ground. This task takes only two to three seconds, so there would have been plenty of time for at least one of the pilots in each cockpit to do this. According to the official report of Flight 93, for example, it took 30 seconds for the hijackers to break into its cockpit.[235] And yet neither pilot entered the hijack code into the transponder. What stronger evidence could there be that there were no hijackers breaking into cockpits?

Alleged Hijackers Show Up Alive: Further evidence that the men accused of hijacking the planes did not do so is supplied by the fact that some of them, such as Waleed al-Shehri, said to have been one of the men who hijacked American Flight 11, later showed up alive. About two weeks after 9/11, the BBC reported that "the same Mr. Al-Shehri [as the one named a hijacker by the FBI] has turned up in Morocco, proving clearly that he was not a member of the suicide attack."[236] Defenders of the official story, including the BBC itself five years later, tried to debunk this story as a mere case of mistaken identity, claiming that al-Shehri's photograph had not been released at the time he spoke to the press.[237] But that was not true, as shown by the original BBC story and additional facts.[238] Several more of the 19 men also pointed out the inconvenient fact that they were still alive.[239]

Planted Evidence: However, one might well ask, if there were no hijackers on the flights, how do we explain the evidence that there *were?* The answer: By providing good reasons to believe that it was planted or otherwise fabricated. I will illustrate such reasons in terms of four types of alleged evidence for Muslim hijackers on the planes: Reported cell phone calls from the airliners; the reported phone calls from Barbara Olson; the passports reportedly found at the crash sites; and a headband reportedly found at one of these sites.

Reported Cell Phone Calls from the Airliners: For most people, the main evidence that the planes had been taken over by Muslim hijackers was provided by reported phone calls from the planes, with cell phone calls playing an especially important role. Shortly after the attacks, for example, a *Washington Post* story, referring to United Flight 93, said:

> The plane was at once a lonesome vessel, the people aboard facing their singular fate, and yet somehow already attached to the larger drama, connected again by cell phones.[240]

Another story in the *Post* said:

> [P]assenger Jeremy Glick used a cell phone to tell his wife, Lyzbeth, . . . that the Boeing 757's cockpit had been taken over by three Middle Eastern-looking men. . . . Glick's cell phone call from Flight 93 and others like it provide the most dramatic accounts so far of events aboard the four hijacked aircraft.[241]

According to a story about a "cellular phone conversation" between flight attendant Sandra Bradshaw and her husband:

> She said the plane had been taken over by three men with knives. She had gotten a close look at one of the hijackers. . . . "He had an Islamic look," she told her husband.[242]

About fifteen of the reported phone calls from the planes were believed to have been made on cell phones. This information came from the recipients, who gave reasons to believe that the callers had used cell phones. The strongest evidence was provided by Deena Burnett, who told the FBI, according to its report, that she had received "a series of three to five cellular phone calls from her husband."[243] She was certain that her husband had used his cell phone, she said, because she had recognized his number on her phone's Caller ID.[244] But these calls were reportedly made when the planes were above 30,000 feet, and cell phone calls from airliners at such altitudes—as pilots and scientists pointed out—were impossible in 2001, given the cell phone technology available at the time.[245] It would appear, therefore, that the reported calls from Tom Burnett, along with all of the other reported high-altitude cell phone calls, had somehow been faked.

Reported Phone Calls from Barbara Olson: The most important of all the reported phone calls were those attributed to Barbara Olson, the wife of US Solicitor General Theodore "Ted" Olson and a well-known commentator on CNN. On 9/11, Ted Olson told CNN and the FBI that his wife had called him from American Flight 77, the airliner that supposedly struck the Pentagon. She had called him twice, he said, reporting that "all passengers and flight personnel, including the pilots, were herded to the back of the plane" by hijackers, who were armed with "knives and cardboard cutters."[246]

One problem with this story was that it would require us to believe that a few rather small men—"The so-called muscle hijackers," the 9/11 Commission pointed out, "were not physically imposing, as the majority of them were between 5'5" and 5'7" in height and slender in build"[247])—armed only with knives and boxcutters, could have held off sixty-some passengers and crew members, who included pilot Charles "Chic" Burlingame, a former navy pilot who was a weightlifter and a boxer.[248]

A second problem involved the type of phone used by Barbara Olson. Ted Olson himself expressed uncertainty: He told the FBI, according to its report, that he did not know "if the calls were made from her cell phone or the telephone on the plane";[249] and in his public statements, he sometimes suggested that she had used a cell phone,[250] while at other times he said she must have used an onboard phone.[251]

Both positions, however, were impossible. On the one hand, the plane would have been too high for cell phone calls, because her first call, according to the 9/11 Commission, occurred "between 9:16 and 9:26AM," at which time Flight 77, the official report says, would have been somewhere between 25,000 and 14,000 feet.[252] Unsurprisingly, therefore, a 2004 FBI report ruled out the cell phone option, saying: "All of the calls from Flight 77 were made via the onboard airphone system."[253] On the other hand, American Airlines' Boeing 757s did not have onboard phones. This information, which was provided by an American Airlines representative in 2004, was confirmed in 2006 by another AA representative, who said: "[W]e do not have phones on our Boeing 757. The passengers on flight 77 used their own personal cellular phones to make out calls during the terrorist attack."[254]

It would appear, therefore, that there was no way in which Barbara Olson could have called her husband from American Flight 77, so his report must have been untrue—a conclusion that, we will see below, the FBI came to support.

Passports at the Crash Sites: Another purported proof that the nineteen Muslim men identified as the hijackers were on the planes was provided by passports reportedly found at the crash sites. But these passports were almost definitely planted, as two examples will illustrate. One of them involved the passport of Satam al-Suqami, said to have been a hijacker on American Flight 11, which crashed into the North Tower.[255] The FBI claimed that his passport was found on the street later in the day. But for this to be true, the passport would have had to survive the collapse of the North Tower, which for some reason pulverized almost everything in the building except its steel into fine particles of dust. This story did not pass the giggle test: "[T]he idea that [this] passport had escaped from that inferno unsinged," remarked a British commentator, "would [test] the credulity of the staunchest supporter of the FBI's crackdown on terrorism."[256]

A second example involved the passport of Ziad Jarrah, the alleged pilot of United Flight 93, which supposedly crashed in Pennsylvania.[257] Jarrah's passport was reportedly found on the ground at the crash site, even though there was virtually nothing else at the site to indicate that an airliner had crashed there.[258] The reason for this absence of wreckage, we were told, was that the plane had been headed downward at 580 miles per hour and, when it hit the spongy Pennsylvania soil, it buried itself entirely in the ground—"as if a marble had been dropped into water," a *New York Times* writer explained.[259] Besides being asked to swallow that, we are supposed to imagine that, just before the plane buried itself in the ground, Jarrah's passport escaped from his pocket or luggage and the cockpit, just in time to fall to the ground where it could be discovered.[260]

A Red Headband at the Site: The FBI also reportedly found a red headband at the Pennsylvania crash site. This was significant because some of the reported phone calls from the planes described the hijackers as wearing red headbands. According to Jeremy Glick's wife, for example, he reported that "the Boeing 757's cockpit had been taken over by three Middle Eastern-looking men. . . wearing red headbands.[261] But former CIA agent Milt Bearden, who had helped train the Mujahideen fighters in Afghanistan, pointed out that, whereas al-Qaeda is a Sunni organization, the red headband is a uniquely Shi'a adornment.[262] Many of us remember that, shortly after the invasion of Iraq, some leading figures of the Bush administration were unaware of the difference between Shi'a and Sunni Muslims. Did one of those people decide that the hijackers would be described as wearing red headbands?

Hani Hanjour as Pilot of American Flight 77: The claim that the planes were taken over and flown by Muslim hijackers is further disproved by the absurdity of the claim that Hani Hanjour took control of American Flight 77 and flew it into the Pentagon. Hanjour was known to be a terrible pilot. According to a *New York Times* story entitled "A Trainee Noted for Incompetence," one of Hanjour's instructors said: "He could not fly at all."[263] A couple of months before 9/11, moreover, a flight instructor, who had gone up with him once in a single-engine plane, refused to do it again, considering it too dangerous.[264]

According to the official story, nevertheless, Hanjour was able, the first time he had flown a giant airliner, to do so with almost super-human skill. The day after the attacks, before Hanjour had been identified as the pilot of the plane that approached the Pentagon, a *Washington Post* story said: "[T]he unidentified pilot executed a pivot so tight that it reminded observers of a fighter jet maneuver."[265] This trajectory would have been so difficult for a Boeing 757 that pilots with years of experience flying these planes have said they could not have done it. "The idea that an *unskilled* pilot could have flown this trajectory," said one of them, "is simply too ridiculous to consider."[266]

The Choice of Wedge 1 to Target: Even if Hanjour, or some other al-Qaeda operative, *could* have executed that maneuver, moreover, there is every reason to believe that he would not have done so. This maneuver was necessary only because the target was the side of Wedge 1, but this would have been about the least desirable target for al-Qaeda operatives. They surely would have wanted to kill Secretary of Defense Donald Rumsfeld and the Pentagon's top brass, who were on the opposite side of the Pentagon; al-Qaeda operatives would have wanted to cause as much death and destruction as possible, but Wedge 1, and it alone, had been renovated to make it less vulnerable to attack; and the renovation was not quite complete, so this area was only sparsely occupied. Al-Qaeda masterminds, being brilliant enough to outfox the most sophisticated defense system in history, would have known that they could cause far more destruction and kill far more people—including the most important ones—simply by having the plane hit a much easier target: the roof above the offices of the Pentagon's top officials.[267]

Secret Service Failure to Hustle Bush to Safety: Further evidence that the airliners were not under the control of al-Qaeda pilots, or any foreign terrorists for that matter, was provided by the behavior of the Secret Service detail with President Bush while he was at a school in Sarasota, Florida. Upon being told after his arrival about the first plane hitting the World Trade Center, Bush dismissed it as an accident.[268] But after word was received about the second plane, it would have been obvious that "America [was] under attack"—which is reportedly what Bush's chief of staff whispered in his ear.[269] And yet Bush's Secret Service detail allowed him to remain at the school for another 30 minutes, thereby making him—along with everyone else at the school, including the Secret Service agents themselves—an easy target for another hijacked airliner planning to strike a high-value target. Had the Secret Service thought Bush was in any danger, they would have followed their standard protocol in such situations, which, as the *St. Petersburg Times* put it, was to "hustle Bush to a secure location."[270]

Evidence for a Military Stand-Down
Although the official 9/11 conspiracy theory says that the airliners were able to hit their targets because of mistakes made by FAA and military personnel (for which no one was ever punished or even publicly reprimanded), the alternative theory holds that there was a plan within the US military to prevent the airliners from being intercepted.

Standard Operating Procedures: According to the best-supported version of this theory, there was a stand-down order, canceling standard operating procedures. This view is based on the fact that the FAA and the military have worked out such procedures, according to which any airplane in the United States showing signs of an in-flight emergency is normally intercepted within about 10 minutes, combined with the fact that, on the morning of 9/11, this did not happen.

The official account of 9/11 maintains that the system simply failed in relation to all four planes. For example, the FAA knew by 8:21 that American Flight 11 was not responding to radio messages and had gone radically off course, and yet 25 minutes later, when this airliner slammed into the North Tower, military interceptor jets had not even taken off. Another example: The FAA notified the military at 9:24 that American Flight 77 had turned around and was headed back toward Washington, and yet when it struck the Pentagon 14 minutes later, no interceptor jets were anywhere near. Given the speed with which fighters on alert normally intercept troubled aircraft, the failures on 9/11 are understandable only on the assumption that those standard procedures were suspended.[271]

LAX Security Heard Discussing Stand-Down Order: The deduction that there must have been a stand-down has been supported by testimony from Charles E. Lewis, who had worked on security systems at Los Angeles International Airport (LAX) prior to 9/11. Having rushed back to the airport that morning in case his expertise was needed, he listened to very upset LAX security officers getting information about the attacks on their walkie-talkies. At first, they were upset because they heard that the attacks had succeeded due to FAA failure to notify the military. They soon became even more upset upon learning that the military *had* been informed but had not responded, because it had been "ordered to stand down." Asking who had issued this order, they were told that it had come "from the highest level of the White House."[272] With President Bush down in Florida, that would have meant Vice-President Dick Cheney.

Cheney's Confirmation of a Stand-Down Order: That Cheney had, in fact, issued a stand-down order was inadvertently reported by Secretary of Transportation Norman Mineta during his testimony to the 9/11 Commission. Speaking of an exchange he had witnessed in the bunker under the White House—officially known as the Presidential Emergency Operations Center, or PEOC—where Vice-President Cheney was in charge, Mineta said:

> During the time that the airplane was coming in to the Pentagon, there was a young man who would come in and say to the Vice President, "The plane is 50 miles out." "The plane is 30 miles out." And when it got down to "the plane is 10 miles out," the young man also said to the Vice President, "Do the orders still stand?" And the Vice President turned and whipped his neck around and said, "Of course the orders still stand. Have you heard anything to the contrary?"[273]

As to what these "orders" were, Mineta assumed, he said, that they were to shoot the plane down. But there was no shootdown of the aircraft that approached the Pentagon. Also, given the fact that two hijacked airliners had already crashed into high-value targets, the expected orders in relation to any unidentified aircraft approaching the Pentagon would have been to shoot it down. So if those had been the orders, the young man would have had no reason to ask whether they "still stand." The only reasonable interpretation, therefore, is that Mineta had witnessed the vice-president confirming a previously given stand-down order. (Further evidence for this interpretation will be given in the section headed "A Degenerating Research Program?")

The Destruction of the World Trade Center

For science-oriented members of the 9/11 Truth Movement, the strongest case for rejecting the government's 9/11 conspiracy theory is provided by evidence that its account of the collapse of the Twin Towers and WTC 7—according to which all three buildings came down because two of them were struck by airliners—could not possibly be true. Here are some of those reasons:

The Total Collapse of the Twin Towers and WTC 7: Prior to 9/11, steel-frame high-rise buildings had never suffered total collapse from any cause other than controlled demolition by means of pre-set explosives and incendiaries. NIST claims that the Twin Towers and WTC 7 were brought down by gravity after they were weakened by fire. But fires in the South and North Towers lasted only 56 and 102 minutes, respectively, whereas fires in other steel-frame buildings have lasted 10, 17, and 18 hours without inducing even partial collapse.[274]

NIST claims, to be sure, that the Twin Towers come down partly because of the airplane impacts, which (allegedly) severed some of the steel columns, thereby creating big holes, which then caused each building's top section to fall down on the lower section, causing it to collapse.[275]

In actual fact, however, the top sections did not come down as solid units, but instead disintegrated in mid-air, so there were no discernible "jolts" when the top sections encountered the lower sections.[276] In an analysis of the North Tower collapse, moreover, mechanical engineer Gordon Ross asked what would have happened—assuming that the "collapse [was] driven only by gravity"—even if the top section as a solid unit had in fact fallen onto the lower section. So much energy would have been absorbed by the lower structure, he concluded, that "vertical movement of the falling section would [have been] arrested . . . within 0.02 seconds after impact," so that it "would not [have] continue[d] to progress beyond that point."[277]

Building 7 of the World Trade Center, moreover, also suffered total collapse, even though it was not hit by a plane. Its collapse, therefore, had to be attributed solely to its fires, even though this building merely had some localized fires, lasting at best only a few hours, on six of its 47 floors. And yet, as mentioned already, even buildings that have become towering infernos, with fires lasting up to 18 hours, have not collapsed, even partially.

The official accounts of the World Trade Center are rendered extremely implausible, therefore, solely by virtue of the fact that these three buildings suffered total collapse. But there are even more decisive reasons for calling these accounts false.

Horizontal Ejections from the Twin Towers: The destruction of the Twin Towers began with huge explosions near the top, which ejected material out horizontally. Included in this material were massive sections of steel columns that were hurled out 500 to 600 feet, a few of which implanted themselves in neighboring buildings, as can be seen in videos and photographs.[278] This feature of the destruction of the Twin Towers provides virtually irrefutable evidence against the official account, according to which the only force available, beyond that supplied by the airplane impacts and the resulting fires, was gravitational attraction, which pulls things straight down. Engineer Dwain Deets, mentioned above in Chapter 4, has said that these "massive structural members being hurled horizontally" is one of the factors that "leave no doubt" in his mind that "explosives were involved."[279]

Vertical, Symmetrical Collapses: WTC 7 was supported by 82 vertical steel columns, and yet it came straight down, in an almost perfectly symmetrical collapse. This means that all of its 82 steel columns failed simultaneously. Structural engineer Kamal Obeid, saying that for this to have occurred without the use of explosives would have been an "impossibility,"[280] has thereby expressed the view of the 1,200-plus members of Architects and Engineers for 9/11 Truth. The same point applies to the Twin Towers, each of which was supported by 287 steel columns, including 47 massive core columns. After the initial explosions at the top, each building came down in a vertical, symmetrical collapse, which means that all 287 columns failed simultaneously. The official account of the World Trade Center is made absurd by these vertical collapses alone—but there are still more contradictory facts.

WTC 7 in Absolute Free Fall: Scientists and engineers in the 9/11 Truth Movement have long pointed out that WTC 7 accelerated downward at the rate of free-fall, or at least close to it. Prior to its final report on WTC 7, however, NIST had claimed that the time required for the building to collapse "was approximately 40 percent longer than the computed free fall time."[281] Shyam Sunder, the lead investigator for NIST, even explained why the building could not have come down in free fall (assuming the truth of NIST's non-demolition theory of the collapse): An object in free fall, he pointed out during a "technical briefing" on WTC 7 given in August 2008, "would be an object that has no structural components below it." The top floor could not possibly have come down in free fall, in other words, because all the steel and concrete in the lower floors would have offered "structural resistance."[282]

In response, David Chandler, a high-school physics teacher, put a video on the internet showing that, for over two seconds, WTC 7 had come down in absolute (not merely virtual) free fall.[283] In its final report, NIST acknowledged this fact, saying that for 2.25 seconds, the building descended "at gravitational acceleration."[284] Leaving no room for ambiguity, NIST said in an accompanying document that, for this 2.25-second period, the descent of WTC 7 was characterized by "gravitational acceleration (free fall)."[285]

NIST acknowledged, therefore, that the top floor of the building, while coming straight down through a region that had, only seconds earlier, been occupied by steel-and-concrete floors supported by 82 steel columns, encountered *zero resistance*.

While acknowledging this empirical fact, however, NIST retained its previous theory, according to which the building had been brought down by fire, not explosives, incendiaries, or some combination thereof. But this theory, Sunder had previously explained, is inconsistent with free fall. In the final version of its report, accordingly, NIST removed the multiple assurances, which had been contained in its draft report, that its account of WTC 7's collapse was "consistent with physical principles."[286] NIST implicitly acknowledged, in other words, that its WTC 7 report violated laws of physics.

In my 2009 book *The Mysterious Collapse of World Trade Center 7: Why the Final Official Report about 9/11 Is Unscientific and False*,[287] I emphasized that NIST, by admitting free fall—evidently in response to Chandler's presentations—had contradicted Sunder's statement, given in the August "technical briefing," that free fall would have been impossible. How did NIST respond? By removing the video and transcript of that technical briefing from the internet.[288]

Melted and Sulfidized Steel: Three professors in the Fire Protection Engineering Program at Worcester Polytechnic Institute (WPI), studying a piece of steel recovered from WTC 7 and another piece from one of the Twin Towers, made a startling discovery, which a 2002 article in WPI's magazine described thus:

> A one-inch column has been reduced to half-inch thickness. Its edges—which are curled like a paper scroll—have been thinned to almost razor sharpness. Gaping holes—some larger than a silver dollar—let light shine through a formerly solid steel flange. This Swiss cheese appearance shocked all of the fire-wise professors, who expected to see distortion and bending—but not holes.[289]

One reason for their shock had been stated earlier in the article: "[S]teel—which has a melting point of 2,800 degrees Fahrenheit—may weaken and bend, but does not melt during an ordinary office fire." Another reason was that the steel, these professors wrote, had thinned as a result of sulfidation, after which they added: "No clear explanation for the source of the sulfur has been identified."[290]

A *New York Times* story referred to this discovery as "perhaps the deepest mystery uncovered in the investigation."[291] The article by the three WPI professors, which was published as an appendix in the 2002 FEMA report on the World Trade Center, concluded by saying: "A detailed study into the mechanisms of this phenomenon is needed."[292] But when NIST issued its 2005 report on the Twin Towers, it simply ignored this phenomenon. And then in 2008, when it issued its report on WTC 7, NIST again failed to mention this phenomenon. NIST thereby implicitly admitted that its theory, according to which fire was the only source of heat, could not account for this melted and sulfidized steel.

NIST could have easily accounted for this phenomenon, however, with the hypothesis that the steel had been melted by thermate, which is thermite—an incendiary—to which sulfur, which lowers the melting point of steel, has been added. Doing this, however, would have violated the government's, and hence NIST's, not-to-be-questioned assumption, according to which the three buildings came down solely because al-Qaeda hijackers had crashed airliners into two of them.[293]

Metallic Particles in the WTC Dust: The WTC dust was found to contain metallic particles that can be explained—and evidently *only* explained—by the hypothesis that incendiaries and/or explosives were used. For example, the RJ Lee Group, which was hired by Deutsche Bank to prove to its insurance company that its building had been contaminated by dust from "the WTC Event," reported that "iron and other metals were melted during the WTC Event, producing spherical metallic particles."[294] The melting point of iron is 2,800°F, at least 1,000°F higher than the fires could have been. Scientists at the US Geological Survey, moreover, discovered that molybdenum had melted,[295] even though its melting point is 4,753°F.[296] As shown by these and other discoveries, the destruction of the World Trade Center buildings involved extremely high temperatures, which could not have been produced without incendiaries and/or explosives.[297]

Nanothermite: A report by several scientists, including chemist Niels Harrit of the University of Copenhagen, showed that the WTC dust also contained unreacted nanothermite, which—in distinction from ordinary thermite—is a high explosive. This nanothermite existed in the dust in the form of tiny red/gray chips. In calling the chips "unreacted nanothermite," these scientists were pointing to the fact that the chips, besides having all the ingredients of nanothermite, exploded when touched with a flame.[298] Asked whether this is "the smoking gun," Harrit said it is better called "the 'loaded gun,' material that did not ignite for some reason."[299] In light of this discovery, the full significance of NIST's admission that it did not examine the dust for thermite—which is a generic term, covering thermate and nanothermite as well as ordinary thermite—becomes apparent.

Testimonies about Explosions: Further evidence that explosives were used to bring down the buildings was provided by the testimonies, mentioned in Chapter 4, about explosions in the Twin Towers and WTC 7.

Al-Qaeda Theory Ruled Out: The overwhelming evidence that the Twin Towers were brought down with explosives, perhaps in conjunction with incendiaries, rules out the government's al-Qaeda conspiracy theory, for three reasons. First, the fact that the buildings came straight down means that they were subjected to the type of controlled demolition known as "implosion," which is "by far the trickiest type of explosive project," which "only a handful of blasting companies in the world . . . possess enough experience . . . to perform."[300] Al-Qaeda would not have had the needed expertise.

Second, controlled demolition is relatively easy if a building can simply be knocked over sideways. The only reason to go to all the work required for bringing a tall building straight down is to avoid damaging nearby buildings. Had the 110-story Twin Towers fallen over sideways, they would have caused massive destruction in lower Manhattan, destroying dozens of other buildings and killing many thousands of people. Does anyone believe that, even if al-Qaeda operatives had had the expertise to make the buildings come straight down, they would have had the courtesy?

Third, foreign terrorists could not have obtained access to the buildings for all the hours it would have taken to plant incendiaries and explosives. Only insiders could have done this.

To Conclude: Still further evidence against the official conspiracy theory, and thereby in favor of the alternative conspiracy theory, could be provided, including evidence against the government's accounts of the damage to the Pentagon and the downing of United Flight 93. What has been presented above, however, is more than enough to show the falsity of Sunstein's twofold claim that the 9/11 Truth Movement's conspiracy theory is unjustified, because its evidence is "weak or even nonexistent," whereas the government's conspiracy theory, according to which al-Qaeda was responsible for 9/11, is "a justified and true conspiracy theory." As we have seen, the exact opposite is the case.

3. A Degenerating Research Program?

Sunstein also made the following claim:

> Conspiracy theories often display the characteristic features of a "degenerating research program" in which contrary evidence is explained away by adding epicycles and resisting falsification of key tenets.[301]

As Sunstein's footnote to this passage indicates, the concept of a "degenerating research program" was formulated in 1970 by philosopher of science Imre Lakatos,[302] whose distinction between "degenerating" and "progressive" research programs has become influential in philosophy-of-science circles.[303]

In a *progressive* research program, the theory on which the program is based becomes progressively confirmed, as each theory-inspired discovery leads to still further discoveries. In a *degenerating* program, by contrast, the advocates, rather than being led to new confirming evidence, are forced to defend the original theory by explaining away apparently disconfirming evidence—in ways analogous to the addition of epicycles to save the geocentric theory of the universe—and by simply refusing to admit that any evidence, no matter how damning, has falsified the theory.

Although Sunstein's paragraph introducing this notion of degenerating research programs speaks simply of "conspiracy theories," he clearly means it to apply to the 9/11 conspiracy theory in particular, given the fact that it is his "main focus" and "running example." And it does, in fact, apply to it. But not to the conspiracy theory of the 9/11 Truth Movement, which has proven to be a remarkably fruitful and hence progressive research program, as shown by the above summary of evidence and the growing number of professional 9/11 organizations, listed in the previous chapter, that have adopted this theory. Moreover, the very fact that Sunstein felt a need to write this essay, providing a proposal for undermining the movement, suggests his awareness that its "research program" is progressing, not degenerating.

It is, instead, the government's 9/11 conspiracy theory that has turned out to be the degenerating research program. Besides the fact that the Bush–Cheney conspiracy theory has not led to the discovery of any new (true) facts about 9/11, its defenders have used two of the standard methods by which degenerating programs resist admitting that their theory has been falsified by contrary evidence: (1) changing the story, and (2) simply refusing to admit that any of the disconfirming evidence does, in fact, falsify their theory.

Changing the Story

Analogously to adding epicycles, creators and defenders of the official account of 9/11 have often, in the face of evidence contradicting some particular story within the overall account, added new elements to, or otherwise changed, this story. Here are some examples:

Did Atta Drink Vodka at Shuckums on September 7? The day after the 9/11 attacks, the Associated Press published a story based on an interview with Tony Amos, the manager of a bar in Hollywood, Florida, called "Shuckums." Reporting that Amos, having been shown photos of two men, had identified the one signed "Mohamed," this story continued:

> Amos said the two men had each consumed several drinks Friday night [September 7] and had given the bartender a hard time. . . . "The guy Mohamed was drunk, his voice was slurred and he had a thick accent," Amos said. Bartender Patricia Idrissi said the men argued over the bill.[304]

The next day, the *St. Petersburg Times* wrote:

> Tony Amos, the night manager at Shuckums Bar in Hollywood, told the Palm Beach Post that Atta argued with him over his tab. . . ."They were wasted," said [bartender Patricia] Idrissi, who said she directed the two men to a Chinese restaurant a few doors down. They later returned and each ordered about five drinks, she said.[305]

That same day, September 13, a *New York Times* story said:

> Patricia Idrissi would not have noticed [Mohamed Atta] except that he drank Stolichnaya vodka for three hours . . . and then seemed not to want to pay his $48 bar tab.[306]

Three days later, Scotland's *Sunday Herald* gave an account in which Atta used colorful language:

> Last Friday Atta . . . and two other Middle Eastern men were spotted at a bar in Hollywood in Florida called Shuckums. They ran up a bill and started rowing with waitress Patricia Idrissi over the cost of their vodkas and rums. Atta shouted at the manager: "You think I can't pay? I'm a pilot for American Airlines. I can pay my f***ing bill."[307]

A week later, *Newsweek* gave a still more startling account, saying:

> Last week Atta and two of his buddies seem to have gone out for a farewell bender at a seafood bar called Shuckums. Atta drank five Stoli-and-fruit-juices, while one of the others drank rum and Coke. . . . Atta and his friends became agitated, shouting curse words in Arabic, reportedly including a particularly blasphemous one that roughly translates as "F—k God."[308]

This story was in considerable tension with *Newsweek*'s characterization of the hijackers as "a small band of religious zealots,"[309] and especially in tension with the idea that Atta, the ringleader, was a devout Muslim—an idea the 9/11 Commission would later make canonical by saying that Atta had become very religious, even "fanatically so."[310]

This tension was gradually overcome by means of mutations in the Shuckums story. On September 16, the *Washington Post* wrote:

> Atta played video Trivial Pursuit and blackjack with great determination. . . . Al-Shehhi and the other man had about five drinks each, [manager Tony Amos] said. . . . "Al-Shehhi was definitely upset," Amos said. The bartender feared that Al-Shehhi might leave without paying his $48 tab. The manager intervened, asking if there was a problem. Al-Shehhi, glaring, . . . said: "There is no money issue. I am an airline pilot."[311]

The following week, the *Post* contained a still more cleaned-up version, which said:

> Atta played video games, a pursuit out of line with fundamentalist beliefs. But the manager on duty that night has said that he doesn't recall seeing Atta drink alcohol.[312]

Atta, of course, had to drink *something*. This detail was provided in a *Los Angeles Times* story on September 27, which said:

> [Shuckums'] owner, Tony Amos, says Atta sat quietly by himself and drank cranberry juice and played a video game, while Al-Shehhi and the other customer tossed back mixed drinks and argued.[313]

The same week, *Time* magazine—which had earlier run the version of the Shuckums story in which Atta, having had five vodka-and-orange-juice drinks, was "wasted"[314]—carried the new version, writing:

> Atta, Al-Shehhi and another man visited Shuckums . . . Contrary to earlier reports of his carousing, Atta was the only one of the three who didn't drink alcohol. Instead, he downed cranberry juice all night, sugary fuel for the pinball machine . . . that he played for 3 1/2 hours.[315]

Finally, the 9/11 Commission—perhaps feeling uncomfortable about having the "fanatically religious" Atta at a bar, even if he was only drinking cranberry juice—eliminated the September 7 evening at Shuckums altogether. Describing Atta's activities during the week before the attacks, it wrote:

> Atta was still busy coordinating the teams. On September 7, he flew from Fort Lauderdale to Baltimore, presumably to meet with the Flight 77 team in Laurel. On September 9, he flew from Baltimore to Boston.[316]

The Commission's Mohamad Atta was clearly all business.

Incriminating Evidence in Atta's Luggage: Some of the strongest evidence of al-Qaeda's responsibility for the 9/11 attacks was reportedly found in luggage discovered at the airport in Boston after the attacks. This luggage, with Atta's name on it, reportedly contained various incriminating materials, including Atta's last will and testament and a letter about preparing for the mission that was identical to letters reportedly found at the crash site of United Flight 93 and in an automobile rented by one of the hijackers and left at Dulles Airport, thereby connecting the hijackers on three of the flights.[317]

Why was this luggage at the airport? Because, we were told, Atta had taken a commuter flight down from Portland, Maine, that morning in order to catch American Flight 11, and although he made the connection, his luggage did not.

But why was Atta in Portland? Because, although he was already in Boston on September 10, he and Abdullah al-Omari (another member of al-Qaeda) had rented a silver-blue Nissan and driven up to Portland.

This story seemed to make no sense. Why would Atta have been planning to take his will on a plane that he was going to fly into the World Trade Center? And why would Atta have gone up to Portland and stayed overnight? Besides being the ringleader for the operation, he was going to pilot Flight 11. If the commuter flight had been late, he would have been forced to cancel the whole operation, which he had been planning for years. The 9/11 Commission admitted that it could not explain why he would have made this trip.[318]

The story makes no sense because it was a poorly thought-out substitute for the original story, which was that the incriminating material had been found in a white Mitsubishi, which Atta had rented and left in the parking lot at Boston's Logan Airport. According to this story, which was broadcast on September 12 and 13, the hijackers who drove the Nissan to Portland and then took the commuter flight back to Boston were Adnan and Ameer Bukhari.[319]

On the afternoon of the 13th, however, a problem emerged: It was discovered that neither of the Bukharis had died on 9/11: Ameer had died the year before and Adnan was still alive. So the story had to be changed. An Associated Press article on September 14 reported that the Nissan had been driven to Portland by Atta and his companion, but the incriminating materials were still said to have been found in a rented car in the Boston airport, although now it had been rented by "additional suspects," not Atta.[320] The final form of the story evidently first appeared on September 16 in a *Washington Post* story, which said:

> Mohamed Atta. . . is thought to have piloted American Airlines Flight 11, the first to slam into the World Trade Center. A letter written by Atta, left in his luggage at Boston's Logan Airport, said he planned to kill himself so he could go to heaven as a martyr. It also contained a Saudi passport, an international driver's license,

instructional videos for flying Boeing airliners and an Islamic prayer schedule. Officials believe that Atta and Alomari rented a car in Boston, drove to Portland, Maine, and took a room Monday night at the Comfort Inn . . . . They then flew on a short flight Tuesday morning from Portland to Boston, changing to Flight 11.[321]

By October 5, the FBI had supplied a complete chronology of Atta and al-Omari's activities in Portland, complete with videotape evidence of their presence at a Walmart, two ATMs, and the Portland Jetport.[322] The FBI at some point even provided an affidavit, dated September 12, stating that the Nissan found at the Portland Jetport had been rented by Mohamed Atta, and that "American Airlines personnel at Logan discovered two bags [checked to passenger Atta] that had been bound for transfer to AA11 but had not been loaded onto the flight."[323]

Were the FBI agent and the judge who signed this affidavit on September 12 aided by a precognitive vision, in which they saw the story that would emerge only several days later? In any case, the authorities had successfully replaced a story that was contradicted by empirical facts by a story that was merely incoherent.

Flight Manifests with Alleged Hijackers' Names: As mentioned above, the passenger manifests for the four 9/11 flights did not contain the names of the alleged hijackers, even though they had supposedly purchased tickets. In 2004 or 2005, this problem was seemingly over-come by the appearance of passenger manifests that do contain the names of the 19 men.[324]

There are three problems with these manifests, however, which suggest that they are late fabrications. One problem is the very fact that they did not show up until several years later, after their absence had been noted by the 9/11 Truth Movement. A second problem is the fact that the FBI did not include them in the evidence it presented to the Moussaoui trial, although it surely could have included them if it had considered them authentic.[325] A third problem is that these purported manifests included names of men who had not been iden-tified as hijackers until some days after 9/11. The manifest for American Flight 11, for example, contains the names of Waleed and Wail al-Shehri, even though these brothers were replacements for the Bukhari brothers, who, as we saw above, were not removed from the list until September 13. So these could not be the passenger manifests issued on September 11.[326]

Getting Rid of Impossible Cell Phone Calls: According to news reports during the first few years after 9/11, as we saw earlier, there were said to have been many cell phone calls from the airliners, with about ten such calls from United 93 alone. Some of those calls were reported by Deena Burnett, about whom the FBI's report says: "Burnett was able to determine that her husband was using his own cellular telephone because the caller identification showed his number."[327] These calls came, however, when Flight 93's altitude would have been between 34,300 and 40,700 feet.[328] As we saw earlier, scientist A. K. Dewdney demonstrated in 2003 that cell phone calls at this height would have been impossible in 2001. Perhaps not surprisingly, therefore, the FBI changed the story.

This change was evidently made in 2004, as illustrated by a new account of a 12-minute phone call reportedly made by American 11 flight attendant Amy Sweeney to Michael Woodward, the manager of the American Flight Services Office in Boston. An affidavit from the FBI agent who interviewed Woodward that same day stated that, according to Woodward, Sweeney had been "using a cellular telephone."[329] This affidavit had, moreover, become public knowledge through an Associated Press story of October 2001, which said:

> An American Airlines employee received a cell phone call from a flight attendant aboard doomed Flight 11 shortly before it crashed into the World Trade Center, according to newly unsealed court documents. . . . The FBI cited its interview with the American Airlines employee in an affidavit.[330]

But when the 9/11 Commission discussed this call in its report, which appeared in July 2004, it declared, in a note at the back of the book, that Sweeney had used an onboard phone.[331]

Behind that change was an implausible new story told by the FBI earlier in 2004: Woodward, not having a tape recorder in his office, had repeated Sweeney's call verbatim to Nancy Wyatt, a colleague in his office, who had in turn repeated it to another colleague at American headquarters in Dallas, who had recorded it. This recording, which was discovered only in 2004, indicated that Sweeney had used a passenger-seat phone, thanks to "an AirFone card, given to her by another flight attendant."[332]

This new story is implausible for many reasons: First, if this relayed recording had really been made on 9/11, we cannot believe that Woodward would have failed to mention it to the FBI agent who interviewed him later that same day. While the agent was taking notes, Woodward would surely have said: "You don't need to rely on my memory, because there is a recording of a word-for-word repetition of Sweeney's statements down in Dallas." Second, if Woodward had repeated Sweeney's statement that she had used "an AirFone card, given to her by another flight attendant," he would not have told the FBI agent later that same day that she had been "using a cellular telephone." Third, a *Los Angeles Times* story of September 20, 2001, said this about the Sweeney-to-Woodward call:

> FBI officials in Dallas, where American Airlines is based, were able, on the day of the terrorist attacks, to piece together a partial transcript and an account of the phone call.[333]

If officials at AA headquarters had a recording of Nancy Wyatt's virtually verbatim account of Michael Woodward's virtually verbatim account of what Amy Sweeney had said, FBI officials in Dallas would not have needed to "piece together a partial transcript." For these reasons, we can only conclude that the FBI invented this story in order to get rid of the 12-minute cell phone call in the original story.

In any case, this new story about the Amy Sweeney call was evidently merely one part of a general change in the FBI's position, through which it no longer affirmed high-altitude cell phone calls. Although this change was evidently made by 2004, it became somewhat widely known only after the Moussaoui trial of 2006, at which the FBI presented evidence about the phone calls from the four airliners.[334] During the trial, an FBI spokesman said: "13 of the terrified passengers and crew members made 35 air phone calls and two cell phone calls."[335] As this statement shows, of the 10 to 12 calls that had been reported by their recipients to have been cell phone calls, only two were now thus identified by the FBI. These were two calls reportedly made at 9:58am, when the plane had descended to 5,000 feet.[336] Moreover, as the FBI's report available on the internet shows, the only cell phone calls now affirmed by the FBI for the four airliners combined are these two low-altitude calls from United 93. The FBI was no longer affirming any technologically impossible high-altitude cell phone calls.

While getting rid of that problem, however, the FBI created a new one: How to explain why so many people had believed that they had been called on cell phones. In particular, if Tom Burnett had actually used a seat-back phone, as the FBI's report now says, why did Deena Burnett see his cell phone number on her Caller ID? The official defenders of the government's conspiracy theory have offered no answer to this question. And for good reason: There is no possible answer except to admit that these calls had been faked, in one way or another. So the question is simply ignored.

Getting Rid of the Impossible Barbara Olson Calls: As we saw earlier, Ted Olson claimed that he had received two calls from his wife, Barbara Olson, who had reportedly been on American Flight 77. This claim became part of the official story: Referring to four "connected calls to unknown numbers" that had been made from this flight, the 9/11 Commission, writing in 2004, said: "[T]he FBI and DOJ believe that all four represent communications between Barbara Olson and her husband's office."[337] In 2006, however, after the fact that Flight 77 had no onboard phones had become known, the FBI's report said that Barbara Olson "attempted" one call, that it was "unconnected," and that it (therefore) lasted "0 seconds."[338] This is quite a change from Ted Olson's claim, according to which he had received two calls from his wife, with the first one lasting "about one (1) minute,"[339] and the second one lasting "two or three or four minutes."[340]

Al-Suqami's Passport Discovered—Revised Version: As we saw above, credulity was severely strained by the FBI's claim that it had discovered the passport of Satam al-Suqami on the street *after* the collapse of the North Tower. By 2004, when the 9/11 Commission was discussing this alleged discovery, the story had been modified to say that "a passer-by picked it up and gave it to a NYPD detective shortly before the World Trade Center towers collapsed."[341] So, rather than needing to survive the collapse of the North Tower, the passport now merely needed to escape from al-Suqami's pocket or luggage, escape from the plane's cabin, avoid being destroyed or even singed by the instantaneous jet-fuel fire, and then escape from the building so that it could fall to the ground. This modification did little if anything to make the story more credible.

Cheney to the PEOC—Revised Timeline: As we saw earlier, Secretary of Transportation Norman Mineta, during open testimony to the 9/11 Commission, reported an exchange in the PEOC under the White House during which Vice President Cheney seemed to confirm a previously given stand-down order. The 9/11 Commission's damage-control revisions involved the following elements:

—First, whereas Mineta had described a conversation that occurred before the Pentagon was struck—at about 9:25 or 9:26, he estimated—the 9/11 Commission claimed that Cheney did not even enter the underground corridor leading to the PEOC until 9:37, after which he paused in the corridor to telephone President Bush, at which time Cheney learned about the strike on the Pentagon (which reportedly occurred at 9:38) and "saw television coverage of the smoke coming from the building."[342]

—Second, the Commission said that Cheney did not enter the PEOC itself until almost 10:00, "perhaps at 9:58."[343]

—Third, Mineta's testimony about the exchange between Cheney and the young man was simply not mentioned in *The 9/11 Commission Report*, and the video of Mineta's giving this testimony was removed from the 9/11 Commission's video archive.[344]

—Fourth, that exchange, in which the young man told Cheney about an incoming plane and repeatedly asked what should be done, was replaced by a story about an exchange that occurred later: "At 10:02, the communicators in the shelter began receiving reports from the Secret Service of an inbound aircraft. . . . At some time between 10:10 and 10:15, a military aide told the Vice President and others that the aircraft was 80 miles out. Vice President Cheney was asked for authority to engage the aircraft. . . . The Vice President authorized fighter aircraft to engage the inbound plane. . . . The military aide returned a few minutes later, probably between 10:12 and 10:18, and said the aircraft was 60 miles out. He again asked for authorization to engage. The Vice President again said yes."[345]

According to this new story, the order was for the military to engage, not to stand-down. And the exchange occurred not only after the Pentagon had been struck but also after United 93 had crashed, which occurred a few minutes after 10:00. Having the exchange come after this crash was important because of multiple reports that United 93 was shot down and that this had occurred after Cheney—at about 9:45, according to counterterrorism chief Richard Clarke—had issued shootdown authorization.[346]

The new story, therefore, got Cheney off the hook for both the Pentagon strike and the crash of United 93: Not having arrived in the PEOC, where he took charge of the administration's response to the attacks, until long after the Pentagon was struck, he could not have confirmed a stand-down order while he was there. And, not having given the shoot-down authorization until about 10:15, he could not have authorized a shoot-down order for United 93.

The only problem with the new story was that it contradicted an enormous amount of testimony, including that of David Bohrer (his photographer), Condoleezza Rice, and Richard Clarke (in addition to that of Mineta).[347] It even contradicted testimony of Cheney himself, who told Tim Russert on NBC's *Meet the Press* five days after 9/11:

> [A]fter I talked to the president [from my office] . . . I went down into . . . the Presidential Emergency Operations Center. . . . [W]hen I arrived there within a short order, we had word the Pentagon's been hit.[348]

Cheney himself, therefore, said that he had entered the PEOC prior to the Pentagon attack, not 20 minutes afterwards, as the 9/11 Commission would claim. For all these reasons, we can safely conclude that the Commission's new timeline for Dick Cheney was false.

Why the Airliners Were Not Intercepted—The New Official Story: Aside from its revision of the Cheney timeline, the 9/11 Commission's most important revision, and the one to which it devoted the most space, was its creation of a new explanation of why the hijacked airliners had not been intercepted. According to the first explanation, as we saw earlier, the FAA had notified the military about the troubles being experienced by all four airliners, but not in time for the military to make the interceptions. Between 2001 and 2004, however, the 9/11 Truth Movement showed convincingly that, even if the FAA had been as tardy as the military claimed, the airliners should still have been intercepted; I summarized these arguments in *The New Pearl Harbor*. 9/11 Commission co-chairs Kean and Hamilton even agreed, writing in their 2006 "inside story" book:

> [I]f the military had had the amount of time they said they had . . . and had scrambled their jets, it was hard to figure how they had failed to shoot down at least one of the planes.[349]

As this statement implies, the military had given false testimony, according to Kean and Hamilton, saying that they had had more time than they really did. And this allegedly false information, for which the military and the FAA shared responsibility, "created the opportunity for people to construct a series of conspiracy theories that persist to this day."[350] At the core of these false conspiracy theories, Kean and Hamilton said, was "the notion that the military . . . had issued a 'stand down' order on 9/11, thus permitting the attacks to occur."[351]

The antidote for this conspiracy theory, they said, is the new, improved timeline, which was provided in *The 9/11 Commission Report*. According to this new timeline, the FAA notified the military about American Flight 11 at about when they had said (which did not, the 9/11 Commission insists, provide time for an interception), but the FAA did not notify the military about Flights 175, 77, and 93 until after they had crashed—which explains why the military did not intercept them.

This would, of course, provide an excellent explanation—if it were true. But there are many reasons to believe that it is not. Take American Flight 77, about which the military had, according to the old story, been notified at 9:24. The new story says that the FAA did not notify the military until 9:34 (four minutes before the Pentagon was struck), and even then said only that Flight 77 was lost, not that it had been hijacked.

This new story is contradicted by an enormous amount of evidence, one piece of which is an FAA memo that was read into the 9/11 Commission's record and then ignored. This memo, written before the military had challenged the 9:24 notification time, said that this time was far too late, because it was only the *formal* notification time: "before the formal notification," this memo said, "information about [American Flight 77] was conveyed continuously during the phone bridges."[352] Commissioner Richard Ben-Veniste, after reading this memo into the record, emphasized its main point: that the military had been advised of Flight 77's troubles "substantially earlier than the formal notification of hijacking."[353] When the 9/11 Commission issued its report, however, it said that the FAA, far from having notified the military about Flight 77's hijacking *before* 9:24, did not notify it at all: "[The military] never received notice that American 77 was hijacked."[354]

For this and many other reasons, which I have laid out at considerable length elsewhere,[355] the 9/11 Commission's new explanation for the failures to intercept, like its other new stories, appears to have been a lie.

Refusing to Admit Falsification

Besides rewriting history to erase disconfirming stories from the record, the defenders of the official conspiracy theory have repeatedly refused to admit that a large body of evidence contradicting their theory has already, in fact, falsified it. This body of evidence, which the government has not sought to deny or explain away, includes the following facts:

—The FBI's page on Osama bin Laden as a "Most Wanted Terrorist" does not name him as wanted for 9/11, because, an official spokesman admitted, "the FBI has no hard evidence connecting Bin Laden to 9/11." The White House has not explained why, if it has hard evidence, the FBI evidently does not know about it.

—The idea that the 9/11 attacks were orchestrated by "radical Islam" is further contradicted by the fact that the behavior of at least many of the alleged hijackers showed them to be anything but devout Muslims. The government has not explained why an attack carried out (allegedly) by men who drank, took cocaine, and hired lap dancers and prostitutes could be portrayed as an attack by representatives of Islam.

—None of the eight pilots squawked the hijack code, even though there would have been more than enough time. The government has given no explanation as to why these pilots would not have performed this quick and simple act, if indeed men were trying to break into the cockpits.

—Ted Olson's claim that he was called twice by his wife, Barbara Olson, from American Flight 77 is not supported by the FBI's report on phone calls from this plane. No explanation of this contradiction has been offered.

—The FBI report on phone calls from United Flight 93 now says that Tom Burnett used a seat-back phone to call his wife, Deena Burnett, although she had reported seeing his cell phone number on her telephone's Caller ID. There has been no explanation of this contradiction.

—There has also been no explanation as to why the al-Qaeda hijackers were wearing red headbands if, as former CIA officer Milt Bearden says, these are worn by Shi'a, but not Sunni, Muslims.

—Another mystery unexplained is how Hani Hanjour, known to be incapable of safely flying a single-engine plane, could have flown a Boeing 757 through a trajectory declared by some experienced 757 pilots to be too difficult even for them. (The authors of the *Popular Mechanics* book about 9/11 volunteered a solution to this mystery, saying that Hanjour flew most of the route on autopilot, "steer[ing] the plane manually for only the final eight minutes of the flight."[356] It was precisely during this period, however, when he reportedly performed the trajectory.

—The government has never explained why the Secret Service allowed the president to remain at the school in Florida for 30 minutes after the second attack on the World Trade Center, which was reportedly taken as evidence that terrorists in hijacked airliners were going after high-value targets. The White House, as we saw, did try to claim that Bush had left the *classroom* more quickly than he actually did, but there has been no attempt to claim that he left the school earlier—even though the fact that the Secret Service allowed him to remain there seemed to falsify the claim that it knew unknown terrorists were using hijacked airliners to strike high-value targets. As Philip Melanson, the author of a book about the Secret

Service,[357] said in 2004: "[T]he procedure should have been to get the president to the closest secure location as quickly as possible."[358]

—With regard to the time at which Vice-President Cheney reached the PEOC, there has been no attempt to explain the contradiction between the 9/11 Commission's claim, according to which he did not get there until almost 10:00AM, and the testimony of Norman Mineta and even Cheney himself (on *Meet the Press* five days after 9/11), according to which he arrived there before the attack on the Pentagon.

—There has been no attempt to explain why, if explosives did not bring the Twin Towers down, over 100 members of the Fire Department of New York reported explosions going off in the buildings before and during their collapses.

Accordingly, while Sunstein correctly says that degenerating research programs are typically guilty of "resisting falsification of key tenets," it is, contrary to his suggestion, the defenders of the Bush–Cheney conspiracy theory, rather than the leaders of the 911 Truth Movement, who have manifested this behavior.

4. Sunstein's Fifth Thesis Understood Esoterically

Sunstein' fifth thesis, if taken in the sense that most readers would understand it, is clearly false. It is so obviously false that Sunstein, being a highly respected law professor who has taught at both Chicago and Harvard, surely could not have meant it to be understood in that sense—that is, as referring to the 9/11 Truth Movement. He would surely not have written an article concerning a movement about which he was ill-informed. Therefore, being well-informed about the 9/11 Truth Movement, he would have known (1) that its conspiracy theory is *not* demonstrably false, *not* unjustified because devoid of evidence, and *not* an example of a degenerating research program, and (2) that the government's 9/11 conspiracy theory does exemplify these characteristics.

If we accept the idea that Sunstein's essay contained an esoteric message, we can see it as pointing towards this twofold truth by omission: Sunstein must have been aware of a good deal of the evidence provided by the 9/11 Truth Movement against the government's theory, and thereby for its own theory. And yet he made no attempt to refute this evidence. Did he not thereby provide a hint that this evidence was irrefutable?

We can, therefore, see Sunstein's fifth thesis as a clever way to get across this twofold point. That is, by virtue of having a good understanding of human psychology, Sunstein would have known that, by writing an article that stated the exact opposite of the truth, he would stimulate members of the 9/11 Truth Movement to spell out, more explicitly than they had before, the fact that the Bush–Cheney administration's 9/11 conspiracy theory is trebly in trouble, because:

—It is unjustified, not being supported by any evidence that can withstand scrutiny.

—It is demonstrably false and has, in fact, been demonstrated to be false.

—It has long been the basis for a degenerating research program, which can seem unfalsified to much of the public only because its proponents—who include much of the mainstream press—have revised disproven elements of it or, when this was impossible, simply refused to acknowledge the falsification.

CHAPTER 6
THE 9/11 CONSPIRACY THEORY
AS HARMFUL

Sunstein's sixth thesis says:

9/11 conspiracy theorists, being extremists, are likely to become violent, "with terrifying consequences." Even if not, the 9/11 conspiracy theory "can still have pernicious effects from the government's point of view, . . . by inducing unjustifiably widespread public skepticism about the government's assertions, or by dampening public mobilization and participation in government-led efforts," or by "undermin[ing] democratic debate."[359]

Sunstein is concerned, he says, with conspiracy theories that are "false, harmful, and unjustified."[360] In the previous chapters, we looked at his claim that the conspiracy theory of the 9/11 Truth Movement is unjustified and false. In the present chapter, we examine his claim that it is harmful.

This claim, more precisely, seems to be that this theory is *dangerous*—that is, *potentially* harmful—not that it has already proven itself to be (actually) harmful. In one place, in fact, Sunstein says that it is "potentially harmful" (instead of simply "harmful"), and he sometimes writes "false and dangerous" (instead of "false and harmful").[361] However, because Sunstein has generally used the term "harmful," I will also use it, with the understanding that Sunstein used it to mean *potentially* harmful.

In any case, this sixth thesis—that the 9/11 Truth Movement's conspiracy theory is (potentially) harmful—constitutes a necessary link in Sunstein's argument, which concluded that the government should have agents infiltrate this movement with the intent to break it up. In order to justify such action by the government against groups of citizens exercising their First Amendment right of free speech, Sunstein needed to portray this movement as dangerous, and he certainly tried.

1. Extremism

The key concept in this effort is "extremism." The "principal claim" of his argument, Sunstein says, "involves the potential value of *cognitive infiltration of extremist groups*."[362] To justify infiltration of the 9/11 Truth Movement, therefore, he has to characterize groups belonging to this movement as "extremist."

That is clearly his intent: Given the fact that this movement provides the "main focus" and "running example" of his essay, he obviously means his statements about extremist groups to apply preeminently to 9/11 groups. But this dimension of his argument is problematic at best.

One problem is that he never defines "extremism" or "extremist." Although he has a section labeled "Definitional Notes," he offers no definition of "extremism," in spite of its being one of his essay's key concepts. Also, although authors generally define their technical terms upon their first use, the first passage by Sunstein using this term simply says:

> Many extremists fall in this category [of having crippled epistemologies]; their extremism stems not from irrationality, but from the fact that they have little (relevant) information, and their extremist views are supported by what little they know.[363]

That is all he says, evidently taking it for granted that his readers share his intuitive understanding of what constitutes extremism.

A further problem is that, because he leaves the meaning of this term unexpressed, he necessarily provides no justification for classifying groups belonging to the 9/11 Truth Movement as "extremist." He simply presupposes, it appears, that this is an unproblematic characterization.

A partial explanation for this presupposition may be that he derived his argument's basic concept, "crippled epistemology," from an essay by Russell Hardin entitled "The Crippled Epistemology of Extremism." Perhaps he assumed that readers would go to this article to find out what he meant by "extremism."

2. From Extremism to Violence

In any case, to see that Sunstein's characterization of the 9/11 Truth Movement as extremist is *not* unproblematic, we need only to look at his next step, in which he says that groups who hold the 9/11 conspiracy theory, being extremists, are likely to become violent.

This causal connection is expressed in a passage in which he argues that crippled epistemologies are likely to lead to violence:

> If the most trustworthy . . . information justifies conspiracy theories and (therefore) extremism, and (therefore?) violence, then terrorism is more likely to arise.[364]

The question mark after the second "therefore" evidently indicates that, although extremist beliefs do not necessarily lead to violence, they tend to do so.

In any event, we can see here why it is terribly problematic for Sunstein to make such connections without explaining what he means by "extremism." According to one common meaning, extremist beliefs are simply convictions that are out of step with what most people in a given society believe, perhaps because those convictions are widely thought to be contradicted by science. By this conception, people who believe the Earth is flat are extremists, but there is no reason to think that flat-earthers are especially prone to violence. The same is true for those believe that our universe is only a few thousand years old, that Nostradamus correctly predicted the major events in human history since his time, and that we can become immortal through cryogenics. So if the belief that 9/11 was an inside job is "extremist" in the same sense, this fact provides no reason to think that groups holding this belief are more likely than other groups to become violent.

More likely, however, Sunstein is referring to beliefs that are extremist in the sense of attributing conspiracies to the government. The best-known conspiracy theories of this type include the belief that FDR maneuvered the Japanese into attacking Pearl Harbor and then did nothing to prevent the attack, that the CIA was involved in the assassination of JFK, that the FBI was involved in the assassinations of MLK and RFK, that the "Tonkin Gulf incident" never happened, that the moon-landing was a hoax, that the Bush–Cheney administration fabricated the evidence about weapons of mass destruction in Iraq, that it fabricated the connection between Saddam Hussein and al-Qaeda, and that it was responsible for the anthrax attacks.

But groups holding one or more of these theories have not shown a special proclivity to resort to violence. (They seem mainly to write books and articles and, in some cases, to hold annual meetings.) Our experience with these groups, therefore, provides no basis for a prediction that 9/11 truth groups, some of which have existed for many years now, are likely to become violent.

An essential step in Sunstein's argument, therefore, appears not to be justified by historical evidence.

3. Extremism, Justification, and Truth

Another problem is that, similarly to the way in which Sunstein, for the most part, writes as if conspiracy theories are by definition unjustified, he generally writes the same way about extremist beliefs. But just as he admits that some conspiracy theories have been both justified and true, he makes the same concession, even if only in a footnote, with regard to extremist beliefs, acknowledging the twofold point "that some extremism is justified and that the beliefs that underlie extremism may be true."[365] Not all extremists, in other words, have had crippled epistemologies.

It is good that Sunstein makes these acknowledgments. But these concessions to reality undermine his argument. He said at the outset, as we saw, that he is concerned only with conspiracy theories that are "false, harmful, and unjustified."[366] Besides having admitted that the 9/11 conspiracy theory is not false simply by virtue of being a conspiracy theory, he has now admitted that, even if he could make the case for classifying it as an extremist theory, he would not thereby have shown it to be either unjustified or false.

By calling the 9/11 conspiracy theory "extremist," therefore, he has not—even for people who do not challenge the label—shown it to belong to the category of "false, harmful, and unjustified" theories, which the government should seek to undermine.

To provide a (justified!) rationale for such an attempt by the government, therefore, he would need to show the beliefs of the 9/11 Truth Movement to be both false and harmful. However, besides providing no evidence to support his claim that these beliefs are false, as we saw in the previous chapter, he also provides no evidence, as we have now seen, to support his claim that the 9/11 Truth Movement is harmful.

He seeks to portray it as such, nevertheless, by suggesting frightening possibilities.

4. Frightening Possibilities

"Some false conspiracy theories create serious risks," Sunstein says, and "in extreme cases, they create or fuel violence."[367] Given the fact that the 9/11 conspiracy theory is his running example and main focus, he thereby implies that it is—or at least is likely to become—one of these extreme cases.

Perhaps anticipating the objection that the recognized leaders of the 9/11 Truth Movement—people such as activist Carol Brouillet, architect Richard Gage, chemists Niels Harrit and Kevin Ryan, computer scientist A.K. Dewdney, economist Michel Chossudovsky, Japanese Senator Yukihisa Fujita, physicists David Chandler and Steven Jones, poet Peter Dale Scott, and Janice Matthews, the long-time director of 911Truth.org—are not likely to advocate violence, he says:

> [C]onspiracy theories have had large effects on behavior. And even if only a small fraction of adherents to a particular conspiracy theory act on the basis of their beliefs, that small fraction may be enough to cause serious harms.

As to why, Sunstein writes:

> [Some commentators] argue that technological change has driven down the costs of delivering attacks with weapons of mass destruction, to the point where even a small group can pose a significant threat. If so, and if only a tiny fraction of believers act on their beliefs, then as the total population with conspiratorial beliefs grows, it becomes nearly inevitable that action will ensue.[368]

Sunstein has hence sought to move his readers to the point where they would believe that, if the 9/11 Truth Movement is allowed to keep growing, it is "nearly inevitable" that some of its members will orchestrate an attack employing nuclear, biological, or chemical weapons of mass destruction.

Sunstein, however, has provided no reason to think of such an attack originating from the 9/11 Truth Movement as a realistic possibility, let alone a "nearly inevitable" eventuality. His scary scenario rests solely on his characterization of groups belonging to the 9/11 Truth Movement as "extremist"—a term he did not even bother to define.

It is possible, to be sure, that as more and more people become aware of the evidence that the official account of 9/11 is false, and thereby become aware that the 9/11 attacks were orchestrated by members of our own government in order to provide a pretext for a "war on terror," some individuals who have picked up these beliefs from the 9/11 Truth Movement, whether directly or indirectly, will resort to violence as a consequence.

But people are moved to violence by all sorts of beliefs, such as the belief that abortion is wrong, that gay marriage is wrong, or that one has been laid off from one's job unfairly. That such incidents occur does not provide the government with a justification for trying to stop groups from advocating gay rights or abortion rights or trying to prevent employers from laying off people when their companies are losing money.

Likewise, some acts of violence that can plausibly be attributed to beliefs advocated by the 9/11 Truth Movement would provide no justification for taking special measures against groups belonging to it—not only for the reason just given, but also because Sunstein's targets are supposed to be limited to conspiracy theories that are false as well as harmful. So even if he could point to some acts of violence to make his case that the 9/11 Truth Movement is harmful, he would also need to show that it is false. And he has not, as we have seen, even made the effort to demonstrate this.

Such considerations will not, to be sure, prevent the government and its lapdogs in the press from seizing upon any act of violence committed by someone who shares some of the 9/11 Truth Movement's beliefs as evidence that the movement is dangerous.

For example, during the first week of March 2010, while I was completing the first draft of this chapter, a shooting occurred at the Pentagon. A *New York Times* story about it began:

The gunman who opened fire at an entrance to the Pentagon on Thursday, injuring two police officers, harbored a deep-seated anger toward federal authorities and may have believed that the government staged the Sept. 11 attacks, officials said Friday.

The remainder of the story showed that this belief, which he "may" have held, was only one of a number of factors that could have led to his act of violence:

> The gunman, John Patrick Bedell, 36, who was killed by the officers, made copious—and often rambling—postings and recorded lectures on the internet in the past few years. In them he raged against what he saw as a totalitarian federal government, which he faulted for its handling of monetary policy, public education and private property rights.
>
> Reb Monaco, 65, a longtime friend of Mr. Bedell's, said: "From what I gather from the family, he's been on a downhill spin for a while. And they were very, very concerned about him."
>
> Mr. Monaco added that Mr. Bedell, who was unmarried, a regular marijuana smoker and living with his parents, seemed to slide into a deep paranoia in the past couple of years. . . .
>
> On Friday, the police here were trying to determine whether Mr. Bedell's views on the 1991 death of a Marine officer, Col. James E. Sabow, in El Toro, Calif., played a role in his attack on the Pentagon officers. Colonel Sabow's death, which was officially ruled a suicide, is the subject of numerous dark theories about military cover-ups, claiming that he was murdered because he was about to expose covert military operations in Central America involving drug smuggling.
>
> Mr. Bedell wrote on the Web that he was "determined to see that justice is served" in the death of Colonel Sabow and that to uncover the truth behind the death would be "a step toward establishing the truth of events such as the Sept. 11 demolitions."[369]

So, although Bedell was mentally ill and was evidently upset with the federal government for a wide range of reasons, the *Times'* story was written so as to suggest that his act of violence was likely due to a belief that the government had been responsible for the 9/11 attacks. The 9/11 Truth Movement will have great difficulty defending itself against this kind of biased journalism.

This movement will also find it difficult to defend itself if infiltrators are ordered, after becoming accepted members of the 9/11 Truth Movement, to perpetrate acts of violence, perhaps "with terrifying consequences."

The fact will remain, nonetheless, that the history of the movement prior to the time that Sunstein's essay was written provided no basis for his claim that violence issuing from it was "nearly inevitable."

5. Other Pernicious Effects

Having ineffectively tried to portray the 9/11 Truth Movement as potentially harmful in the sense of being likely to turn violent, Sunstein then articulated what seemed to be his real concern. Even if the 9/11 conspiracy theory does not produce violent action, he said:

[It] can still have pernicious effects from the government's point of view, either by inducing unjustifiably widespread public skepticism about the government's assertions, or by dampening public mobilization and participation in government-led efforts.[370]

Widespread Skepticism about Government Claims

Of these two possible "pernicious effects," the first one—that the 9/11 Truth Movement might induce "widespread public skepticism about the government's assertions [about 9/11]"—is, of course, exactly what the movement is attempting to do, using its constitutionally protected right of free speech to make its case.

Sunstein says that such skepticism would be *unjustifiable*. As we have seen, however, he has provided no basis for this assertion. As a lawyer, he surely understands that one cannot convince people to resist a particular conclusion—such as the conclusion that the government was complicit in the 9/11 attacks—simply by telling them that this conclusion is unjustifiable. One must provide evidence.

For example, I have published eight books (prior to this one) that argued for this allegedly unjustifiable conclusion. In addition to books by other authors, there have also been several scientific papers, published in peer-reviewed journals, that support this conclusion by showing that the official reports on the World Trade Center cannot possibly be true, given the fact that they contradict some basic principles of physics and chemistry.[371] If Sunstein wanted to convince people that the conclusion for which these books and papers argue is unjustifiable, the best way to do this would be to point to government-supported rebuttals of these books and papers. But he does not, perhaps in part because there have been no effective rebuttals.

In the face of this situation, it would seem that Sunstein should be enlisting reputable scientists to provide these rebuttals. In their absence, his claim that our conclusions are unjustifiable is—of course—unjustified.

Dampening Public Mobilization

A second way in which the 9/11 Truth Movement can be harmful without being violent, Sunstein suggests, is by "dampening public mobilization and participation in government-led efforts." The major "public mobilization" resulting from 9/11 has, of course, been the "war on terror" (which thus far has resulted primarily in the US-led wars in Afghanistan and Iraq). This so-called war on terror can be considered justified, if at all, only if the official account of 9/11 is true. One of the major purposes of the 9/11 Truth Movement is to show that these wars are *not* justified by showing the official account to be false. We hope thereby to dampen the mobilization and participation in these wars, which we consider immoral and illegal.

We want, accordingly, to be "harmful" to this particular government-led effort in precisely the way Sunstein fears—just as those who told the truth about the Vietnam war were harmful to *that* government-led effort. If Sunstein and his friends in high places consider the wars in Afghanistan and Iraq—or at least the war in Afghanistan—to be justified, they should try to make a better case for this claim than the proponents of the war in Vietnam made for their claim.

Given the fact that they have not even tried to do this by refuting the arguments of the 9/11 Truth Movement, we can only suspect that this is because they know that no such refutation is possible.

Undermining Democratic Debate

Sunstein suggests, finally, a third nonviolent but pernicious effect of the 9/11 conspiracy theory. Having said, "Some false conspiracy theories create serious risks," he continues: "They . . . undermine democratic debate."[372] Given the fact that the 9/11 conspiracy theory is his main focus and running example, Sunstein must be saying that this theory in particular undermines democratic debate. This is a very bizarre claim, especially given the history of the 9/11 Truth Movement's attempts to generate debate.

Even apart from this history, Sunstein's claim is very strange. How could democratic debate be undermined by a claim that the government's account of some event is false? Such a claim by its very nature is an *invitation* to debate. Of course, if members of the 9/11 Truth Movement had made their claim about 9/11 and then turned down all offers to debate it, there would be some basis for Sunstein's charge. But the refusal to debate has come entirely from the other side.

In 2006, for example, Edward Haas, a member of the 9/11 Truth Movement, reported a telephone conversation he had with Michael Newman, a spokesman for NIST. After pointing out that "more than half of all Americans now believe the US government has some complicity if not culpability regarding 9/11," Haas suggested that "a possible method to reconcile the division in the United States between the government and its people" might be to have a series of nationally televised debates between the scientists who worked on the NIST report and scientists who question this report. Before he could get his suggestion fully out, Haas reported, he "was abruptly interrupted and told that none of the NIST scientists would participate in any public debate."[373]

Haas later attempted to organize a debate. He first obtained an agreement from seven leading members of the 9/11 Truth Movement to participate in a televised debate that would take place in Charleston, South Carolina, on September 16, 2006. These members included an attorney, a former member of the US Air Force, and five professors (of physics, mechanical engineering, economics, philosophy of science, and philosophy of religion). Haas then invited the scientists responsible for the NIST report on the Twin Towers plus the members of the 9/11 Commission to come to Charleston, all expenses paid.

The NIST scientists did not even respond to the invitation. After Haas sent several more invitations to them, he received a message from Newman saying: "The project leaders of the NIST World Trade Center investigation team respectfully decline your invitations to participate in the National 9/11 Debate on September 16, 2006." Haas then asked Newman if there was a better date or location, to which Newman replied: "The members of the NIST WTC Investigation

Team has [*sic*] respectfully declined your invitation to participate in the National 9/11 Debate. A change in venue or date will not alter that decision."[374]

The invitation was also refused by all ten members of the 9/11 Commission, even though the co-chairmen, Thomas Kean and Lee Hamilton, published a book that same year in which they listed five negative characteristics of conspiracy theorists, one of which was that they have "disdain for open and informed debate."[375]

Finally, hoping to get anyone with some official or even semi-official status to debate, Hass sent an invitation to James B. Meigs, the editor-in-chief of *Popular Mechanics*, which had in March 2005 published an article entitled "9/11: Debunking the Myths," followed in 2006 by its expansion into a book, *Debunking 9/11 Myths*. The editors of this book, Brad Reagan and David Dunbar, were also invited. In his letter of invitation, Haas, besides pointing out that all expenses would be covered, added:

> I have noted that *Popular Mechanics* is now touting itself as the final answer that debunks 9/11 myths. The question now is will the people behind and responsible for the book titled *Debunking 9/11 Myths*, people such as yourself, stand firmly behind your work and participate in the National 9/11 Debate?

Haas never received a reply from any of these individuals.[376]

Moreover, I have written several books about 9/11, all of which by their very nature were invitations to debate, but these invitations went unanswered. My second one was a critique of *The 9/11 Commission Report*,[377] but no member of the Commission wrote a response, whether publicly or privately, or challenged me to a debate. My 2007 book *Debunking 9/11 Debunking* is subtitled *An Answer to Popular Mechanics and Other Defenders of the Official Conspiracy Theory*. Among those "other defenders" are Thomas Kean and Lee Hamilton, the co-chairs of the 9/11 Commission, and Philip Zelikow, its executive director, but neither Kean, nor Hamilton, nor Zelikow, nor anyone from *Popular Mechanics* responded. Also, my 2008 book *9/11 Contradictions* is subtitled *An Open Letter to Congress and the Press*, but no member of Congress responded and no member of the mainstream press wrote a review of the book or even mentioned it in print.

If "democratic debate" is in trouble in this country (and it is), it is not the fault of the 9/11 Truth Movement.

6. An Esoteric Reading of Sunstein's Sixth Thesis

The absurdity of Sunstein's claims about the dangers presented by the 9/11 conspiracy theory, when taken at face value, suggest that his real target must not have been the 9/11 Truth Movement. When read with eyes alert to a possible hidden or esoteric meaning, Sunstein's previous theses have suggested the actual target must have been the 9/11 conspiracy theory that was promulgated by the Bush–Cheney administration: It is the one that is based on a crippled epistemology; it is the one that is unjustified and demonstrably false; and it is the one that has resulted in a degenerating research program. The present thesis, when read for a possible hidden, too-dangerous-to-express-openly meaning, can be seen as adding the point that this same conspiracy theory is harmful.

Violence and Terror

That this might be Sunstein's real meaning is suggested if we look at his first-expressed concern in his sixth thesis—*9/11 conspiracy theorists, being extremists, are likely to become violent, with "terrifying conse-quences"*—with our eyes open for a deeper meaning. When under-stood in terms of its surface meaning, as referring to the recognized leaders of the 9/11 Truth Movement, this claim, as we saw, is ridiculous. Even if it is taken to refer to people who might be influenced by this movement, there is no reason to expect more violence to result from its beliefs than from those of many other controversial movements.

This claim is perfectly correct, however, if taken to refer to the government's 9/11 conspiracy theory, which was used by extremists in the Bush–Cheney administration to invade and occupy two countries. It is widely agreed that each invasion has resulted in over a million deaths, and Dr. Gideon Polya, who asks how many deaths have resulted from the invasions—not simply from military activity but all deaths that would not have occurred without the invasions—puts the figure for Iraq at 2.3 million and that for Afghanistan as 4.5 million deaths.[378] Whether we accept Polya's estimates or the more standard ones, the 9/11 conspiracy theory promoted by the Bush–

Cheney administration has resulted in an enormous amount of death and destruction.

With regard to "terrifying consequences": Think how terrifying it would be to live in a country where you could not hold a wedding or a funeral without fear that missiles from a drone would strike your party at any minute.

In the eight years from 9/11 to September 11, 2009, by contrast, the conspiracy theory promoted by the 9/11 Truth Movement resulted in little if any violence, terrorism, and death. And if some violence does begin to result, it will be insignificant in comparison with that which has resulted from the government's conspiracy theory. Does this contrast not suggest that the "extremists" about whom Sunstein is concerned must be those who have used the Bush–Cheney 9/11 conspiracy theory to promote US interests in Afghanistan, Iraq, and elsewhere?

Hardin's Essay

The truth of this interpretation becomes even more likely when we look at the essay on which Sunstein's argument is most heavily dependent: "The Crippled Epistemology of Extremism," by Russell Hardin.

The "extremists" about which Hardin is primarily concerned, he tells us at the outset, are *fanatical nationalists*. Saying that his key concepts will be *fanatical politics*, *nationalism*, and the *epistemology of extremism*, he writes: "I will suggest how crippled epistemology leads to fanaticism, which may in turn lead to fanatical nationalism."[379]

So, although at the surface level it seems that Sunstein's discussion of epistemologically crippled extremism is directed at the 9/11 Truth Movement—which has been opposing America's nationalistic projects in Afghanistan and Iraq—his reference to Hardin's essay allows discerning readers to see that his real target must be a movement that promotes and actualizes fanatical nationalism, not one that opposes it.

Once this is realized, can we doubt that his target must be the coalition of fanatical nationalists who used the Bush–Cheney administration's demonstrably false conspiracy theory for imperialistic purposes—namely, the neoconservatives, usually called simply "neocons"? This neocon movement, which achieved enormous power and influence when the Bush–Cheney administration was installed in 2001, included ideologues such as Elliott Abrams, John Bolton, Dick Cheney, Zalmay Khalilzad, Charles Krauthammer,

William Kristol, Lewis "Scooter" Libby, Richard Perle, Donald Rumsfeld, Paul Wolfowitz, and Albert Wohlstetter (who reportedly provided a model for "Dr. Strangelove"[380]).

The fanaticism of these people was revealed in their writings. After the fall of the Soviet Union, for example, Krauthammer argued that the United States, being the "unchallenged superpower," should be "unashamedly laying down the rules of world order."[381] Several other neocons, including Cheney, Perle, Wohlstetter, and Wolfowitz, began calling for the overthrow of Saddam Hussein in the early 1990s and continued this call throughout the decade.[382] In 1992, which was Cheney's final year as secretary of defense, he oversaw the writing of a document that has been called "a blueprint for permanent American global hegemony" and Cheney's "Plan . . . to rule the world."[383] In 1997, Kristol formed a neocon organization called the Project for the New American Century (PNAC), which reaffirmed "the basic tenets" of the 1992 Cheney document.[384] In September 2000, shortly before the Bush–Cheney administration took office, PNAC produced a document calling for the US to use its military power to produce an "American peace"—a *Pax Americana*. Its proposals to transform the world, it added, would likely take a long time "absent some catastrophic and catalyzing event—like a new Pearl Harbor."[385]

And when this new Pearl Harbor came the following September, it was exploited to the hilt. As one commentator wrote in 2005, the neocons "have taken full advantage of the nation's outrage over 9/11 to advance their already fully formed drive for empire."[386] "[T]he traumatic effects of the 9/11 terrorism," wrote another, "enabled the agenda of the neocons to become the policy of the United States of America."[387]

Iraq, as we have seen, had been on this agenda for a decade. Afghanistan was also on it before the 9/11 attacks: In July 2001, having found that the Taliban had refused their ultimatum—"Either you accept our offer of a carpet of gold, or we bury you under a carpet of bombs"[388]—representatives of the Bush administration reportedly said that "military action against Afghanistan would go ahead . . . before the snows started falling in Afghanistan, by the middle of October at the latest."[389] (Given the date of the 9/11 attacks, the Pentagon was indeed ready to begin its military action in Afghanistan on October 7.)

In order to carry out their agenda, it was not sufficient for these extremists to orchestrate the 9/11 attacks and make them appear to be the work of Osama bin Laden's al-Qaeda organization. They also had to claim, in order to provide a justification for attacking Afghanistan, that the Taliban had refused to turn over bin Laden. The truth, however, was that the Taliban had agreed to turn him over if the Bush administration would only provide proof of his responsibility for the 9/11 attacks—a request that the Bush administration rejected.[390]

In order to get the backing of the American people to attack Iraq, this administration told two more lies. One of these was that Saddam Hussein had played a role in the 9/11 attacks. The second lie, as Cheney formulated it in August 2002, was that "there is no doubt that Saddam Hussein now has weapons of mass destruction . . . [and] is amassing them to use . . . against us."[391] Although the administration later claimed that this false charge was based on bad intelligence, the truth was that, as pointed out above in Chapter 2, the Bush–Cheney administration had "the intelligence and facts fixed around the policy [of going to war]." Both lies came to be accepted by about 70 percent of the American people.[392]

These neocons are clearly perfect specimens of the type of extremists with which Hardin's essay was primarily concerned, namely, fanatical nationalists. In order to serve US imperial interests, they were ready to kill thousands of American citizens on 9/11, frame Muslims for the crime, then tell more lies in order to attack and occupy two Muslim nations in operations that have killed millions of their citizens. Nationalism does not get much more fanatical than this.

In Hardin's discussion of how epistemologies can become crippled, he says that when "a crippled epistemology leads to fanaticism," this fanaticism "then leads to the urge for governmental control or nationalism." Explaining why, he says:

> It is only through gaining control of a state . . . that a fanatical group could expect to exclude contrary views and thereby maintain the crippled epistemology of their followers. With the power of the state behind them, they can coerce.[393]

In referring readers to Hardin's essay, was Sunstein not leading us to see that, when people have crippled epistemologies, it is often a condition imposed upon them by their political leaders, who have used the power of the state to "exclude contrary views"—namely, all views except their own—from the public discussion? Was he not leading them to see that, insofar as citizens have only "a sharply limited number of (relevant) informational sources," this is likely because their political leaders have used their coercive power to prevent them from learning about other sources of information?

That this was Hardin's point, at least, is made even clearer in the following passage:

> Belief is not a matter of choice or decision. Commonly, it happens to us because the facts compel us. . . . [A]mong the facts that compel us are the testimony of others around us and, perhaps especially, those over us. . . . [F]anatics understand this and they therefore often want . . . the power to coerce and influence others.[394]

It would seem that Sunstein, by referring us to Hardin's essay, was pointing out that, by getting a like-minded, controllable person installed in the Oval Office, the neocons were able to use the president's "bully pulpit" to get most of the American people to believe their lies about 9/11, Afghanistan, and Iraq, and hence to support their wars of fanatical nationalism.

This was especially the case, Sunstein may have expected us to recall, during the first few years after 9/11, when the tendency of mainstream reporters to act as stenographers and megaphones—simply writing down White House statements and repeating them to the public—was intensified, because any questioning was seen as almost treasonous. For example, explaining to London's *Guardian* why he and other journalists had not been asking the administration tough questions on the "war on terrorism," then CBS anchor Dan Rather said:

> "[T]here was a time in South Africa that people would put flaming tyres around people's necks if they dissented. And in some ways the fear is that you will be necklaced here, you will have a flaming tyre of lack of patriotism put around your neck," he said. "Now it is that fear that keeps journalists from asking the toughest of the tough questions. . . . And the current administration revels in that, they relish that, and they take refuge in that."[395]

The Bush–Cheney administration had the power to effect almost any policy it wished.

Further elaborating on the way in which fanatics, once they take control of a state, can build up their power by keeping the people ignorant, Hardin's essay continues:

> Hampering open discussion cripples the epistemology of the populace and makes it more readily susceptible to the blandishments of fanatics. Counter to the slogan, Knowledge is power, very nearly the opposite is true for fanatics. Suppressing knowledge is the route to power.[396]

Published in 2002, Hardin's essay thereby accurately described how the Bush–Cheney administration was able to exercise almost dictatorial control of American policy for several years.

By getting their people in positions of power, the neocons were able to control the information flow to the public. They were able, for example, to get the press to suppress most of the reports that contradicted the administration's account of what happened on 9/11. They were then able to make sure that the official reports put out by NIST and the 9/11 Commission supported this account. In these and related ways, they were able to keep the people ignorant of the true facts and thereby to share, at least to a sufficient degree, their own fanatical nationalism. This dynamic illustrated one of Hardin's central points: that the "epistemology of nationalism" is usually based on "woeful ignorance."[397]

Accordingly, given the fact that Sunstein points his serious readers to Hardin's essay, we can reasonably infer that his primary concern, at the deeper level, is with the fact that the neocon-led Bush–Cheney administration used its control of the nation's coercive powers to cripple the public's epistemology, thereby making it possible to get a majority of the public to accept the administration's false conspiracy theory about 9/11 and to support its nationalistic wars in Afghanistan and Iraq.

Finally, Sunstein's charge that the 9/11 conspiracy theory undermines democratic debate, which is silly when taken to mean the 9/11 Truth Movement's theory, is entirely true when taken to refer to the false conspiracy theory purveyed by the Bush–Cheney administration. Democratic debate presupposes that citizens are in possession of accurate information about the issues at hand. No meaningful debate can occur when the leaders systematically lie to the citizens, crippling their epistemologies. Democratic debate, hence democracy itself, has been completely undermined by the false conspiracy theory put out by the Bush–Cheney administration and supported by the official reports and, thus far anyway, the mainstream press.

In the following chapters, we will see proposals for dealing with this problem.

CHAPTER 7
THE DUTY TO UNDERMINE THE 9/11 CONSPIRACY THEORY

According to Sunstein's seventh thesis:

"Conspiracy theories turn out to be unusually hard to undermine," but "[i]f government can dispel [false and harmful] conspiracy theories," such as the 9/11 conspiracy theory, "it should do so."[398]

This thesis presupposes Sunstein's statement of the basic problem faced by those in power: "Imagine a government facing a population in which a particular conspiracy theory is becoming widespread."[399] In this situation, Sunstein's seventh thesis says, the government has a duty to stop the spread of this theory. In elaborating on this thesis, Sunstein wrote:

> Our focus throughout is on demonstrably false conspiracy theories, such as the various 9/11 conspiracy theories, not ones that are true or whose truth is undetermined. Our ultimate goal is to explore how public officials might undermine such theories, and as a general rule, true accounts should not be undermined.[400]

Many readers will find the final part of this passage—"as a general rule, true accounts should not be undermined"—disconcerting: Under what conceivable conditions, they will ask, does Sunstein believe that true accounts should *ever* be undermined? Sunstein is presupposing, to recall, a "well-motivated government," meaning one that would seek "to eliminate conspiracy theories . . . if and only if social welfare is improved by doing so."[401] When would such a government seek to undermine a true theory, thereby seeking to spread a false account? In a footnote, Sunstein refers to this as an "interesting question."[402]

In any case, leaving that interesting question aside, we can agree with Sunstein's general thesis: The government, when it can, should seek to undermine conspiracy theories that are both harmful and demonstrably false.

Sunstein does raise a possible objection to this thesis: If the government simply ignores a particular conspiracy theory, people will likely infer from its silence "that the theory is too ludicrous to need rebuttal," whereas "to rebut the theory may be to legitimate it" by moving it to "the zone of claims that . . . are in some sense worth discussing."[403]

However, Sunstein counters, simply ignoring a theory can also be dangerous, because people may infer that "the government is silent because it cannot offer relevant evidence to the contrary."[404] Also, drawing on the notion of synergistic gains, Sunstein adds the following consideration:

> [R]ebutting many conspiracy theories can reduce the legitimating effect of rebutting any *one* of them. When government rebuts a particular theory while ignoring most others, the legitimating effect arises at least in part because of . . . the inference . . . that government has picked the theory it is rebutting out of the larger set because this theory, unlike the others, is inherently plausible . . . . The more theories government rebuts, the weaker is the implicit legitimating signal sent by the very fact of rebuttal.[405]

In the original version of Sunstein's paper, moreover, this statement was followed by a practical suggestion about how to implement this proposal:

> Practically speaking, government might do well to maintain a more vigorous countermisinformation establishment than it would otherwise do, one that identifies and rebuts many more conspiracy theories [than] would otherwise be rebutted.[406]

Sunstein concludes, accordingly, that the government should seek to rebut all or at least most of the harmful and demonstrably false conspiracy theories circulating at any given time. This argument will probably win widespread assent.

1. Taking the Seventh Thesis at Face Value

A problem arises, however, because Sunstein—we are beginning, of course, with the exoteric reading of his seventh thesis—uses this general principle to claim that the government should seek to undermine conspiracy theories articulated by the 9/11 Truth Movement (such as the theory that the WTC buildings were brought down by explosives and the theory that the Pentagon was not struck by an airliner flown by an al-Qaeda pilot). This claim is problematic because Sunstein has not shown such theories to be false, as we have seen, or to be harmful or dangerous in the sense of being especially likely to give rise to violence.

Sunstein has correctly pointed out, to be sure, that these theories can be "harmful" in the sense of undermining government policies that have been based on the Bush–Cheney interpretation of 9/11, such as the wars in Iraq and Afghanistan. But given the widespread agreement that the war in Vietnam ended when it did only because of what we might now call the "Vietnam War Truth Movement," not many Americans would look kindly on an effort to break up the 9/11 Truth Movement simply because it wanted to bring the wars in Iraq and Afghanistan to an end.

Americans who disagree with the 9/11 Truth Movement would, to be sure, welcome an attempt by the government to undermine it by providing evidence to demonstrate its beliefs to be false. But the government has made no attempt to do this. As we will see in the following chapters, moreover, Sunstein himself does not even recommend that it try.

In sum: Although Sunstein is correct that the government should seek to undermine conspiracy theories that are harmful as well as demonstrably false, he has not—due to his failure to show the ideas espoused by the 9/11 Truth Movement to be either harmful (in the sense in which this claim would commonly be understood) or false—provided any basis for his claim that the government should seek to undermine this movement's central ideas. All the more has he not provided any support for such an effort employing means other than evidence and rational argumentation.

2. Reading for a Hidden Meaning

In the previous chapters, we found that Sunstein's theses, when understood literally, made no sense, but that when they were understood in terms of a hidden, esoteric meaning, they made perfect sense. The same is true of his seventh thesis, if understood to mean that the government should seek to undermine the official 9/11 conspiracy theory, which—as we have seen in previous chapters—is demonstrably false as well as being extremely harmful.

This interpretation may, at first glance, seem to be self-contradictory: The official theory is by definition the government's theory: How could Sunstein have expected the government to undermine its own theory?

We must recall, however, that Sunstein's paper—including the final version of it, which was published in a journal in 2009—was placed online in 2008, which was the final year of the Bush–Cheney administration. Given the growing unpopularity of that administration along with Republicans in general, Sunstein would have been expecting it to be replaced by a Democratic administration, which would be free to expose the falsity of the Bush–Cheney administration's 9/11 conspiracy theory.

By recognizing that context, we can better appreciate why the paper may have been written with two levels of meaning. In 2008, while the Bush–Cheney administration was still in power, it would not have been prudent for Sunstein to indicate, in a statement about which there could be no doubt as to its true meaning, that the 9/11 theory promoted by that administration belonged to the class of false and harmful conspiracy theories. Doing so would have been especially imprudent if Sunstein had hoped for a position in the next administration in which he would be able to undermine that theory, because the slightest expression of doubt about the Bush–Cheney administration's conspiracy theory has been taken, by Democrats as well as Republicans and the mainstream press, as proof of unfitness for public office.[407]

To most eyes, therefore, the paper had to contain a proposal for undermining the theories associated with the 9/11 Truth Movement. Those with eyes to see a deeper meaning, however, could understand Sunstein to be sending a signal: that it was time to start a process of undermining the 9/11 conspiracy theory that had been foisted onto Congress and the public by the Bush–Cheney administration.

CHAPTER 8
INOCULATING THE PUBLIC

The eighth thesis in Sunstein's argument says:

In seeking to undermine the 9/11 conspiracy theory, the government should take a twofold approach: besides dealing with the theory's demand side, by seeking to inoculate the public against it, the government should also address the theory's supply side, by seeking to "debias or disable its purveyors."[408]

In discussing this thesis, we begin, of course, with Sunstein's meaning when his statements are taken at face value.

1. Thesis Eight Understood Exoterically

The twofold approach suggested in this thesis is Sunstein's answer to the question as to which audience the government should address in seeking to prevent the 9/11 conspiracy theory from spreading. He wrote:

> Should governmental responses be addressed to the suppliers, with a view to persuading or silencing them, or rather be addressed to the mass audience, with a view to inoculating them from pernicious theories?[409]

In beginning his answer, Sunstein wrote:

> Of course these two strategies are not mutually exclusive; perhaps the best approach is to straddle the two audiences with a single response or simply to provide multiple responses.[410]

The problem with this suggestion, Sunstein cautioned, is that "pitching governmental responses to the suppliers of conspiracy theories" will generally be unsuccessful, because the hard-core conspiracy theorists, who supply these theories, are generally resistant to contrary evidence, especially when offered by the government. Because of this difficulty, Sunstein continued:

> [M]any officials dismiss direct responses to the suppliers of conspiracy theorists [*sic*] as an exercise in futility. . . . Thus officials address their responses to the third-party mass audience, hoping to stem the spread of conspiracy theories by dampening the demand rather than by reducing the supply.[411]

But, Sunstein countered, "giving up on the hard core of conspiracy theorists" is not a good idea, because "the hard core may itself provide the most serious threat."[412]

Accordingly, he argued, the government needs to direct its efforts to the hard-core conspiracy theorists as well as to the public, but it needs to use different approaches for these different audiences. The distinctive approach to the hard-core conspiracy theorists advocated by Sunstein, along with his more extensive explanation for its necessity, will be reserved for the following two chapters. The remainder of the present chapter is devoted to Sunstein's ideas about inoculating the public against the 9/11 conspiracy theory.

Maintaining a Free, Open Society
In a section headed "An Open Society as the First-Line Cure," Sunstein says:

> The first-line response to conspiracy theories is to maintain an open society, in which those who might be tempted to subscribe to such theories . . . are exposed to evidence and corrections. Nongovernmental organizations, including the media, can and do work hard to respond to such theories. . . . [I]n free societies, conspiracy theories are generally dislodged by the media and other non-governmental actors.[413]

This argument is problematic.

One problem is that, if Sunstein's meaning is that the US media can generally be counted on to dislodge government-sponsored conspiracy theories as well as anti-government theories, then he would be presupposing a type of free press that, as we saw in Chapter 2, we do not have.

A second problem is that, although Sunstein has granted that anti-government conspiracy theories are sometimes true, he here writes as if they should all be dislodged by the media. That would be the case only if the media's task were to refute all anti-government theories, whether they be true or false. But if that is explicitly acknowledged to be the media's task, then the fact that we do not have a free press is out in the open—we simply accept the fact that we have a press that is the government's lapdog, not its watchdog.

In a recent essay in a symposium on State Crimes Against Democracy, Laurie Manwell, having referred to Alexis de Tocqueville's emphasis on the necessity of a free press for the maintenance of self-government, wrote:

> The right to dissent with the majority opinion, and the necessity to have this dissenting discourse within the public sphere, must be protected.[414]

But the 9/11 Truth Movement's dissenting discourse has definitely *not* been allowed into the public sphere. Rather, as Manwell says, "the U.S. government's account of 9/11 [is] parroted by the mainstream media."[415] These mainstream media then refuse to permit leading members of the 9/11 Truth Movement to present their evidence against this account. We have, therefore, "information widely reported by the mainstream media, government, and 9/11 Commission," on the one hand, and "dissimilar information presented by less-well-known alternative media, dissenting experts, scholars, and whistleblowers," on the other.[416] Although this may be Sunstein's conception of a free and open society, it certainly was not de Tocqueville's.

In a truly open society, in which the media provided opportunities for the leading critics of the government's 9/11 conspiracy theory to make their case, PBS or one of the commercial television networks would be able to run a series with programs such as:

—A debate between authors of *The 9/11 Commission Report*, such as Thomas Kean, Lee Hamilton, and Philip Zelikow, and critics of that report, such as Peter Dale Scott and myself.

—Architect Richard Gage making his presentation on the World Trade Center, which convinces virtually everyone who sees it that all three buildings were brought down by incendiaries and explosives.

—Chemist Niels Harrit describing his reasons for concluding that one of the substances used for this purpose was nanothermite.

—Members of the Fire Department of New York describing explosions that were going off in the Twin Towers before and during the collapses (as described in their oral histories recorded by the Fire Department of New York).

—A debate between some authors of NIST's reports on the Twin Towers and WTC 7, including lead investigator Shyam Sunder, and some critics of that report, such as physicists David Chandler and Steven Jones, chemists Kevin Ryan and Niels Harrit, and engineers Dwain Deets and Tony Szamboti.

—Former Air Force Lt. Col. Robert Bowman, who was an interceptor pilot before earning a Ph.D. in engineering and becoming head of the US Air Force's "Star Wars" program, explaining why he rejects the military's explanation for its failure to intercept the airliners on 9/11.

—Former Air Force and United Airlines pilot Russ Wittenberg debating some member of the 9/11 Commission on the question: Could Hani Hanjour have flown a Boeing 757 through the trajectory said to have been taken by American Flight 77 in order to strike the Pentagon?

—A debate between Philip Zelikow, former executive director of the 9/11 Commission, and a member of the Truth Movement, such as myself, on whether the evidence for the existence of al-Qaeda hijackers stands up to scrutiny.

—Former CIA analyst William Christison (prior to his death this year) explaining why he, reluctantly and painfully, came to the conclusion that the 9/11 attacks were arranged by our own government.

If we truly had the free and open society of which Sunstein speaks, a series such as this would have already been shown by now. If such a series had been aired, the percentage of Americans who still believe the Bush–Cheney conspiracy theory would be far smaller than it is now.

Insofar as this point is self-evident, we can see that a truly free press would not, in spite of Sunstein's apparent confidence to the contrary, serve to undermine the claims of the 9/11 Truth Movement while strengthening those of the government. The effect would be exactly the opposite.

With this point, we return to the falsity of Sunstein's claim that the 9/11 Truth Movement has served to "undermine democratic debate." Democratic debate about 9/11 has instead been prevented by defenders of the Bush–Cheney administration's 9/11 conspiracy theory.

Employing "Independent" Experts to Win Hearts and Minds

Although Sunstein would surely not grant that point, he does acknowledge that the maintenance of a free and open society would not suffice to undermine the 9/11 Truth Movement. The government would also need to take additional steps, he holds, to win the battle for hearts and minds, which he describes as a three-sided game:

> [C]onspiracy theorizing is a multi-party game. Government is faced with suppliers of conspiracy theories. . . . [T]hose two players are competing for the hearts and minds of third parties, especially the mass audience of the uncommitted.

Sunstein then suggests, however, that the government would have a better chance of winning if it added a fourth set of players:

> Expanding the cast further, one may see the game as involving four players: government officials, conspiracy theorists, mass audiences, and independent experts—such as mainstream scientists—whom government attempts to enlist to give credibility to its rebuttal efforts.[417]

One can only wonder, however, where the government would find these "independent experts." To qualify as such, people would need to be (1) degreed or certified in a relevant profession, (2) familiar with the relevant evidence, and (3) not dependent upon the government for their livelihoods. How many people fulfilling these criteria would publically support the Bush–Cheney conspiracy theory, given the types of evidence against it mentioned in Chapter 5?

As we saw in Chapter 4, growing numbers of natural scientists (including physicists and chemists) and professionals in the relevant fields (including architects, engineers, firefighters, intelligence officers, military officers, and pilots) are rejecting the official account of 9/11. The people listed in that chapter illustrate the fact that, *among scientists and professionals in the relevant fields who have studied the evidence, the weight of scientific and professional opinion is now overwhelmingly on the side of the 9/11 Truth Movement.* Whereas thousands of such people have publicly supported the stance of this movement, there are virtually no scientists or professionals in the relevant fields who have gone on record in support of the official story—except for individuals whose livelihoods would be threatened if they refused to support it. (This caveat is important, because, as Upton Sinclair famously observed: "It is difficult to get a man to understand something, when his salary depends upon his *not* understanding it!"[418]) Except for such people, virtually everyone who has expertise in a relevant field, and who has studied the relevant evidence, rejects the official conspiracy theory.

It is unlikely, therefore, that the government would be able to find many truly independent experts who would publicly support the official account of 9/11.

"Independent" in Name Only? That Sunstein himself is aware of this problem is suggested in a later passage, in which he indicates that the "independent experts" would not truly be independent. Having suggested that the government's chances for success will be improved if "it enlists credible independent experts in the effort to rebut the [9/11 conspiracy] theories," he added this revealing passage:

> There is a tradeoff between credibility and control, however. The price of credibility is that government cannot be seen to control the independent experts. Although government can supply these independent experts with information and perhaps prod them into action from behind the scenes, too close a connection will prove self-defeating if it is exposed—as witnessed in the humiliating disclosures showing that apparently independent opinions on scientific and regulatory questions were in fact paid for by think-tanks with ties to the Bush administration.[419]

It would seem, therefore, that Sunstein means for the "independent experts" only to *appear* to be independent: "government cannot be *seen* to control [them]." In reality, however, it would be doing so, supplying them with their talking points ("information") and prodding them into action. Moreover, in speaking about *enlisting* these experts, Sunstein seems to mean *paying* them: The only problem with the Bush administration's practice of paying experts to express their "apparently independent opinions on scientific and regulatory questions," in Sunstein's mind, seems to be the fact that these financial arrangements were "exposed."

Is it not interesting that, although Sunstein recognizes that this disclosure was humiliating for the parties involved, he apparently feels no embarrassment in letting people know that he is proposing essentially the same arrangement? Doing something unethical is, evidently, problematic only if one gets caught.

Be that as it may, Sunstein's admission here—that the government would be able to get testimonial support from nongovernmental experts only by surreptitiously enlisting them—gives the lie to his claim that it is the 9/11 Truth Movement's evidence that is "weak or even nonexistent."

Popular Mechanics *as "Independent" Experts:* As an illustration of his claim that the 9/11 Truth Movement's conspiracy theory is "self-sealing"—in the sense of making itself virtually invulnerable to correction, even when this correction is offered by (apparently) independent experts—Sunstein states:

> Conspiracy theorists may . . . fold independent third-party rebuttals into their theory by making conspiratorial claims of connection between the third party and the government. When the magazine *Popular Mechanics* offered a rebuttal of 9/11 conspiracy theories, conspiracists claimed that one of the magazine's reporters, Ben Chertoff, was the cousin of Homeland Security Secretary Michael Chertoff and was spreading disinformation at the latter's behest.[420]

In the footnote to this passage, Sunstein wrote: "In fact, the two [Ben and Michael Chertoff] may be distant relatives, but had never met."[421] In saying this, however, Sunstein evidently simply took the word of James Meigs, the magazine's editor-in-chief, and there is good reason to believe that he was hiding the truth.

The possible relationship between the two men was reported by 9/11 researcher Christopher Bollyn in a story entitled "9/11 and

Chertoff: Cousin Wrote 9/11 Propaganda for PM."[422] Curious about a familial relationship, Bollyn reported that he first asked Benjamin Chertoff whether he was related to Michael Chertoff, the head of Homeland Security, to which the younger Chertoff said, "I don't know," then told Bollyn to direct all further questions to the *Popular Mechanics'* publicist (as if he or she would know more about this than Benjamin himself). Instead, however, Bollyn telephoned Benjamin's mother and asked whether her son was related to the new Secretary of Homeland Security, to which she replied, according to Bollyn: "Yes, of course, he is a cousin."[423]

However, in the afterword to the *Popular Mechanics* book about 9/11, editor-in-chief Meigs gave the impression that there was some doubt about this. After commenting about "the odd coincidence that Benjamin Chertoff, then the head of the magazine's research department, has the same last name as the then newly appointed head of the Department of Homeland Security, Michael Chertoff," Meigs wrote:

> Christopher Bollyn phoned Ben's mother, who volunteered that, yes, she thinks Michael Chertoff might be a distant cousin.[424]

Given Meigs's transmutation of her reported reply, "Yes, of course," into "yes, she thinks," and of her reported "he is a cousin" into "Michael Chertoff might be a distant cousin," Sunstein should not have treated Meigs as a trustworthy reporter. But he did, endorsing Meigs's further comment that "it's possible that Ben and Michael Chertoff are distantly related" and his assurance that, "In fact, Ben and Michael Chertoff have never spoken."

It would appear from the foregoing that not only were Ben Chertoff and James Meigs anxious to deny that the former had any relationship to Michael Chertoff and hence to the Bush–Cheney administration, but that Sunstein was eager to support their denial, accepting Meigs's dubious statements without checking them out.

It is interesting in this light that the published version of Sunstein's paper deleted a reference to *Popular Mechanics* that was present in the provisional draft. In that draft, the statement about "independent experts" as one of the "four players" said:

> [O]ne may see the game as involving four players: government offi-
> cials, conspiracy theorists, mass audiences, and independent
> experts—such as mainstream scientists or the editors of *Popular
> Mechanics*—whom government attempts to enlist to give credibil-
> ity to its rebuttal efforts.[425]

In the published version of the paper, this statement is exactly the
same, except that the phrase "or the editors of Popular Mechanics"
has been deleted. It would seem that Sunstein, in the preliminary
draft, had inadvertently revealed that the government had "enlisted"
the editors of *Popular Mechanics* to serve as "independent experts."

2. An Esoteric Reading of Thesis Eight

As we have seen, it is difficult to take the surface meaning of
Sunstein's eighth thesis as expressing his true intentions. Although
he claims to believe that the 9/11 Truth Movement's theories could
be considerably undermined by means of an open society with a free
press, he has to know this to be the opposite of the truth: that if this
movement's dissenting opinions could be openly presented in the
mainstream media, the official story of 9/11 would be quickly discredited. Should his sophisticated readers, who also know this to be the
case, not take this as one more clue that the true meaning of Sunstein's
essay is not expressed at the surface level?

Sunstein provided an even clearer indication, it would seem, with
his talk about enlisting support from experts who are only *apparently*
independent. Did Sunstein not thereby reveal his awareness that the
Bush–Cheney conspiracy theory is not believed by many, if any, independent experts who are familiar with the evidence? (What architect,
physicist, or structural engineer could believe, for example, that fire
could cause a steel-frame building to collapse in free fall?) Did Sunstein
not thereby again signal his sophisticated readers that his real target is
not the "9/11 conspiracy theory" as normally understood?

Still another clue as to a hidden purpose in Sunstein's essay, it
would seem, occurs in his discussion of *Popular Mechanics*. Although
he appears to be defending this magazine against the suspicion, fueled
by the presence of Ben Chertoff on its staff, that it had been enlisted
by the Bush administration to support the official story, Sunstein let

his careful readers—those who would compare his published essay with the preliminary draft—know that the services of *Popular Mechanics* had indeed been enlisted by the government.

If Sunstein's real goal was to undermine the Bush–Cheney administration's conspiracy theory, how would we understand the present thesis, according to which the government should take a twofold approach: (1) dampening the demand for this theory by inoculating the public against it, on the one hand, and (2) using a different approach in relation to its purveyors, on the other? Saving the discussion of the latter approach until the final two chapters, I will here deal with the former.

Sunstein's secret plan, it would seem, would be to begin letting the American public know, very gradually, that the conspiracy theory they were sold on 9/11 and the days immediately thereafter—which was then reinforced by the reports issued by the 9/11 Commission and NIST—is false.

This realization needs to dawn on people gradually so that the shock will not be so great as to incapacitate them personally and the nation as a whole. People who have accepted the official story for so many years cannot just be told, suddenly, that it was all a lie, especially if they have lost loved ones in the wars that have been justified by that lie. They cannot simply be informed one day that they were betrayed not only by Bush and Cheney—which in itself would no longer be much of a shock—but also by the Department of Justice, the FBI, the CIA, the Pentagon, and various other branches of government. Nor can they suddenly be told that the major media, which they have relied upon for their news, agreed to cover up facts that contradicted the official story. The revelation of the truth would need to be gradual—hence the metaphor of "inoculation."

The Washington Times

By coincidence, a story that could be regarded as a step in this gradual revelation appeared the very week that I was writing this chapter. On February 19, 2010, Architects and Engineers for 9/11 Truth held a press conference in San Francisco to announce that its petition, which calls for a new investigation of the destruction of the World Trade Center, had been signed by 1,000 professional architects and engineers. Although no members of the mainstream press showed up physically at the event, its proceedings were streamed on the internet, and a non-dismissive article about the event appeared a few days later in the *Washington Times*. It began:

> A lingering technical question about the Sept. 11 terrorist attacks still haunts some, and it has political implications: How did 200,000 tons of steel disintegrate and drop in 11 seconds? A thousand architects and engineers want to know, and are calling on Congress to order a new investigation into the destruction of the Twin Towers and Building 7 at the World Trade Center.

This account, which appeared in Jennifer Harper's "Inside the Beltway" column, then continued:

> "In order to bring down this kind of mass in such a short period of time, the material must have been artificially, exploded outwards," says Richard Gage, a San Francisco architect and founder of the nonprofit Architects & Engineers for 9/11 Truth.
>
> Mr. Gage, who is a member of the American Institute of Architects, managed to persuade more than 1,000 of his peers to sign a new petition requesting a formal inquiry. . . .
>
> He is particularly disturbed by Building 7, a 47-story skyscraper, which was not hit by an aircraft, yet came down in "pure free-fall acceleration."
>
> He also says that more than 100 first-responders reported explosions and flashes as the towers were falling and cited evidence of "multi-ton steel sections ejected laterally 600 ft. at 60 mph" and the "mid-air pulverization of 90,000 tons of concrete & metal decking."
>
> There is also evidence of "advanced explosive nano-thermitic composite material found in the World Trade Center dust," Mr. Gage says. The group's petition at www. ae911truth.org is already on its way to members of Congress.
>
> "Government officials will be notified that 'Misprision of Treason' . . . is a serious federal offense, which requires those with evidence of treason to act," Mr. Gage says.[426]

There are several features of this article by Jennifer Harper that set it apart from the mainstream press's previous treatment of 9/11 Truth events. First, she raised a serious technical question: How could an enormous steel-frame building disintegrate and come down so fast?

Second, she reported that 1,000 architects and engineers had signed a petition asking for a new investigation to answer this and related questions. Third, rather than referring to Richard Gage as a "conspiracy theorist," she pointed out that he belongs to the American Institute of Architects. Fourth, she mentioned the destruction of WTC 7, about which many Americans were still unaware, and pointed out that it was not hit by an airplane (thereby indicating that, even if one believes the Twin Towers were brought down by airliners, this explanation cannot apply to this third building). Fifth, she mentioned that over 100 first-responders reported explosions going off in the Twin Towers. Sixth, she mentioned the fact that heavy sections of steel were ejected out horizontally as far as 600 feet. Seventh, she cited the fact that much of the buildings' concrete was pulverized in mid-air. Finally, she mentioned the discovery of explosive nanothermite in the WTC dust.

In short, besides presenting Richard Gage as a credible person who had persuaded 1,000 architects and engineers to sign his petition, she mentioned five facts about the destruction of the World Trade Center that probably at least half of the American public had never heard before.

That the public will be receptive to such information, once it appears in the mainstream media, is illustrated by the fact that this article remained the most read story on the *Washington Times* website for several days after it appeared.[427]

American Behavioral Scientist

For another example of the kind of publication that would begin providing a gradual revelation, we can look at the symposium on State Crimes Against Democracy (SCADs), in which the previously quoted paper by Laurie Manwell appeared. Far from appearing in some publication that could be dismissed as a purveyor of conspiracy theories, it appeared in the *American Behavioral Scientist*, which since its founding 50 years ago has become a highly respected and influential journal, indexed in major database services around the world.

Defining SCADs as "concerted actions or inactions by government insiders intended to manipulate democratic processes and undermine popular sovereignty," one of the symposium's authors— Professor Lance deHaven-Smith of the Reubin Askew School of Public Administration and Policy at Florida State University—

pointed out that "antidemocratic conspiracies in high office do, in fact, happen":

> The congressional hearings on Watergate, the Church Committee's discoveries about illegal domestic surveillance, and the special prosecutors' investigations of Oliver North and Scooter Libby revealed that public officials at the highest levels of American government can and sometimes do engage in conspiracies to manipulate elections, wiretap and smear critics, mislead Congress and the public, and in other ways subvert popular sovereignty.

Professor deHaven-Smith then explained the reason for the presence of this symposium in a major social science journal:

> Certainly, such crimes and the criminogenic circumstances surrounding them warrant scientific inquiry, not only to better understand elite politics but also to identify institutional vulnerabilities so that protections can be established or strengthened. The challenge for scholars is to engage in serious, unblinkered study of the subject without contributing to mass paranoia or elite incivility.[428]

What makes this inquiry an example of the kind of inquiry that (the esoteric) Sunstein would evidently want is the fact that it treats 9/11 as an instance of this category of criminality.

For example, the abstract for the introductory essay begins by speaking of the "ellipses of due diligence riddling the official account of the 9/11 incidents." The essay itself says: "The official account of 9/11 bears the imprimatur of . . . illusory authority. . . . The official commentary on 9/11 reveals glaring gaps and not a few bright line contradictions."[429]

Another essay, comparing Newton's laws with George Orwell's "secret doctrine that $2 + 2 = 4$,"[430] says:

> Professor Steven Jones found himself forced out of [a] tenured position for merely reminding the world that physical laws, about which there is no dissent whatsoever, contradict the official theory of the World Trade Center Towers' collapse.[431]

This essay's author then pointed out that, if NIST's account of why these buildings collapsed is accepted, "the specifications of design for all skyscrapers *ought*, in the public interest, to be subjected to major review." NIST's account also requires, he added, a revision of the physical laws regarding the behavior of steel that have long been presupposed in the engineering sciences.[432] His point, of course, was that no scientists or engineers believe that these laws need to be revised, so that the contradiction between NIST's account of the destruction of the World Trade Center, on the one hand, and some elementary principles of physics, on the other—a contradiction that has been expressed by artist Mark Dotzler in a piece of artwork titled "The Split"[433]— means that all architects and engineers aware of this contradiction should be joining Jones in publicly rejecting NIST's report.

Conclusion

Whereas the story in the *Washington Times* should help the general public begin to realize that the official account of 9/11 was a lie, so that the event itself must have been an inside job (a "state crime against democracy"), this *American Behavioral Scientist* symposium should help the academic world in particular to begin looking critically at the 9/11 events, no longer regarding them as off-limits to scientific and other types of academic investigations.

These two publications came, of course, long after Sunstein's essay was written. But they can be seen as examples of the kinds of publications that would begin to achieve the purposes suggested by Sunstein's essay when understood to have a hidden level of meaning.

If such studies and news reports continue to appear, the truth about 9/11 will gradually become an accepted reality, so that we, in the not-too-distant future, will hear Bryan Williams begin his evening report on NBC News by saying: "As we all know now, the 9/11 attacks were not orchestrated by Muslims from abroad but by members of our own government," and we will see Katie Couric on CBS News asking Sarah Palin: "When did you first realize that 9/11 was an inside job?" Sunstein's secret plan for undermining the false 9/11 conspiracy theory will have succeeded.

CHAPTER 9
HARD-CORE CONSPIRACY THEORISTS AS UNTEACHABLE

The ninth thesis in Sunstein's argument says:

Although one might think that the government could use credible public information to cure the 9/11 conspiracy theory's purveyors of their false beliefs, this approach will not work, because this theory has "a self-sealing quality," which makes its purveyors "resistant to correction," especially by "contrary evidence offered by the government."[434]

The full title of Sunstein's essay, to recall, is "Conspiracy Theories: Causes and Cures." Having discussed the nature and causes of conspiracy theories in his first six theses, Sunstein in the later ones proposes cures. Following his proposals for dealing with the general public in the previous thesis, he in this one explains why the same treatment—"providing credible public information"—will not achieve the government's goal in relation to the theories' hard-core suppliers, which is to "persuade, debias, or silence those suppliers."[435]

1. Sunstein's Ninth Thesis: The Surface Level

This ninth thesis is a critical step in Sunstein's argument, understood exoterically, because this thesis provides the justification for the proposal that has been responsible for most of the negative reaction to his essay—his proposal to have government agents infiltrate groups that are spreading theories designated "harmful and demonstrably false" by the government. Without the present thesis, Sunstein would have no response to the most obvious objection to this proposal, which might be phrased thus:

Mr. Sunstein: You have been a professor at two of the country's premiere institutions of higher learning. As a professor, you know that the best cure for misinformation is better information. If people are making false accusations because they are ignorant of the facts, the proper solution is to convince them of their errors by giving them the truth. If they do not believe you at first, you provide convincing evidence. Instead of using a discredited FBI technique—sending infiltrators into movements that are spreading false conspiracy theories—why don't you propose a method befitting a Chicago-cum-Harvard professor: providing educational materials? You might even bring the leading 9/11 conspiracy theorists to Harvard for a seminar, so that they could be disabused of their false beliefs.

The purpose of Sunstein's ninth thesis is to forestall any such objection by stating that this method would be ineffective. In his words:

> The most direct governmental technique for dispelling false (and also harmful) beliefs—providing credible public information—does not work, in any straightforward way, for conspiracy theories. This extra resistance to correction through simple techniques is what makes conspiracy theories distinctively worrisome.[436]

Why do proponents of conspiracy theories manifest this "extra resistance to correction"? Sunstein gives two answers.

One answer is that they are "especially resistant to contrary evidence offered by the government."[437] The reason for this is obvious: Insofar as 9/11 conspiracy theorists believe that the 9/11 attacks were perpetrated and covered up by forces within the government, they will be suspicious of any "information" provided by agents of that government.

Biased Assimilation and Knowledge

But Sunstein also suggests that conspiracy theorists—and this is his second reason for calling them extra resistant to correction—are "likely to be especially biased assimilators." That is, they may assimilate evidence with the potential to correct their views, but they assimilate it in such a biased way that their views remain the same.[438]

However, insofar as Sunstein's argument here is directed to the 9/11 Truth Movement, it is circular: He presupposes that the theories held by the members of this movement are false, so he takes the fact that they will not change their minds as evidence that they are "biased assimilators" who are "resisting" the truth. The circular nature of this argument is shown by the existence of another category of people who are also extremely resistant to changing their minds—people who have knowledge.

Knowledge, to recall, is *justified true belief*. I know, for example, that I went to high school in Hermiston, Oregon. I know this because I *remember* it and also have all sorts of evidence, such as my high school annual. It would be very difficult, probably impossible, for anyone to convince me that I was wrong.

Likewise, many people today are in position to know that the Earth is billions of years old and is not flat. If Sunstein tried to convince them that they were wrong, he would find them extremely resistant to his proffered corrections.

The point of these illustrations is that the behavior of people with knowledge is in one respect indistinguishable from that of biased assimilators who hold false beliefs: they both refuse to be budged from their beliefs. The very fact that the hard-core members of the 9/11 Truth Movement are "resistant to correction," therefore, may simply mean that their beliefs constitute knowledge. To argue that their resistance shows them to be biased assimilators is to beg the question.

That Sunstein is guilty of this question-begging assumption is shown by an incident he cites in relation to this claim:

> When the National Institute of Standards and Technology issued a fact sheet to disprove the theory that the World Trade Center was brought down by a controlled demolition, the government spokesman stated that "[w]e realize this fact sheet won't convince those who hold to the alternative theories that our findings are sound. In fact, the fact sheet was never intended for them. It is for the masses who have seen or heard the alternative theory claims and want balance."[439]

Sunstein simply accepts as true the contrast implied by this NIST spokesman—that while NIST's information will persuade the masses, because they are *unbiased* assimilators of information, it will not convince conspiracy theorists, because they are *biased* assimilators.

What Sunstein fails to acknowledge is that many members of the 9/11 Truth Movement, such as its scientists, architects, engineers, and firefighters, have very good reasons for rejecting the claims made in

NIST's "fact sheet," because they know that NIST ignored relevant evidence, fabricated data, and provided explanations that violate basic principles of physics. Insofar as these professionals resist NIST's "facts," they do so not because of unwarranted bias but because of their knowledge. From this perspective, one could argue that NIST wrote its so-called fact sheet for "the masses" because it was counting on them to be *ignorant* assimilators.

True Conspiracy Theories

The fallaciousness of Sunstein's argument is also shown by his acknowledgment that some conspiracy theories have proven to be true. There was a time when it was simply a theory that the Nixon White House had authorized illegal activities in the Watergate Hotel, that the CIA had used LSD and other mind-altering drugs in Project MKULTRA, that the Bush administration had fabricated a relationship between Saddam Hussein and Osama bin Laden, and that the Bush administration had lied in claiming to believe that Saddam had weapons of mass destruction. But now these conspiracies are publicly acknowledged facts. Many of those who first argued for the existence of these conspiracies, stubbornly refusing to be dissuaded from their beliefs, did so because they knew some facts that most people did not. The truly biased assimilators were those who were exposed to these facts but did not draw the correct conclusions.

Sunstein has provided no reason to believe that the situation is different with regard to the 9/11 Truth Movement's theory, which would mean that the biased assimilators are those who have not allowed the evidence presented by this movement to change their initial view about 9/11, according to which the attacks were orchestrated by al-Qaeda.

2. Sunstein's Ninth Thesis: Its Possible Deeper Meaning

As with the previous theses, it seems that Sunstein could not have meant the surface level of this ninth thesis to convey his true meaning. Given the fact that both he and his sophisticated readers knew that the 9/11 Truth Movement's "hard core"—its leadership—consists of architects, engineers, firefighters, intelligence officers, scientists, military veterans, and other professionals, Sunstein surely would not have expected these readers to take seriously his claim that such people are resistant to correction because they are biased assimilators. Instead, he would have expected these readers to realize that, in refusing to be "corrected" by "information" provided by defenders of the official conspiracy theory, the leaders of the 9/11 Truth Movement are simply, in effect, repeating the reply of the 18th-century preacher who said: "I cannot permit your ignorance, however vast, to take precedence over my knowledge, however limited."[440]

If so, Sunstein would have expected his sophisticated readers to understand that, by speaking of the 9/11 conspiracy theory as having a "self-sealing quality," he was referring to the Bush–Cheney conspiracy theory, and that by describing the hard-core 9/11 conspiracy theorists as biased assimilators, he was referring to those who have accepted that false theory.

The Official Theory's Self-Sealing Quality

In order to support the point about the self-sealing nature of the official conspiracy theory, Sunstein could have simply referred to examples, summarized above in Chapter 5, of ways in which defenders of the official theory have refused to admit that this theory has been falsified by the massive amount of evidence contradicting it. If asked for still more examples of its self-sealing quality, Sunstein could have added the following examples:

—The 9/11 Commission reaffirmed the FBI's list of al-Qaeda hijackers in spite of the fact that Waleed al-Shehri and some of the other men on this list showed up alive after 9/11.

—Besides the fact that the flight manifests issued by the airlines shortly after the attacks had no Arab names on them, and that the later purported manifests with hijackers' names were not included in the FBI's evidence for the Moussaoui trial, a FOIA-obtained autopsy list for American Flight 77 also contained no Arab names. There has been no explanation as to how these facts can be squared with the official story.

—NIST maintained that the WTC buildings were brought down by fires, not explosives and/or incendiaries, in spite of the fact that various scientific studies, including one by the US Geological Survey, reported finding particles in the World Trade Center dust showing that various metals, including iron and molybdenum, had been subjected to extremely high temperatures, several times higher than the fires could have provided.

—NIST maintained its non-demolition theory in spite of the presence of large amounts of nanothermite in the WTC dust.

—In the draft version of its report on WTC 7, NIST claimed that this building's descent was not even close to free fall. But after physicist David Chandler demonstrated that the top floor had come down in absolute free fall for over two seconds, NIST in its final report acknowledged this fact. In doing so, however, NIST did not change its theory, even though its lead investigator, Shyam Sunder, had previously explained (during the "technical briefing" on WTC 7) that this theory did not allow for the possibility of free fall. NIST assimilated this new information by simply removing the multiple assurances in its draft report that its account of WTC 7's collapse was "consistent with physical principles."[441] NIST thereby ended up (explicitly) claiming that its report is true while (implicitly) admitting that it is not consistent with physics. To deal with the contradiction between its admission of free fall and Sunder's explanation, at the technical briefing, that free fall would have been impossible, NIST simply removed the video and transcript of this technical briefing from the internet.[442] A theory cannot get more self-sealing than this.

The Truly Biased Assimilators

If challenged to show that the official defenders of the Bush–Cheney conspiracy theory have been biased assimilators, Sunstein could appeal to many examples, such as the following:

Swiss-Cheese Steel: Three professors at Worcester Polytechnic Institute, as we saw earlier, reported finding a piece of steel from WTC 7 that had melted so severely as to have gaping holes in it. In an appendix to the FEMA report, these professors wrote: "A detailed study into the mechanisms [that caused] this phenomenon is needed."[443] Arden Bement, who was the director of NIST when it took on the WTC project, said that NIST's report would address "all major recommendations contained in the [FEMA] report."[444]

But when NIST issued its report on WTC 7, it did not mention this piece of steel with the Swiss-cheese appearance. Compounding its fraud, NIST even claimed that not a single piece of steel from WTC 7 had been recovered.[445]

No Girder Shear Studs: As part of its explanation as to how fire caused WTC 7 to collapse, NIST claimed that a crucial girder had failed because it, like the other girders in this building, was not connected to the floor slab with sheer studs. NIST wrote: "Floor beams . . . had shear studs, but the girders that supported the floor beams did not have shear studs.[446] However, NIST's *Interim Report on WTC 7*, which was published in 2004, had reported that the girders as well as the beams had shear studs.[447] NIST here proved itself to be a biased assimilator— even of information that it itself had provided at an earlier time.

NIST's Raging 5:00PM Fire on Floor 12: NIST's distortion of its own information about girder shear studs was not an isolated incident. In its final report on WTC 7, NIST claims—as an essential element in its theory as to how fire brought the building down at 5:21—that big fires covered much of the 12th floor's north face at 5:00PM. But NIST's 2004 *Interim Report on WTC 7* had contained the following information: "Around 4:45PM, a photograph showed fires on Floors 7, 8, 9, and 11 near the middle of the north face; Floor 12 was burned out by this time."[448] Other photographs even show that the 12th floor fire had virtually burned out as early as 4:00.[449] NIST again assimilated information from its own earlier report in a biased way—if such a mild term can be used for an outright distortion.

Testimonies about Explosions: As mentioned earlier, testimonies of explosions going off in the Twin Towers were given by many people, including 118 members of the Fire Department of New York.[450] But NIST, dismissing the idea that explosives might have brought the buildings down, said: "There was no evidence (collected by . . . the Fire Department of New York) of any blast or explosions in the region below the impact and fire floors."[451] In response, physicist Steven Jones and other scholars, employing a federal law that required NIST to respond to a "request for correction," filed such a request in which they quoted many of the FDNY testimonies about explosions in the Twin Towers, including some that spoke specifically of explosions "in the region below the impact and fire floors." They then stated: "An unbiased NIST investigation would consider these multiple, credible, mutually supporting, publicly available reports of explosions inside the Twin Towers."[452]

In reply, NIST wrote: "NIST reviewed all of the interviews conducted by the FDNY of firefighters (500 interviews). . . . Taken as a whole, the interviews did not support the contention that explosives played a role in the collapse of the WTC Towers."[453] In other words, whereas NIST had originally claimed that there were *no testimonies whatsoever* supportive of the idea that explosions had brought the buildings down, it was now saying that, although there were some such testimonies, *there were not enough of them* (while not specifying how many *would* have been enough). Whether or not Sunstein had this incident in mind, it certainly provides a perfect example of the biased assimilation by conspiracy theorists to which he has objected.

Molten Metal: Another example is based on the fact that many people at Ground Zero reported molten metal in the rubble—which most of them described as molten *steel*. For example, firefighter Philip Ruvolo said: "You'd get down below and you'd see molten steel, *molten* steel, running down the channel rails, like you're in a foundry, like lava."[454] Similar reports were given by other witnesses, including Leslie Robertson, a member of the engineering firm that designed the Twin Towers,[455] Dr. Ronald Burger of the National Center for Environmental Health,[456] and Dr. Alison Geyh of The Johns Hopkins School of Public Health, who headed up a scientific team that went to the site shortly after 9/11 at the request of the National Institute of Environmental Health Sciences.[457] However, when John Gross, one of the principal authors of NIST's reports, was asked about the molten steel, he challenged the "basic premise that there was a pool of molten steel," adding: "I know of absolutely no . . . eyewitness who has said so."[458] The most biased way to "assimilate" evidence, of course, is simply to deny its existence.

Conclusion

Sunstein's ninth thesis, when understood (exoterically) to refer to the leaders of the 9/11 Truth Movement, obviously involves a complete mischaracterization. But if taken as a coded way of referring to the hard-core suppliers of the official conspiracy theory about 9/11, this thesis, which says that the simple provision of public information will not serve to "persuade, debias, or silence those suppliers," is amply justified by historical experience.

CHAPTER 10
COGNITIVE INFILTRATION AS THE BEST SOLUTION

Sunstein's tenth thesis, which has been the focus of most of the criticism his essay has evoked, can be formulated thus:

> Because the government in an open society cannot (normally) "ban 'conspiracy theories'" or "tax . . . those who disseminate such theories," the best approach is for the government to "engage in *cognitive infiltration of the groups that produce conspiracy theories.*"[459]

To begin with the first part of this thesis: The word "normally" is inserted parenthetically to take account of the fact that Sunstein does not completely rule out these two options. In response to a question he raises—"What can the government do about conspiracy theories?"—Sunstein lists five possibilities:

> (1) Government might ban "conspiracy theories," somehow defined. (2) Government might impose some kind of tax, financial or otherwise, on those who disseminate such theories. (3) Government might itself engage in counterspeech, marshaling arguments to discredit conspiracy theories. (4) Government might formally hire credible private parties to engage in counterspeech. (5) Government might engage in informal communication with such parties, encouraging them to help.[460]

Then, in response to a second question—"what *should* it [government] do?"—Sunstein says of the above five "instruments":

> Each instrument has a distinctive set of potential effects, or costs and benefits, and each will have a place under imaginable conditions. Our main policy claim here is that government should engage in *cognitive infiltration of the groups that produce conspiracy theories*, which involves a mix of (3), (4), and (5).[461]

Most Americans will be relieved to see that Sunstein excluded the first two options from his list of recommended actions.

However, some of the strongest criticism has been evoked by his statement that even those two options "will have a place under imaginable conditions." For example, Glenn Greenwald, saying that this passage shows "what an extremist Cass Sunstein is," wrote (as we saw in the introduction):

> I'd love to know the "conditions" under which the government-enforced banning of conspiracy theories or the imposition of taxes on those who advocate them will "have a place." That would require, at a bare minimum, a repeal of the First Amendment. Anyone who believes this should, for that reason alone, be barred from any meaningful government position. [462]

In the provisional draft of his article, Sunstein had said a little more about the "conditions" under which those possibilities might have a place, writing:

> The most direct response to a dangerous conspiracy theories [*sic*] is censorship. That response is unavailable in an open society, because it is inconsistent with principles of freedom of expression. We could imagine circumstances in which a conspiracy theory became so pervasive, and so dangerous, that censorship would be thinkable. [463]

Given the fact that, as Sunstein explicitly said in that provisional draft, the 9/11 Truth Movement's conspiracy theory was its "main focus," he seemed to be saying that this theory in particular could become "so pervasive, and so dangerous," that the government would be right to make any advocacy of this theory illegal, even though this law would be, he acknowledged, "inconsistent with principles of freedom of expression."

It is indeed troubling, to say the least, that a preeminent constitutional scholar would allow for such a possibility. To expand on Greenwald's point, do not citizens need to ask: Which is more dangerous, people who believe 9/11 was an inside job, or people occupying influential positions within our government who can calmly contemplate canceling the First Amendment?

However, given the fact that Sunstein did not actually recommend these First Amendment–canceling options, I will move on to the options he did recommend—which, as we saw in the Introduction, critics have found disturbing, even fascistic.

The Tenth Thesis: Surface Meaning

Of the five options Sunstein mentioned, the first two, as we have seen, were ruled out as not permissible—at least normally—in a free society. The third option, according to which government would be directly involved in "marshaling arguments to discredit conspiracy theories," was recommended by Sunstein, as we saw in Chapter 8, for dealing with the general public. But Sunstein's ninth thesis declared this option largely ineffective for trying to silence those who have been supplying 9/11 conspiracy theories.

Sunstein's "Distinctive Tactic"
The exclusion of those first three options for dealing with hard-core conspiracy theorists leaves only the fourth and fifth options, according to which government would "hire credible private parties to engage in counterspeech" and would also "engage in informal communication with such parties, encouraging them to help." Those two options are then combined into what Sunstein calls "a distinctive tactic for breaking up the hard core of extremists who supply conspiracy theories," namely:

> [C]ognitive infiltration of extremist groups, whereby government agents or their allies (acting either virtually or in real space, and either openly or anonymously) will undermine the crippled epistemology of believers by planting doubts about the theories and stylized facts that circulate within such groups, thereby introducing beneficial cognitive diversity.[464]

On the basis of past experiences, it can be anticipated that this harmless-sounding "cognitive diversity" would have effects that would be anything but harmless. It would produce antagonisms, fights, broken friendships, and divisions, perhaps even the complete disbanding of the groups. The language Sunstein uses the most, in fact, is "breaking up":

He speaks of "breaking up the tight cognitive clusters of extremist theories, arguments and rhetoric that are produced by the hard core"; of "weakening or even breaking up the epistemological complexes that constitute these networks and groups;" and of "breaking up the hard core of extremists who supply [9/11] conspiracy theories."[465]

The ultimate goal of the government's infiltrators, it seems, would be the destruction of the 9/11 Truth Movement.

With regard to whether these government and government-hired agents would infiltrate 9/11 groups physically (in real space), or only virtually (through websites and chat rooms), Sunstein recommends both.[466]

On the question of whether they would operate openly or anonymously, Sunstein recommends primarily the latter, due to the self-sealing nature of conspiracy theories and the bias of their advocates:

> Because conspiracy theorists are likely to approach evidence and arguments in a biased way, they are not likely to respond well, or even logically, to the claims of [people they know to be] public officials.[467]

In the most effective form of infiltration, therefore "government officials would *participate anonymously or even with false identities*" in 9/11 websites and chat rooms; they would also join 9/11 groups, participating in the activities.[468]

Risks

Sunstein cautions, however, that joining groups physically would be risky: "Perhaps agents will be asked to perform criminal acts to prove their bona fides."[469] In saying this, Sunstein is, of course, drawing on his descriptions of 9/11 conspiracy theorists, discussed in Chapter 6, as "extremists" who are likely to resort to violence, "with terrifying consequences." But this is absurd. Does he imagine, for example, that when people apply to join Architects and Engineers for 9/11 Truth, Richard Gage will insist that they "prove their bona fides" by blowing up a building?

To be sure, that fantasy—that agents would be asked to perform criminal acts—is not the only risk Sunstein mentions. His more complete statement says:

Perhaps agents will be asked to perform criminal acts to prove their bona fides or (less plausibly) will themselves become persuaded by the conspiratorial views they are supposed to be undermining.[470]

Does Sunstein really believe that this second ominous possibility is less plausible? Or is this his warning, given his awareness of the persuasiveness of the 9/11 Truth Movement's case, about the more serious danger involved in carrying out this proposal?

In any case, Sunstein points to yet another risk that would be involved in "tactics of anonymous participation," namely:

[T]hose tactics may be discovered or disclosed, with possibly perverse results. If the tactic becomes known, the conspiracy theory may become further entrenched, and any genuine member of the relevant groups who raises doubts may be suspected of government connections.[471]

Sunstein quickly adds, however, that the results of disclosure might not actually be perverse (from the government's perspective):

Another possibility is that disclosure of the government's tactics will sow uncertainty and distrust within conspiratorial groups and among their members; new recruits will be suspect and participants in the group's virtual networks will doubt each other's bona fides. To the extent that these effects raise the costs of organization and communication for, and within, conspiratorial groups, the effects are desirable, not perverse.[472]

Evaluation
Now that we have Sunstein's proposal before us, we can ask various evaluative questions.

Befitting? One question to ask is whether this is a proposal befitting "the pre-eminent legal scholar of our time," who has taught at the prestigious law schools at the universities of Chicago and Harvard. Does it not sound more like a proposal that would arise out of FBI headquarters?

Aware that critics would compare his suggestion to the FBI's Counter Intelligence Program (COINTELPRO), Sunstein suggests that there is little similarity: After advocating "cognitive infiltration of extremist groups," he adds: "By this we do not mean 1960s-style infiltration with a view to surveillance and collecting information, possibly for use in future prosecutions."[473]

The distinction, however, seems less than crystal clear. The infiltrators would of necessity be engaged in "surveillance and collecting information." And who would have confidence in Sunstein's assurance that this material would not be used for "future prosecutions"? Skepticism with regard to Sunstein's own thoughts seems especially appropriate in light of his apparent openness to suspending the First Amendment—by either banning conspiracy theories (thereby making criminals out of anyone the government designates a "conspiracy theorist") or fining people who continue to espouse them (in which case the information gathered by the infiltrators would surely be used to identify and fine them and then arrest those who did not pay the fines).

Moreover, the instructions given to COINTELPRO agents, as we saw in Chapter 2, were to "expose, disrupt, misdirect, discredit, or otherwise neutralize" these organizations. How different is this from the language of Sunstein, whose agents would be told to "undermine," "break up," "disable," and "silence"? The similarities are further indicated by the above-quoted passage, in which Sunstein calls "desirable" tactics that "sow uncertainty and distrust within conspiratorial groups."

Legal? As we saw in Chapter 2, the FBI's COINTELPRO was eventually declared illegal because it violated the rights of free speech and association. Given its strong similarities to that program, Sunstein's proposal would seem to be equally illegal.

Glenn Greenwald pointed out, furthermore, that there is another reason for considering Sunstein's proposal illegal, namely, that it appears to violate "long-standing statutes prohibiting government 'propaganda' within the U.S., aimed at American citizens." Greenwald cited in this connection a report prepared for Congress in 2005 by the Congressional Research Service, which states that no government agency may use funds for "covert propaganda," which is defined by the Government Accountability Office (GAO) as "government communications that fail to disclose that they are paid for with appropriated funds." Spelling it out even more clearly, this report says that the prohibition against covert propaganda "prohibits executive agencies from attempting to persuade or deceive the public through surreptitious means."[474]

Given the fact that this is exactly what Sunstein's program proposes, it would clearly be illegal.

Moreover, besides being illegal from the point of view of Congress and the GAO, Sunstein's proposal even violates what George W. Bush's Office of Legal Council (OLC) stated in 2005 in the aftermath of the scandal involving Armstrong Williams (which arose when it became known that the Bush administration had paid him to endorse "No Child Left Behind"). Bush's OLC, reaffirming earlier opinions, wrote:

> [M]ost appropriations statutes enacted since 1951 have contained general prohibitions on the use of appropriated funds for "publicity or propaganda purposes." Over the years, GAO has interpreted "publicity or propaganda" restrictions to preclude use of appropriated funds for, among other things, so-called "covert propaganda." . . . Consistent with that view, OLC determined in 1988 that a statutory prohibition on using appropriated funds for "publicity or propaganda" precluded undisclosed agency funding of advocacy by third-party groups. We stated that "covert attempts to mold opinion through the undisclosed use of third parties" would run afoul of restrictions on using appropriated funds for "propaganda."[475]

Sunstein's essay proposes precisely that: "covert attempts to mold opinion through the undisclosed use of third parties."

It is clear for more than one reason, therefore, that Sunstein's plan would be illegal as well as unbefitting.

Necessary? Sunstein advocated this approach, as we saw, as a way to address what he portrayed as the basic problem, as expressed in a statement quoted in Chapter 7: "Imagine a government facing a population in which a particular conspiracy theory is becoming widespread."[476] Having made clear that he was thereby speaking only of theories that are both harmful and demonstrably false, Sunstein declared it the government's duty to do what it could to prevent any such theory from becoming more widespread. The necessity of arranging cognitive infiltration of groups spreading this theory, in order to achieve this goal, was concluded on the basis of the following argument:

—The government should try to undermine the 9/11 conspiracy theory.

—The government should try to silence the suppliers of this theory, as well as trying to inoculate the public against it.

—The government cannot silence the suppliers by banning conspiracy theories or fining their advocates.

Therefore, the best solution is to infiltrate conspiracy groups with agents who, while being on the government payroll, generally conceal this fact.

However, even if one accepts this argument's three premises, its conclusion would follow only if there were no other way to achieve the goal—the further spread of the theory—and this is not the case.

For example, Professor Mark Crispin Miller has pointed to another and arguably better approach by saying:

> If Sunstein (and his allies) gave a hoot about the truth, they'd try to test those dreaded "theories" in the most effective way—not by setting up a covert force of cyber-moles, but by joining all the rest of us in calling for a new commission to look into 9/11, airing all the evidence that's been so long ignored and/or suppressed, and entertaining all those questions that the first commission either answered laughably or just shrugged off. That would be the democratic way to deal with it.[477]

This is clearly another alternative for achieving Sunstein's goal. If that goal is to prevent the theory advocated by the 9/11 Truth Movement from becoming more widely accepted by the American people, and if this theory is "demonstrably false," as Sunstein says, then there would be no need to try to silence the 9/11 conspiracy theorists. *The government would only need to discredit their theory so publicly and severely that it would win no new converts and would even lose many of its previous converts.*

An excellent way to do this would be through a new investigation, carried out by credible, independent people and mandated to answer all the questions that have been raised by the 9/11 Truth Movement. If Sunstein is right in saying that this movement's theories are demonstrably false, then the questions raised by this movement will be easily answered, and the investigation will demonstrate to the American people, and also people around the world, the falsity of the claim that 9/11 was an inside job.

There is also another alternative, which would be faster and less expensive: a series of televised debates between defenders of the competing conspiracy theories. With regard to the destruction of the World Trade Center, for example, an architect, an engineer, a fire-fighter, a physicist, and a chemist who support the official conspiracy theory could debate people from the same fields who have advocated the alternative theory. Analogous debates could be set up for other issues, such as the failures to intercept the airliners, the evidence for hijackers on those airliners, the Pentagon attack, and the fate of United 93. If the alternative theory is "demonstrably false," as Sunstein says, then these debates should demonstrate this fact to the public.

Sunstein's controversial approach is, therefore, unnecessary, because there are at least two alternative approaches, each of which has the advantage of being legal and democratic. The best approach, indeed, would be to combine these two approaches. The televised debates could be arranged quickly—within a matter of weeks—so that the spread of the 9/11 Truth Movement's "false and harmful" theory could be stopped almost immediately. Then the new investigation, by publishing a report that thoroughly answers all the lingering questions, could put the final nails in the coffin, preventing this terrible conspiracy theory from ever rising again.

Sunstein was evidently led by faulty logic to think that his illegal proposal was necessary: Although he recognized, as we saw earlier, that the government could inoculate the public against the alternative theory by "marshaling arguments to discredit [it]," he declared that this approach would not work in relation to hard-core conspiracy theorists, due to the self-sealing nature of their theories. His logical error was to assume that, in order to stop the spread of their theory, the government would need to *silence* them, whereas in reality it would only need to *discredit* them. So the method that he as a professor has used to defeat false views—marshalling arguments against them—is the only method that the government needs to use. It should rely on the power of truth, not COINTELPRO-like tactics.

Assuming that the surface meaning of Sunstein's essay conveys his true thoughts about these matters, he should enthusiastically endorse this suggestion.

2. The Tenth Thesis: Its Possible Deeper Meaning

As we have seen in previous chapters, however, Sunstein's essay contains numerous clues that its surface meaning must *not* reflect his true purpose in writing it. His defense of his tenth and final thesis contains even more such clues.

Clues to a Possible Deeper Meaning
One clue is provided by his hint that, if the 9/11 Truth Movement keeps growing, the government might need to take the extraordinary step of banning it. What message would this send to his careful, well-informed readers among the elite? Perhaps something like the following:

> *You know as well as I that the evidence for the Bush–Cheney admin-*
> *istration's 9/11 conspiracy theory is weak to nonexistent. You know that*
> *this theory is, in fact, demonstrably false. You know that the evidence*
> *for the position of the 9/11 Truth Movement is overwhelming, so that*
> *as more and more people become aware of it, this movement is going to*
> *continue to grow. It will soon become so widespread that the president*
> *will not be able to justify policies by appealing to al-Qaeda's attack on*
> *America without evoking snickers, which may soon evolve into outright*
> *laughter. We don't want senior White House reporters laughing at the*
> *president while TV cameras are running! The only way to prevent this*
> *eventuality, given the fact that you cannot discredit this movement's*
> *"conspiracy theory" in the public forum, would be to ban this theory.*
> *This would be an unthinkable violation of the First Amendment. But*
> *this is what you will need to do if you persist in trying to defend the*
> *Bush–Cheney administration's absurd claim that al-Qaeda pulled off*
> *the attacks. So I'm pleading with you: Bite the bullet! Tell the American*
> *people the truth! As to why you waited so long, you can surely come up*
> *with a plausible cover story.*

A perhaps even clearer clue to Sunstein's true meaning is provided by the fact that his "distinctive tactic" for breaking up the 9/11 Truth Movement would be illegal. As a scholar of the Constitution, Sunstein would obviously know this. He also perhaps gave a hint about this by inviting a comparison of his approach with the FBI's tactics in the 1960s that were ruled illegal. As "the pre-eminent legal scholar of our time," could Sunstein have been seriously proposing a tactic that had been declared illegal by Congress and even the legal counsel for the Bush White House?

The outrage expressed by Glenn Greenwald and other critics, one could suspect, would have been exactly what the esoteric Sunstein wanted. This outrage would tell America's ruling class that the period during which their preferred policies could be justified by the Bush–Cheney conspiracy theory is over, because the only way they could prevent the continued growth of the 9/11 Truth Movement would be to destroy this movement through the use of tactics that, by violating both the US Constitution and positive law, would evoke so much outrage as to make the country ungovernable.

Sunstein's Apparent Logical Error

Seen in this light, Sunstein's "logical error," criticized above, was not a slip on his part. Careful readers, he would surely have known, would realize that he was aware that the options he considered were not exhaustive—that another option would be for the government to stop the spread of the 9/11 Truth Movement's conspiracy theory by simply demonstrating its falsity in a public forum, perhaps through televised debates. By seeming to overlook this obvious option, Sunstein can be read as reminding his knowing readers that it was not a *real* option, because no such demonstration would be possible. The only way to defeat the 9/11 Truth Movement, therefore, would be to destroy it by using means that would entail the abrogation of the Bill of Rights, most obviously the First Amendment.

Accordingly, Sunstein would have signaled the elite members of his intended audience, it is time to allow the truth about 9/11 to come out. The process will surely be embarrassing and painful, he would likely add, but necessary, because there is no way to keep up the pretense without descending into fascism.

Cognitive Infiltration

If the goal of the esoteric Sunstein was to undermine the Bush–Cheney administration's 9/11 conspiracy theory, how would we understand his proposal to have government agents engage in cognitive infiltration of groups providing this theory?

To understand what he may have had in mind, we need to remember that "the US government" is far from monolithic. There are many branches and agencies, and the leadership of some of these branches and agencies have very different ideas and values than the leadership of other branches and agencies. The legislative and executive branches, for example, often have different ideas. And the differences between the CIA and the FBI are well known, as are those between the Pentagon and the State Department. One of the government's branches or agencies might, therefore, have agents "cognitively infiltrate" another one in order to try to change its thinking.

In light of this possibility, we could understand that, writing in 2008, Sunstein may have been thinking of the next president and how he—assuming it was going to be his friend Barack Obama—might deal with the dilemma created by his inheritance of the Bush–Cheney administration's absurd conspiracy theory about 9/11.

On the one hand, if the new president continued to endorse this theory indefinitely, he would increasingly lose credibility with the American people, as they became increasingly aware of the falsity of that theory, and with political leaders around the world who know the theory to be false (some of whom have joined Political Leaders for 9/11 Truth).

On the other hand, this theory had been publicly endorsed by Congress, the Pentagon, the Department of Justice and its FBI, the Department of Homeland Security, and the CIA, the NSA, and the other intelligence agencies. It had even been endorsed by all the major newspapers, news magazines, and TV networks. The new president could not simply announce that the Bush–Cheney conspiracy theory was a lie, because this would be to let the American people know that all of these organizations had either been duped or had been lying to them—either of which would induce in them a loss of faith in their institutions, and that could lead to chaos.

The new president, therefore, would need to move slowly and subtly, gradually preparing these various organizations to begin revealing the truth in a way that would not create a national crisis of confidence.

Done correctly, in fact, the revelations could begin to increase the public's confidence in its government and the mainstream news media—confidence that has declined precipitously in recent years. America's political leaders and news media, the people would see, were finally leveling with them. The 35 percent or more of the population who already knew, or at least believed, the official story to be a lie would be immediately encouraged. And although much of the remainder of the population might initially react with disbelief or despair, the disbelief would be quickly overcome once the president and news media began systematically laying out the facts, and the despair would soon turn to hope—that the United States would quit lying to its people and begin acting more in line with its professed ideals.

As to the role cognitive infiltration would play in bringing about this transformation, the president would know that minds in all of these organizations, which had been supporting the Bush–Cheney conspiracy theory, would need to be changed. Some people in these organizations would need to be provided with evidence against the truth of the Bush–Cheney administration's 9/11 conspiracy theory. But the main target would be people in leadership positions, most of whom would already know this theory to be false. Many of these leaders, such as those in the Pentagon, the Department of Homeland Security, and the intelligence agencies, would be loath to give up the theory (publicly), because it has been so good for their budgets. A central purpose of the infiltrators would be to introduce cognitive diversity within these leadership circles, creating doubt as to whether continuing to support the Bush–Cheney conspiracy theory would really be good for those organizations, especially now that this theory is being increasingly discredited.

Understood in this way, we can see that Sunstein's warning about risks were not pure fantasy. Although his worry that agents might "be asked to perform criminal acts to prove their bona fides" is absurd in relation to professional organizations belonging to the 9/11 Truth Movement, it might be a genuine concern for agents seeking to infiltrate the CIA, the FBI, or the Pentagon.

In any case, infiltrators would also, Sunstein probably assumed, need to be sent into the headquarters of the major media, to help stimulate thinking about how, after having supported the Bush–Cheney administration's false interpretation of 9/11 for so many years, to begin revealing the truth. This would clearly need to be handled delicately in order to retain, and hopefully increase, the public's trust in those media.

But the public would not be the only concern: The major media could not be effectively targeted in isolation from their corporate owners. Indeed, the owners of the giant corporations, along with the elite class more generally, might well be the most important target for the cognitive infiltrators. In advocating the "cognitive infiltration of extremist groups," Sunstein may well have had in mind bankers and corporate owners who, while already being obscenely wealthy, continue to promote policies, both at home and abroad, to increase their own wealth at the expense of much poorer people in this and other countries and at the expense of the planet itself (as illustrated by the BP oil well blowout in the Gulf of Mexico). In equating these "extremist groups" with "the groups that produce conspiracy theories," moreover, Sunstein may well have been assuming that the 9/11 attacks, along with the plan to blame Muslims for them, originated in these elite circles (so that people who were clearly involved at the operational level, such as Cheney and Rumsfeld, were carrying out orders from above).

Given the fact that our country is now more a plutocracy than a democracy, Sunstein would have known that the truth about 9/11 would not be allowed to become public until the country's elite class, or at least a significant portion of it, had decided that the revelation had become necessary. Accordingly, insofar as members of the elite class had for the most part either accepted the Bush–Cheney administration's 9/11 conspiracy theory or, while knowing it to be false, accepted the idea that pretending to believe it promoted their interests, this class's thinking would be where cognitive diversity would most be needed. Sunstein could have been thinking of the shared thinking of the various networks and groups making up this class when he spoke of "weakening or even breaking up the epistemological complexes that constitute these networks and groups."

If so, the task of the infiltrators from the executive branch would be to introduce doubts into the thinking of members of the elite class—doubts either about the truth of the Bush–Cheney conspiracy theory or about the wisdom of continuing to promote it—in order to bring this class to the point where it would permit the president and the press to reveal the truth. Not the whole truth, of course, because that would be to reveal elite complicity, but simply the fact that it had been an inside job, carried out by members of the Bush administration and some of its agencies. As usual, the exposure would go only so high, and no higher.

Sunstein as an ethical person and a constitutional scholar would, to be sure, probably prefer that the full truth be revealed. But as a realist, he would know better than to let the perfect be the enemy of the good. Getting out some of the truth about 9/11—enough to reverse the destructive policies that have been based on the Bush–Cheney conspiracy theory—would need to suffice for now. The task of overcoming plutocracy would have to be assigned to a much longer-term project.

―――――

Insofar as we accept the above-described esoteric meaning of Sunstein's essay, we can see him as a great, self-sacrificing American, willing to risk his reputation in order to undermine the Bush–Cheney administration's 9/11 conspiracy theory, which has been used as a pretext for two illegal and immoral wars and also for eroding the US Constitution. As a constitutional scholar, Sunstein would naturally see the protection of our Constitution, especially its precious Bill of Rights, as his supreme duty, so that his temporary loss of reputation, caused by his apparent willingness to recommend illegal and even unconstitutional acts, would seem a small price to pay.

CONCLUSION
INTERPRETING THE ESOTERIC
INTERPRETATION

At the end of the Introduction, I indicated that my proffered esoteric interpretation of Sunstein's essay should be taken "seriously but not literally." In this conclusion, I explain what I meant.

On the one hand, the so-called esoteric interpretation, rather than being taken literally, should be understood more as irony or satire. To have intended it literally, I would need to believe that this "interpretation" brings out a level of meaning that was intended, whether consciously or unconsciously, by Sunstein himself, and I do not believe that. One implication is that the "rather harsh criticisms" of his essay by Glenn Greenwald and others, which I quoted in the Introduction, are ones that I share.

On the other hand, I used this so-called "interpretation" to make a serious point: namely, that Sunstein's essay is filled with statements and references that contradict various elements in his argument. When the author of an argumentative essay makes self-contradictory statements, this is usually a sign that something is seriously wrong with the position being argued. Why? Because when authors are defending positions that are false, they find it very difficult to deny the true state of affairs completely, so that contradictions often creep in as implicit acknowledgments of reality. Self-contradictions are, therefore, often signs of the falsity of the argument being made.

My explication of a hidden level of meaning in Sunstein's essay, radically different from the surface meaning, was in part simply a way of calling attention to the existence of statements and references in the essay that contradicted—or at least pointed to evidence that contradicted—the main thrust of his argument.

The "esoteric interpretation" also served another purpose: It allowed me to show that those contradictions could be portrayed as adding up to a coherent alternative position. Indeed, I put the brief note at the end of the Introduction, indicating that my "esoteric interpretation" should not be taken literally, because pre-publication reviewers warned that, without this note, many readers might believe that Sunstein actually intended his essay to convey this deeper meaning—or at least that I *thought* he did.

The position expressed in what I called the esoteric level is, of course, the position that I, as a member of the 9/11 Truth Movement, wish that Sunstein *had* intended to communicate.

But it is also the position that I believe Sunstein *should* have taken, assuming the following two conditions: (1) that he had studied the evidence sufficiently to be ready to evaluate the credibility of the two 9/11 conspiracy theories before he wrote his article—which he should have done: no good lawyer would go to court without knowing the evidence for both sides; and (2) that he had thought through the implications of the various statements and references that contradict the main thrust of his article.

Sunstein's Self-Contradictions: A Review

By way of summarizing and concluding this book, I will review those statements and references that, although not actually indicative of an esoteric level of meaning, do contradict the main thrust of Sunstein's essay, thereby suggesting that, to achieve a self-consistent position, he would have needed to revise his position rather drastically.

Conspiracy Theories Defined (Chapter 1): In this chapter, we saw that Sunstein supported his tendentious title—which indicates that conspiracy theories, like illnesses, need "cures"—by giving a one-sided definition, according to which a "conspiracy theory" is "an effort to explain some event or practice by reference to the machinations of powerful people." This definition allowed Sunstein to write as if conspiracy theories were typically formulated by people with anti-government biases. It also entailed that people who believe that 9/11 was orchestrated by individuals in the Bush–Cheney administration are "conspiracy theorists," while those who believe that it was orchestrated by al-Qaeda are not.

But then Sunstein admitted that his definition was not inclusive, because "many conspiracy theories involve people who are not especially powerful." Why, then, had he not given a generic definition of conspiracy theories—one that would include conspiracy theories about both powerful and not-so-powerful people?

Because, he suggested, formulating such a definition was probably not possible. But he then referred readers to an excellent article on conspiracy theories by philosopher Charles Pigden, which contains such a definition: "[A] conspiracy theory is simply a theory that posits a conspiracy—a secret plan on the part of some group to influence events by partly secret means." There was, accordingly, no excuse for his one-sided definition.

Sunstein further contradicted the main thrust of his article, the title of which suggests that conspiracy theories as such are illnesses that need to be cured, by pointing out that "some conspiracy theories have turned out to be true." Sunstein then did even more damage to his argument by advising readers to consult Pigden's article with regard to that point and its "philosophical implications." Readers who do consult this article will find it saying that "conspiracy theories as such are no less worthy of belief than theories of other kinds." With this recommendation, therefore, Sunstein had completely undermined the claim implied by his article's title, namely, that "conspiracy theories" are a special breed of theories for which we need to discover both "causes" and "cures."

Conspiracy Theories in America as Usually False (Chapter 2): We next examined Sunstein's claim that conspiracy theories about political leaders in the United States are usually false, because we have a well-motivated government, so its officials would rarely if ever engage in nefarious conspiracies, and because we have a free press, which would quickly expose any such conspiracies that did occur.

But then Sunstein pointed out that US political leaders have, in fact, proposed and even engaged in a number of nefarious conspiracies. Although he mentioned only four—Watergate, MKULTRA, Operation Northwoods, and the campaign to convince Americans that Saddam Hussein was involved in the 9/11 attacks—these were such as to remind informed readers of many more. Sunstein's claim about our free press was undermined by the fact that most of these conspiracies were revealed only many years later, if ever.

Sunstein further undermined his claims about our well-motivated government and our free press with his reference to William Pepper's book, which shows beyond reasonable doubt that various government agencies were involved in the assassination of Martin Luther King, Jr., after which the press failed to inform the public about the trial and its results.

The 9/11 Conspiracy Theory Defined (Chapter 3): In the third chapter, we saw, Sunstein equated the 9/11 conspiracy theory with the theory that "U.S. officials knowingly allowed 9/11 to happen or even brought it about." That equation, however, presupposed Sunstein's definition of conspiracy theories in general, according to which they are about powerful people, and Sunstein, as we saw, admitted that many conspiracy theories are about people who are not powerful.

This acknowledgment made it possible, in turn, to acknowledge that there are *two* 9/11 conspiracy theories, one of which is the government's own theory, according to which the attacks were orchestrated by al-Qaeda followers of Osama bin Laden. And, indeed, Sunstein even explicitly stated this: "The theory that Al-Qaeda was responsible for 9/11 is," Sunstein wrote, a "conspiracy theory."

With these acknowledgments, Sunstein had moved far from the general thrust of his article, expressed in its title, according to which "conspiracy theories" are aberrant views for which we need to discern the "causes" and then devise "cures." Given Sunstein's recognition that the government's al-Qaeda theory is a "conspiracy theory" as fully as is the theory that 9/11 was an inside job, a major portion of his article should have been devoted to the question: How can we determine which of these theories is more justified by the relevant evidence and hence more likely to be true?

9/11 Conspiracy Theorists as Epistemic Cripples (Chapter 4): We next looked at Sunstein's analysis of the basic "cause" of conspiracy theories: that people accept these theories, in spite of the fact that the evidence for them is "weak or even nonexistent," because they have "crippled epistemologies." It appears that this causal analysis must have been worked out prior to Sunstein's acknowledgment that some conspiracy theories are true and also his acknowledgment that the government's theory about 9/11 is a conspiracy theory. In order to take this twofold acknowledgment into account, he would have needed to reconsider his claim that "informational isolation" provides an explanation for the acceptance of conspiracy theories in general.

Also, by virtue of his recognition that those who espouse the alternative theory refer to themselves collectively as the "9/11 Truth Movement," along with his awareness that this movement has at least one internet site (911Truth.org) where one could acquire information about it, he implied the need to look concretely at the make-up of this movement, in order to test the plausibility of his claim that its members typically suffer from informational isolation. And, insofar as his readers did use the internet to explore the nature of this movement, they would have seen that its intellectual leadership is provided by architects, engineers, intelligence officers, lawyers, medical professionals, professors, scientists, and other intellectuals and professionals—not people whose beliefs could be explained by informational isolation.

Finally, this contradiction is made even more obvious by his reference to Russell Hardin's essay, "The Crippled Epistemology of Extremism," which says that "sustaining [a] crippled epistemology . . . requires exclusion of knowledge of, and therefore traffic with, most of the rest of the entire world"—which means that Hardin's essay contradicts, rather than supports, Sunstein's claim about the 9/11 Truth Movement.

The 9/11 Conspiracy Theory as Demonstrably False (Chapter 5): We next looked at Sunstein's claim that the 9/11 Truth Movement's conspiracy theory is problematic in three ways: Besides being (1) "demonstrably false" and also (2) "unjustified" because based on evidence that is "weak or even nonexistent," it has (3) resulted in a "degenerating research program." This threefold claim by Sunstein is implicitly contradicted by three features of his essay.

First, he made no attempt to demonstrate the falsity of the 9/11 Truth Movement's theory, or even to tell the reader where such a demonstration could be found.

Second, although Sunstein must have been aware of some of the evidence published by the 9/11 Truth Movement in support of its own theory against that of the government, he made no effort to refute any of this evidence or to tell the reader where to find such refutations.

Third, the very fact that Sunstein wrote this essay, giving advice to "a government facing a population in which a particular conspiracy theory is becoming widespread"—by which he clearly meant the 9/11 Truth Movement's theory—suggests his awareness that this theory is supported by a progressive, rather than a degenerating, research program.

The 9/11 Conspiracy Theory as Harmful (Chapter 6): In this chapter, we looked at a thesis that is essential to Sunstein's claim that government should take extraordinary steps to undermine the 9/11 Truth Movement—namely, that this movement is harmful. He offers two versions of this thesis. The first version characterizes members of this movement as "extremists," who are likely to become violent, "with terrifying consequences."

It is, in fact, only this first version of the thesis that, if sustained, would justify extraordinary steps by the government to break up this movement. And yet Sunstein implicitly contradicted this version: Besides not providing any evidence that the 9/11 Truth Movement is made up of violence-prone people, he did not even explain why these people should be called "extremists."

Moreover, by citing Hardin's essay, "The Crippled Epistemology of Extremism," he implied that he was using the term "extremism" in Hardin's sense, and when we turn to Hardin's essay, we learn that his concern was with the kind of extremism that leads to "fanatical nationalism." The 9/11 Truth Movement, however, is an *international* movement, seeking to expose 9/11 as a false-flag attack carried out for nationalistic purposes. This movement is, therefore, diametrically opposed to the extremism with which Hardin's essay is concerned. Could Sunstein have contradicted himself any more strongly than he did by attempting to use Hardin's essay to support his allegations about the 9/11 Truth Movement?

The contradiction entailed by Sunstein's appeal to Hardin's essay is made even stronger by Hardin's statement that, when "a crippled epistemology leads to fanaticism," this fanaticism "then leads to the urge for governmental control, because "[it] is only through gaining control of a state . . . that a fanatical group could expect to exclude contrary views and thereby maintain the crippled epistemology of their followers." Accordingly, although Sunstein was trying to employ Hardin's concepts to portray the 9/11 Truth Movement as composed of "extremists" with "crippled epistemologies," Hardin's essay actually deals with the kind of extremism embodied in the neocons who took control of the US government in January 2001, when the Bush–Cheney administration began its reign.

Furthermore, by pointing out that "the Bush administration suggested that Saddam Hussein had conspired with Al Qaeda to support the 9/11 attacks"—a suggestion through which the administration obtained the American people's support for attacking Iraq—Sunstein reflected the fact that it is the Bush administration's 9/11 conspiracy theory, not that of the 9/11 Truth Movement, that has led to violence with terrifying consequences.

Perhaps recognizing that he had no evidence for his attempt to portray the 9/11 Truth Movement as harmful or dangerous, in the sense of likely to lead to terrifying violence, Sunstein provided a second version of his thesis about the potentially harmful nature of this movement. This second version consisted of examples of alternative ways in which, even if it did not lead to violence, this movement could nonetheless have "pernicious effects from the government's point of view." It could have such effects, Sunstein said, by inducing "widespread public skepticism about the government's assertions," or by "dampening public mobilization and participation in government-led efforts."

Insofar as Sunstein thereby implicitly admitted that these were the real "dangers" posed by the 9/11 Truth Movement, he contradicted his claim that it is harmful or dangerous in ways that would justify the employment of COINTELPRO-like tactics against it.

The Duty to Undermine the 9/11 Conspiracy Theory (Chapter 7): The next step in Sunstein's argument was to say that the government should seek to prevent "false and harmful conspiracy theories" from becoming widespread, so that, insofar as it can undermine them, the government should do so. He meant this injunction to apply primarily, of course, to his "main focus" and "running example," the 9/11 Truth Movement's conspiracy theory. However, the claim that it is both false and harmful depended on the claims discussed in the previous two chapters, and these claims, as we have seen, were undermined by various self-contradictions in Sunstein's essay. Those contradictions were implicit, therefore, in his seventh thesis, with the consequence that, insofar as this thesis in any way justified a governmental attempt to undermine "the 9/11 conspiracy theory," it would justify only the version of that theory promulgated by the Bush–Cheney administration, which is indeed both false and harmful.

Inoculating the Public (Chapter 8): Having reported Sunstein's recommendation that, in its effort to undermine the 9/11 conspiracy theory, the government should take a twofold approach—seeking to silence this theory's purveyors as well as trying to inoculate the public against its claims—I dealt in Chapter 8 only with the latter approach.

One contradiction in Sunstein's discussion of this approach related to his assurance that having an open press serves to inoculate the public against the views of the 9/11 Truth Movement. If Sunstein really believed this, along with his related claim that these views are "demonstrably false," then he would have recommended public debates between advocates of these views and defenders of the government's 9/11 conspiracy theory, in which the latter could have demonstrated to the public the falsity of the 9/11 Truth Movement's views. But Sunstein made no such recommendation.

Another contradiction was implied by Sunstein's suggestion that the government obtain help in making its case by employing "independent experts" who are independent in name only, being in reality coached and perhaps even paid by the government. If Sunstein truly believed the evidence for the 9/11 Truth Movement's theory to be "weak or even nonexistent" and that the theory itself is "demonstrably false," then no such subterfuge would be necessary: Fully independent architects, engineers, physicists, chemists, and pilots would speak out on their own, without any payment or coaching, to show the falsity of this theory. Sunstein's recommendation implied, therefore, that he knew the truth to be on the other side.

Chapters 9 and 10: In Sunstein's final two theses (as formulated in my summary of his argument), he first argued that the approach used to inoculate the public—simply providing credible public information—will not work to "debias" the hard-core 9/11 conspiracy theorists, because they have a "self-sealing" theory, which makes them resistant to correction, especially correction by the government. In addition, they assimilate information in a biased way.

Accordingly, he argued, another approach must be taken in order to silence the purveyors of this theory. Because we have a free society, the government cannot simply ban this theory, as this would violate its advocates' rights of free speech and assembly. The only way to deal with these purveyors, Sunstein concluded, would be to have government agents infiltrate the 9/11 Truth Movement, generally anonymously. Their task would be to introduce "cognitive diversity," with the aim of "breaking up the hard core of extremists who supply [9/11] conspiracy theories."

The main contradiction in this argument involves a logical error: Sunstein falsely argued that to accomplish the government's goal of stopping the spread of the 9/11 Truth Movement's conspiracy theory, it needed either to persuade ("debias") or to silence its suppliers. Since they cannot be persuaded, Sunstein argued, the government would have to resort to subterfuge to silence them.

The logical error involved treating a non-exhaustive set of options as if it were exhaustive. That is, if there are four possible solutions to a problem, you cannot logically infer from the unworkability of the first two that the third solution is the best; you must also consider the fourth one. But Sunstein, having concluded that the spread of the 9/11 Truth Movement's theory could not be stopped by banning it or by persuading its purveyors to change their minds, concluded that the best solution would be to have agents infiltrate the movement—even though there was a rather obvious fourth alternative: The government could stop the spread of this theory by publicly discrediting it, perhaps by arranging public debates between spokespersons for the competing theories, in which the government's experts could show the "demonstrable falsity" of the alternative theory.

The fact that Sunstein "overlooked" this obvious alternative suggests his awareness that a public debate would show the opposite to be the case: that it is the Bush–Cheney administration's 9/11 conspiracy theory that is demonstrably false.

That is what we have seen, especially in Chapters 4 and 5: that the conclusion that the official story is false is supported by an enormous amount of evidence of various types, including scientific evidence, and that this conclusion is being embraced by growing numbers of people, including scientists and other professional people with relevant types of expertise.

What Sunstein's essay comes down to, therefore, is a proposal to use tactics of questionable decency and legality to undermine a movement that could not be defeated through the normal tools of his trade: evidence and argumentation. Besides being appalled by Sunstein's proposal, those of us in the 9/11 Truth Movement should also be grateful for it. Why? Because this proposal, which is encapsulated in the phrase "cognitive infiltration," almost explicitly acknowledges that the government would be able to undermine the 9/11 Truth Movement only through surreptitious means, not by using evidence and argumentation to discredit it intellectually.

The Truth Movement should, therefore, take Sunstein's proposal to use "cognitive infiltration" to undermine it as a compliment—as a Harvard law professor's recognition that this movement, which claims to speak the truth about 9/11, actually does so. The movement should, accordingly, publicize this phrase, using it to educate the public about this law professor's implicit admission that, if the government had to defend its account of 9/11 in a court of law, it would not have a winnable case.

Concluding Comment: Self-contradictions in an argument, as mentioned earlier, are usually signs that the argument is based on faulty premises and is headed toward a false conclusion. My "esoteric interpretation" was employed in the various chapters as a dramatic way of bringing out the fact that Sunstein's essay is riddled with such contradictions. In this conclusion, I have prosaically spelled out these contradictions, which certainly should create a suspicion that Sunstein's basic premises—that the government's 9/11 conspiracy theory is true while that of the 9/11 Truth Movement is harmful and demonstrably false—do not correspond to reality. This suspicion has been amply confirmed by the evidence cited in the various chapters.

In light of the falsity of Sunstein's argument and the illegality of his proposals, must defenders of the official 9/11 conspiracy theory not ask themselves: If this is the best plan for dealing with the growing influence of the 9/11 Truth Movement that can be devised by "the pre-eminent legal scholar of our time," is it not time to throw in the towel?

Acknowledgments

This book is much better than it otherwise would have been because of enormous assistance received from Elizabeth Woodworth—a former medical librarian who has become my (volunteer) assistant—and Tod Fletcher, who shares with Elizabeth the ability to be equally helpful in relation to big and tiny matters. Both of them, as they have done on previous books and articles, gave excellent advice on substantive matters as well as lending their superb proofreading skills.

I wish, once again, to thank publisher Michel Moushabeck, editor Pamela Thompson, and all the others at Olive Branch Press (of Interlink Books), which has done so much to help the world understand the truth about 9/11. Special thanks to Juliana Spear for coming up with such a striking cover.

As always, my greatest ongoing debt is to my wife, Ann Jaqua, who provides the context in which I can write.

Finally, I cannot resist thanking Cass Sunstein, whose essay "Conspiracy Theories" has provided such an excellent foil for laying out the current nature of the 9/11 Truth Movement, along with the extent and quality of its evidence.

NOTES

1 This office, known as OIRA, is under the Office of Management and Budget (www.whitehouse.gov/omb/inforeg_administrator).

2 "President Obama Announces Another Key OMB Post," White House, April 20, 2009 (www.whitehouse.gov/the_press_office/President-Obama-Announces-Another-Key-OMB-Post).

3 "Cass Sunstein to Leave U. of Chicago for Harvard," *Chronicle of Higher Education,* February 19, 2008 (http://chronicle.com/article/Cass-Sunstein-to-Leave-U-of/40489).

4 Cass R. Sunstein and Adrian Vermeule, "Conspiracy Theories," Preliminary Draft, January 15, 2008. This draft was both Harvard Public Law Working Paper No. 08-03 and University of Chicago Public Law Working Paper No. 199 (http://papers.ssrn.com/sol3/papers.cfm?abstract_id=1084585#%23). This draft can be downloaded. Henceforth cited simply as "Conspiracy Theories," Preliminary Draft.

5 The fact that the article first appeared online on August 18, 2008, is stated at the webpage for this article (see next note).

6 Cass R. Sunstein and Adrian Vermeule, "Conspiracy Theories: Causes and Cures," *Journal of Political Philosophy*, 17/2 (June 2009), 202-27. Henceforth cited simply as "Conspiracy Theories: Causes and Cures."

7 Marc Estrin, "Your Government Appointees at Work: Cass Sunstein Seeks 'Cognitive' Provocateurs," The Rag Blog, January 11, 2010 (http://theragblog.blogspot.com/2010/01/got-fascism-obama-advisor-promotes.html).

8 "Open letter from Cyril Wecht to Cass Sunstein and Adrian Vermeule," Real History Blog, January 26, 2010 (http://realhistoryarchives.blogspot.com/2010/01/open-letter-from-cyril-wecht-to-cass.html).

9 John Stossel, "Stealth Propaganda," Fox Business, January 18, 2010 (http://stossel.blogs.foxbusiness.com/2010/01/18/stealth-propaganda/?test=latestnews).

10 Bill Willers, "An Attack from Harvard Law on the Escalating 9/11 Truth Movement," OpEdNews, February 4, 2010 (www.opednews.com/articles/AN-ATTACK-FROM-HARVARD-LAW-by-Bill-Willers-100203-909.html).

11 Mark Crispin Miller, "Obama's Info Chief Advocates Disinformation and Domestic Covert Ops," OpEdNews, January 15, 2010 (http://www.opednews.com/articles/Obama-s-Info-Chief-advocat-by-Mark-Crispin-Mille-100115-63.html). Miller's statement first appeared on his blog, News from the Underground, January 15, 2008 (http://groups.google.com/group/newsfromunderground/browse_thread/thread/2d58d4b5f052e08b/dfdc18dde3c49f3e?lnk=gst&q=Sunstein#dfdc18dde3c49f3e).

12 Glenn Greenwald, "Obama Confidant's Spine-Chilling Proposal," Salon.com, January 15, 2010 (www.salon.com/news/opinion/ glenn_greenwald/2010/01/15/ sunstein); the statement about being barred is in Update III.

13 "Conspiracy Theories," Preliminary Draft, 3.

14 "Conspiracy Theories: Causes and Cures," 204.

15 Ibid., 224, 219.

16 Shadia B. Drury, *The Political Ideas of Leo Strauss*, updated edition with a new introduction (New York: Palgrave Macmillan, 2005). The accuracy of her interpretation has been endorsed by no less an authority than Laurence Lampert, author of *Leo Strauss and Nietzsche* (Chicago: University of Chicago Press, 1996), who speaks of Drury's "fine skeptical readings of Strauss's texts and acute insights into Strauss's real intentions" (132n).

17 I myself employed Drury's two-level analysis in interpreting Strauss in "Saving Civilization: Straussian and Whiteheadian Political Philosophy," ed. Michel Weber and Will Desmond, *Handbook of Whiteheadian Process Thought* (Frankfurt: Ontos Verlag, 2008), 521–32.

18 Leo Strauss, *What Is Political Philosophy?* (New York: Free Press, 1959), 221–22; quoted in Drury, *The Political Ideas of Leo Strauss*, 19. Strauss presents this passage as an interpretation of Plato's approach, but doing this, Drury argues, is intrinsic to Strauss's way of disguising his true intentions from the vulgar.

19 "Conspiracy Theories: Causes and Cures," 205.

20 "Conspiracy Theories," Preliminary Draft, 17.

21 "Conspiracy Theories: Causes and Cures," 209.

22 "Conspiracy Theories: Causes and Cures," 204.

23 Ibid., 210. In many places, as in the passages partly quoted in this point, the text did not refer specifically to the 9/11 conspiracy theory, but simply to "conspiracy theories." I have made those passages apply to the 9/11 conspiracy theory in particular on the principle that, if this theory is the essay's "main focus" and "running example" (see the text corresponding to notes 13 and 14, above), then the statements about conspiracy theories in general should apply preeminently to the 9/11 conspiracy theory in particular (meaning, as the essay almost always intends, the theory that 9/11 was, at least partly, an inside job).

24 Ibid., 206, 211, 210.

25 Ibid., 220, 226.

26 Ibid., 204, 226.

27 Ibid., 221.

28 Ibid., 207, 210, 223.

29 Ibid., 218 (emphasis in original).

30 See Krista Tippett, "Obama's Theologian," Speaking of Faith (conversation with E. J. Dionne and David Brooks), February 13, 2009 (http:// speakingoffaith.publicradio.org/programs/2009/obamas-theologian/); John Blake, "How Obama's Favorite Theologian Shaped His First Year in Office," CNN, February 5, 2010 (www.cnn.com/2010/ POLITICS/ 02/05/Obama.theologian/index.html).

31 See Reinhold Niebuhr, *The Nature and Destiny of Man*, II: 50, where he said that, with regard to "ideas dealing with the relation of history and super-history . . . , it is important to take Biblical symbols seriously but not literally." One witness to the frequency with which Niebuhr used this phrase is theological ethicist Roger Shinn, who probably knew Niebuhr and his thought as well as anyone, and who wrote: "Niebuhr, confronting the ultimate questions of human life and all reality, held that the human mind could best respond to them in terms of narratives, especially the biblical narratives, taken 'seriously but not literally,' to use his familiar phrase." Roger L. Shinn, "Reinhold Niebuhr as Teacher, Colleague, and Friend," Daniel Rice and Martin E. Marty, eds., *Reinhold Niebuhr Revisited: Engagements with an American Original* (Grand Rapids: Eerdmans, 2009), 3-20, at 12. See also Langdon Gilkey, *On Niebuhr: A Theological Study* (Chicago: University of Chicago Press, 2001), especially Chap. 10.

32 "Conspiracy Theories: Causes and Cures," 205.

33 Ibid., 206n15.

34 Charles Pigden, "Conspiracy Theories and the Conventional Wisdom," *Episteme*, 4 (2007), 219–32, at 219 (these are the essay's opening lines).

35 "Conspiracy Theories: Causes and Cures," 211.

36 Ibid., 205.

37 Ibid., 205.

38 *The American Heritage Dictionary of the English Language* (American Heritage Publishing Co., 1969).

39 David Ray Griffin, *Debunking 9/11 Debunking: An Answer to Popular Mechanics and Other Defenders of the Official Conspiracy Theory* (Northampton: Olive Branch Press, 2007), 8.

40 Pigden, "Conspiracy Theories and the Conventional Wisdom," 222.

41 "Conspiracy Theories: Causes and Cures," 205.

42 Pigden, "Conspiracy Theories and the Conventional Wisdom," 223.

43 "Conspiracy Theories: Causes and Cures," 206.

44 Ibid., 206.

45 Ibid., 206 n. 15.

46 Pigden, "Conspiracy Theories and the Conventional Wisdom," 222.

47 Ibid., 221.

48 Ibid., 219.

49 "Conspiracy Theories: Causes and Cures," 207.

50 Ibid., 207.

51 I have developed and defended this definition (which has become controversial in some philosophical circles) in "Religious Language and Truth," which is Chap. 9 of Griffin, *Reenchantment without Supernaturalism: A Process Philosophy of Religion* (Ithaca: Cornell University Press, 2001), and in "Truth as Correspondence, Knowledge as Dialogical: Pluralism without Relativism," which is Chap. 5 of Griffin, *Whitehead's Radically Different Postmodern Philosophy: An Argument for Its Contemporary Relevance* (Albany: SUNY Press, 2007).

52 "Conspiracy Theories: Causes and Cures," 212.

53 See "Religious Knowledge and Common Sense," which is Chap. 10 of Griffin, *Reenchantment without Supernaturalism*.

54 "Conspiracy Theories: Causes and Cures," 204.

55 Ibid., 209.

56 I say that the distinction is (only) *virtually* obliterated, so that the meanings are (only) *operationally* the same, because truth (properly defined) is "justified true belief," and a belief could be justified in light of all the information that is presently available in the world today and still be false.

57 "Conspiracy Theories: Causes and Cures," 207.

58 Ibid., 210.

59 Ibid., 206, 207, 225, 226.

60 Ibid., 225, 219.

61 Ibid., 219.

62 Ibid., 206.

63 Alex Constantine, "MOCKINGBIRD: The Subversion of The Free Press By The CIA," as "The Alex Constantine Article: Tales from the Crypt: The Depraved Spies and Moguls of the CIA's Operation MOCKINGBIRD" (http://whatreallyhappened.com/RANCHO/POLITICS/MOCK/mockingbird.html). See also Alex Constantine, "Tales from the Crypt: The Depraved Spies and Moguls of the CIA's Operation MOCKINGBIRD," Alex Constantine's Anti-Fascist Encyclopedia, February 5, 2010 (www.antifascistencyclopedia.com/allposts/tales-from-the-crypt-the-depraved-spies-and-moguls-of-the-cias-operation-mockingbird), for the original article plus commentary.

64 *Final Report of the Select Committee to Study Governmental Operations With Respect to Intelligence Activities*, United States Senate: Together with Additional, Supplemental, and Separate Views (1976): Vol. 1 (www.archive.org/details/finalreportofsel01unit): 455 (click *Read Online* on the left margin).

65 Carl Bernstein, "CIA and the Media: How America's Most Powerful News Media Worked Hand in Glove with the Central Intelligence Agency and Why the Church Committee Covered It Up," *Rolling Stone*, October 20, 1977 (http://carl-bernstein.com/magazine_cia_and_media.php).

66 Daniele Ganser, *NATO's Secret Armies: Operation Gladio and Terrorism in Western Europe* (New York: Frank Cass, 2005); for a shorter version, see Ganser, "What We Have Learned about the 'Strategy of Tension': Historical Data from the Cold War Period," in *9/11 and American Empire: Intellectuals Speak Out*, ed. David Ray Griffin and Peter Dale Scott (Northampton: Olive Branch Press, 2006).

67 Steven Kinzer, *Overthrow: America's Century of Regime Change from Hawaii to Iraq* (New York: Times Books [Henry Holt], 2006), Chap. 5, "Despotism and Godless Terrorism"; William Blum, *Killing Hope: U.S. Military and CIA Interventions Since World War II* (Monroe, ME: Common Courage), Chap. 9: "Iran 1953: Making It Safe for the King of Kings."

68 Piero Gleijeses, *Shattered Hope: The Guatemalan Revolution and the United States, 1944-1954* (Princeton: Princeton University Press, 1991); Kinzer, *Overthrow,* Chap. 6, "Get Rid of This Stinker."

69 Mike Cassidy and Will Miller, "A Short History of FBI COINTELPRO," *Albion Monitor*, May 26, 1999 (www.albionmonitor.com/9905a/jbcointelpro.html); "COINTELPRO," Wikipedia (http://en.wikipedia.org/wiki/COINTELPRO# cite_note-pbsco-6); "COINTELPRO Revisited: Spying and Disruption" (http://whatreallyhappened.com/RANCHO/POLITICS/COINTELPRO/COIN-TELPRO-FBI.docs.html). J. Edgar Hoover's words are quoted from his memo of August 25, 1967, to "all offices" of the FBI.

70 Audrey R. Kahin and George McT. Kahin, *Subversion as Foreign Policy: The Secret Eisenhower and Dulles Debacle in Indonesia* (Seattle: University of Washington Press, 1995).

71 "The Gulf of Tonkin Incident, 40 Years Later," National Security Archive Electronic Briefing Book No. 132, ed. by John Prados, August 4, 2004 (www.gwu.edu/~nsarchiv/NSAEBB/NSAEBB132/index.htm); Gareth Porter, "Robert McNamara Deceived LBJ on Gulf of Tonkin, Documents Show," Raw Story, July 8, 2009 (http://rawstory.com/08/news/2009/07/08/robert-mcnamara-deceived-lbj-on-gulf-of-tonkin/).

72 Kahin and Kahin, *Subversion as Foreign Policy*, 225–28; Gabriel Kolko, *Confronting the Third World* (New York: Pantheon, 1988), 180-81; Ralph W. McGehee, *Deadly Deceits: My 25 Years in the CIA* (New York: Sheridan Square Publications, 1983), 57–58; John Stockwell, *The Praetorian Guard: The U.S. Role in the New World Order* (Boston: South End, 1991), 72–73; William Blum, *Killing Hope*, 193–97. On the shooting lists, see Kathy Kadane, States News Service, "Ex-agents Say CIA Compiled Death Lists for Indonesians," which appeared in four major newspapers, including the *San Francisco Examiner*, May 20, 1990 (www.namebase.org/kadane.html).

73 Blum, *Killing Hope*, Ch. 35.

74 Kinzer, *Overthrow*, Chap. 8, "We're Going to Smash Him"; Blum, *Killing Hope*, Chap. 34; Monte Reel and J.Y. Smith, "A Chilean Dictator's Dark Legacy," *Washington Post*, December 11, 2006 (www.washingtonpost.com/wp-dyn/content/ article/2006/12/10/AR2006121000302.html); "Augusto Pinochet," Wikipedia (http://en.wikipedia.org/wiki/Augusto_Pinochet#Arrest_ and_trial_in_Britain).

75 Barbara Honegger, *October Surprise* (Tudor, 1989); Robert Parry, "How Two Elections Changed America," Consortium News.com (November 4, 2009 (www.consortiumnews.com/2009/110409.html), and "The Crazy October Surprise Debunking," November 6, 2009 (www.consortiumnews.com/2009/110609.html).

76 Gary Webb, *Dark Alliance: The CIA, the Contras, and the Crack Cocaine Explosion* (New York: Seven Stories, 1998).

77 Jane Hunter, Jonathan Marshall, and Peter Dale Scott, *The Iran-Contra Connection: Secret Teams and Covert Operations in the Reagan Era* (Boston: South End Press, 1987); "Iran-Contra Affair," Wikipedia (http://en.wikipedia.org/wiki/Iran–Contra_affair).

78 Noam Chomsky, *Deterring Democracy* (New York: Hill and Wang, 1992), 164-65 (quoting *Brecha*, CODEHUCA, "Report of Joint CODEHUCDA-CONADEHUPA Delegation," January–February 1990, San José).

79 Chomsky, *Deterring Democracy*, 159-72; Blum, *Killing Hope*, 305-13.

80 See Chalmers Johnson, *The Sorrows of Empire: Militarism, Secrecy, and the End of the Republic* (New York: Henry Holt, 2004), 230; Craig Unger, *House of Bush, House of Saud: The Secret Relationship between the World's Two Most Powerful Dynasties* (New York & London: Scribner, 2004), 249; and especially John R. MacArthur, *Second Front: Censorship and Propaganda in the 1991 Gulf War*, updated with a new preface (Berkeley: University of California Press, 2004), 58-66.

81 EPA, Press Release, September 18, 2001 (www.epa.gov/wtc/stories/head-line_091801.htm).

82 Gareth Cook and Tatsha Robertson, "Another Worry: Asbestos Dust Poses Threat to Rescue Crews," *Boston Globe*, September 14, 2001 (www.boston.com/news/packages/underattack/globe_stories/0914/Asbestos_dust_ poses_threat_to_rescue_crews+.shtml).

83 See "Insider: EPA Lied About WTC Air," CBS News, September 8, 2006 (www.cbsnews.com/stories/2006/09/08/earlyshow/main1985804.shtml); EPA Office of Inspector General, "EPA's Response to the World Trade Center Collapse," August 21, 2003, Executive Summary and Chapter 2 (www.mindfully.org/Air/2003/EPA-WTC-OIG-Evaluation21aug03.htm); and "White House Edited EPA's 9/11 Reports," by John Heilprin, Associated Press, *Seattle Post-Intelligencer*, August 23, 2003 (http://seattlepi.nwsource.com/ national/136350_epa23.html).

84 See Anthony DePalma, "Illness Persisting in 9/11 Workers, Big Study Finds," *New York Times*, September 6, 2006 (www.nytimes.com/2006/09/06/ nyregion/06health.html?ex=1315195200&en=aaf1bba2e01bc497&ei=5088&partner =rssnyt&emc=rss); Kristen Lombardi, "Death by Dust: The Frightening Link

between the 9-11 Toxic Cloud and Cancer," *Village Voice*, November 28, 2006 (www.911truth.org/article.php?story= 20061204132809573); "Dust and Disease," *News Hour with Jim Lehrer*, PBS, November 21, 2006, available on YouTube as "'60 Percent of Ground Zero Workers Sick" (www.youtube.com/ watch?v=qdS4X4r28Og); "Jonathan M. Samet, Alison S. Geyh, and Mark J. Utell, "The Legacy of World Trade Center Dust," *New England Journal of Medicine*, May 31, 2007 (http://content.nejm.org/cgi/content/full/356/22/2233); a documentary film entitled *Dust to Dust* (www.informationliberation.com/ index.php?id=21627); and Jerry Mazza's review of this documentary, "9/11's Second Round of Slaughter," Online Journal, January 16, 2008 (http://onlinejournal.com/artman/ publish/article_2845.shtml).

85 Peter Hallward, *Damming the Flood: Haiti, Aristide, and the Politics of Containment* (New York: Verso, 2007), Chap. 2, "The First Coup and Its Consequences."

86 Hallward, *Damming the Flood*, Introduction (the quotation is from page xxv) and Chap. 9, "The Second Coup." For an earlier treatment, written right after the coup, see Michel Chossudovsky, "The Destabilization of Haiti," Global Research, February 29, 2004 (www.globalresearch.ca/articles/CHO402D.html).

87 "Conspiracy Theories: Causes and Cures," 225.

88 Mark Crispin Miller, "None Dare Call It Stolen," *Harper's*, August 2005 (http://learning.nwc.hccs.edu:8080/Plone/members/tom.haymes/govt2302/pdfs/050 8harpmillerstolenelect.pdf).

89 Mark Crispin Miller, *Fooled Again* (New York: Basic Books, 2005).

90 David Manning, "The Secret Downing Street Memo: Secret and Strictly Personal—UK Eyes Only," *Sunday Times* (London), May 1, 2005 (www.timeson-line.co.uk/article/0,,2087-1593607,00.html). For discussion, see Ray McGovern, "Proof the Fix Was In," Antiwar.com, May 5, 2005 (www.antiwar.com/mcgovern/ index.php?articleid=5844); Greg Palast, "Impeachment Time: 'Facts Were Fixed,'" May 5, 2005 (http://web.archive.org/web/20050507213030/ www.gregpalast.com/detail.cfm?artid=426&row=0); and John Prados, "Iraq: When Was the Die Cast?" May 3, 2005 (www.tompaine.com/articles/ iraq_when_was_the_die_cast.php).

91 See Alan Cowell, "For Blair, Iraq Issue Just Won't Go Away," *New York Times*, May 2, 2005 (www.nytimes.com/2005/05/02/international/europe/02britain.html); David E. Sanger, "Prewar British Memo Says War Decision Wasn't Made," *New York Times*, June 13, 2005 (www.nytimes.com/2005/06/13/politics/ 13downing.html?_r=1).

92 PEN American Center, March 29, 2006 (www.pen.org/viewmedia.php/ prmMID/633/prmID/172).

93 Chris Gourlay, Jonathan Calvert, and Joe Lauria, "For Sale: West's Deadly Nuclear Secrets," *Sunday Times*, January 6, 2008 (www.timesonline.co.uk/tol/ news/world/middle_east/article3137695.ece); Justin Raimondo, "Nukes, Spooks, and the Specter of 9/11," AntiWar.com, January 8, 2008 (http://antiwar.com/ justin/?articleid=12166), which quoted Luke Ryland, "Sibel Edmonds Case: Front

Page of the (UK) Papers (Finally)" (http://sibeledmonds.blogspot.com/2008_01_01_archive.html).

94 Chris Floyd, "The Bomb in the Shadows: Proliferation, Corruption and the Way of the World," Empire Burlesque, January 8, 2008 (www.chris-floyd.com/component/content/article/3/1401-the-bomb-in-the-shadows-proliferation-corruption-and-the-way-of-the-world.html).

95 Dave Lindorff, "Sibel Edmonds, Turkey and the Bomb: A *Real* 9/11 Cover-Up?" Counterpunch, January 7, 2008 (www.counterpunch.org/ lindorff01072008.html).

96 Project Censored, 1984 (www.projectcensored.org/static/1984/1984-story4.htm).

97 Project Censored, 1997 (www.projectcensored.org/top-stories/articles/9-us-troops-exposed-to-depleted-uranium-during-gulf-war).

98 Project Censored, 1999 (www.projectcensored.org/top-stories/articles/5-u-s-weapons-mass-destruction-linked-to-the-deaths-of-a-half-million-child).

99 Project Censored, 2000 (www.projectcensored.org/top-stories/articles/10-the-us-and-nato-deliberately-started-the-war-with-yugoslavia).

100 Project Censored, 2000 (www.projectcensored.org/top-stories/articles/12-evidence-indicates-no-pre-war-genocide-in-kosovo-and-possible-plot-to-cr).

101 Project Censored, 2000 (www.projectcensored.org/top-stories/articles/8-planned-weapons-in-space-violate-international-treaty).

102 Project Censored, 2001 (www.projectcensored.org/top-stories/articles/6-international-report-blames-us-and-others-for-genocide-in-rwanda).

103 Project Censored, 2003 (www.projectcensored.org/top-stories/articles/5-us-intentionally-destroyed-iraqs-water-system).

104 Project Censored, 2004 (www.projectcensored.org/top-stories/articles/12-bush-administration-behind-failed-military-coup-in-venezuela).

105 Project Censored, 2004 (www.projectcensored.org/top-stories/articles/8-us-british-forces-continue-use-of-depleted-uranium-weapons-despite-negati).

106 Project Censored, 2006 (www.projectcensored.org/top-stories/articles/3-another-year-of-distorted-election-coverage).

107 Project Censored, 2009 (www.projectcensored.org/top-stories/articles/1-over-one-million-iraqi-deaths-caused-by-us-occupation).

108 Project Censored, 2010 (www.projectcensored.org/top-stories/articles/12-mysterious-death-of-mike-connellkarl-roves-election-thief).

109 "Conspiracy Theories: Causes and Cures," 209–10.

110 Ibid., 212.

111 Ibid., 209; emphasis added.

112 Ibid., 209; emphases added.

113 Ibid., 210; emphases added.

114 Ibid., 205.

115 William F. Pepper, *An Act of State: The Execution of Martin Luther King* (New York: Verso, 2003). Although Sunstein did not mention it, a second edition, "updated with a new afterword," was put out by Verso in 2008.

116 In his open letter to Sunstein, cited in the Introduction, Dr. Cyril H. Wecht, pointing out that "the House Select Committee of the U.S. Congress (1977-79) concluded that the WCR [Warren Commission Report] was wrong in its official determination that Lee Harvey Oswald acted alone in plotting and executing the assassination of JFK," challenged Sunstein "to engage in a public debate . . . — anywhere, anytime—relating to the JFK assassination and the WCR" ("Open Letter from Cyril Wecht to Cass Sunstein and Adrian Vermeule").

117 "Conspiracy Theories," Preliminary Draft, 17.

118 "Conspiracy Theories: Causes and Cures," 209.

119 Ibid., 205.

120 Ibid., 205.

121 Ibid., 204.

122 Ibid., 208.

123 Ibid., 206.

124 Ibid., 204.

125 Ibid., 210.

126 Ibid., 210.

127 Ibid., 211.

128 Beyond the problems in Sunstein's alternative account of a crippled epistemology discussed in the text, there is a deeper problem, which lies in the very concept of "crippled epistemologies." Being derived from *episteme*, which is the Greek word for knowledge, and the suffix "ology," which signifies the "study of" or "doctrine of," epistemology means the doctrine or study of knowledge. As such, it is a branch of philosophy. It is, in particular, one of the two major branches of metaphysics; the other is ontology, the study of being. To engage in epistemology is to ask about the nature of knowledge, the difference between knowledge and (mere) opinion, how knowledge is acquired, and so on. To "have an epistemology" is to have a doctrine or theory about such matters. If philosophers would ever say of someone that he or she had a "crippled epistemology," they would mean that this person, probably another philosopher, had a poor theory of knowledge. They would not, in other words, use this phrase to indicate that someone had inadequate knowledge about the world—that this person was, in short, ignorant.

This, however, is how Sunstein uses the term, defining it as having "a sharply limited number of (relevant) informational sources" or as "know[ing] very few things," most of which are wrong.

The confusion inherent in Sunstein's concept of "crippled epistemologies" was taken over from Russell Hardin's essay, "The Crippled Epistemology of Extremism" (in *Political Extremism and Rationality*, ed. Albert Breton, Gianluigi Galeotti, Pierre Salmon, and Ronald Wintrobe [Cambridge: Cambridge University Press, 2002], 3–22). While Hardin is an astute thinker in his field, which is *political* philosophy, he treats the issues involved in epistemology in a careless and confused manner. For one thing, he simply equates "knowledge" and "beliefs," even though beliefs cannot be counted as knowledge unless they are justified—meaning that the person has good reasons for holding them—and also true, meaning that they correspond to reality: Knowledge is *justified true belief*. Hardin knows that this is the standard view in philosophical epistemology, but he dismisses it, saying that what interests him as a social scientist is "the ways people come to hold their beliefs" (4–5). He is, in other words, not interested in epistemology, which is a *normative* discipline, dealing with *knowledge*, but in the sociology of belief-formation. This is an important and fascinating subject, but it is not epistemology, so it is unfortunate that Hardin coined the term "crippled epistemology," because he thereby used a normative discipline's name for a sociological description.

His blurring of the distinction is illustrated in a passage in which, after pointing out that philosophers might say that "those who assert the truth of some particular view have inadequate grounds for their own assertions," Hardin dismisses this concern by saying: "But this is a claim from standard philosophical epistemology. In their own epistemology, [those people] may genuinely suppose that they do have grounds" (10). *Of course* they may suppose this, but this doesn't mean that they actually have good grounds for their beliefs, and it certainly does not mean that they "have an epistemology."

To justify his ignoring of traditional epistemological distinctions and concerns, Hardin says: "Most of us do not have the time or incentive to be deeply committed philosophers or scientists and we need not even suspect that there is anything questionable about our beliefs" (10). That is true. But if one is not interested in epistemology, one should not use the word. If one is interested in the sociology of belief, there is a perfectly good term for this area of interest: "sociology of belief" (often misnamed "sociology of knowledge").

In any case, Hardin's ignoring of necessary distinctions led him to speak of "crippled epistemology" when he was simply talking about a crippled (distorted) process of belief-formation, meaning one that is likely to result in ignorance and hence a false belief-system. It would have been better if Hardin and Sunstein, if they wanted to use the term "crippled," had simply spoken of a "crippled process of belief-formation." This would not have been so catchy, but it would have had the virtue of accuracy.

129 Greenwald, "Obama Confidant's Spine-Chilling Proposal," Salon.com, January 15, 2010 (www.salon.com/news/opinion/glenn_greenwald/2010/01/15/sunstein).

130 "Conspiracy Theories: Causes and Cures," 208.

131 Ibid., 202n1.

132 Ibid., 219, 224.

133 Alfred North Whitehead, *The Principle of Relativity* (Cambridge: Cambridge University Press, 1922).

134 For Whitehead's life and career, see Victor Lowe, *Alfred North Whitehead: The Man and His Work* (Baltimore: The Johns Hopkins University Press), Vol. 1, 1985; Vol. 2, ed. J.B. Schneewind, 1990. On Whitehead's thought, see Victor Lowe, *Understanding Whitehead* (Baltimore: The Johns Hopkins University Press, 1962), and John B. Cobb, "Alfred North Whitehead," in David Ray Griffin et al., *Founders of Constructive Postmodern Philosophy* (Albany: State University of New York Press, 1993), 165–95.

135 I have discussed Hartshorne's philosophy in "Charles Hartshorne's Postmodern Philosophy," David Ray Griffin et al., *Founders of Constructive Postmodern Philosophy* (Albany: State University of New York Press, 1993), 197–231; I have discussed his life and career, as well as his thought, in "Charles Hartshorne," *Handbook of Christian Theologians*, ed. Donald W. Musser & Joseph L. Price (Nashville: Abingdon Press, 1996). For an overview of his thought, see Lewis Edwin Hahn, ed., *The Philosophy of Charles Hartshorne*, The Library of Living Philosophers, Vol. 20 (LaSalle, Ill.: Open Court, 1991), 3–45.

136 David Ray Griffin, *God, Power, and Evil: A Process Theodicy* (Philadelphia: Westminster, 1976; reprinted with a new preface, Louisville: Westminster John Knox, 2004); *Evil Revisited: Responses and Reconsiderations* (Albany: State University of New York Press, 1991).

137 David Ray Griffin, ed., *Deep Religious Pluralism* (Louisville: Westminster/John Knox, 2005).

138 David Ray Griffin, *Religion and Scientific Naturalism: Two Great Truths: A New Synthesis of Scientific Naturalism and Christian Faith* (Louisville: Westminster John Knox Press, 2004).

139 David Ray Griffin, *Unsnarling the World-Knot: Consciousness, Freedom, and the Mind-Body Problem* (Berkeley & Los Angeles: University of California Press, 1998; Eugene: Wipf and Stock, 2008).

140 David Ray Griffin and John B. Cobb, Jr., eds., *Mind in Nature: Essays on the Interface of Science and Philosophy* (Washington, D.C.: University Press of America, 1977); Griffin, *Religion and Scientific Naturalism*, Ch. 8, "Creation and Evolution"; Griffin, *Evolution without Tears: A Third Way beyond Neo-Darwinism and Intelligent Design* (Claremont: Process and Faith, 2006).

141 David Ray Griffin, ed., *Physics and the Ultimate Significance of Time: Bohm, Prigogine, and Process Philosophy* (Albany: SUNY Press, 1986).

142 See, for example, the final two chapters of my *Reenchantment without Supernaturalism: A Process Philosophy of Religion* (Ithaca, N.Y.: Cornell University Press, 2001).

143 Alfred North Whitehead, *Process and Reality: An Essay in Cosmology* (1929), Corrected Edition, ed. David Ray Griffin and Donald W. Sherburne (New York: Free Press, 1978).

144 David Ray Griffin, *The 9/11 Commission Report: Omissions and Distortions* (Northampton: Olive Branch Press, 2005).

145 David Ray Griffin, *Debunking 9/11 Debunking: An Answer to Popular Mechanics and Other Defenders of the Official Conspiracy Theory*, revised and updated edition (Northampton: Olive Branch, 2007), Chap. 4.

146 Ibid., Chap. 2.

147 Ibid., Chap. 3.

148 David Ray Griffin, *The Mysterious Collapse of World Trade Center 7: Why the Final Official Report about 9/11 Is Unscientific and False* (Northampton: Olive Branch, 2009).

149 Griffin, *Debunking 9/11 Debunking*.

150 David Ray Griffin, *The New Pearl Harbor Revisited: 9/11, the Cover-Up, and the Exposé* (Northampton: Olive Branch Press, 2008).

151 *Publishers Weekly,* November 24, 2008 (www.publishersweekly.com/pw/by-topic/1-legacy/15-web-exclusive-book-reviews/article/6017-web-exclusive-reviews-week-of-11-24-2008-.html).

152 See "Professors Question 9/11" (http://patriotsquestion911.com/professors.html).

153 Architects and Engineers for 9/11 Truth (www.ae911truth.org).

154 Firefighters for 9/11 Truth (http://firefightersfor911truth.org).

155 Intelligence Officers for 9/11 Truth (http://IO911truth.org).

156 Journalists and Other Media Professionals for 9/11 Truth (http://mediafor911truth.org).

157 Lawyers for 9/11 Truth (http://l911t.com).

158 Medical Professionals for 9/11 Truth (http://mp911truth.org).

159 Pilots for 9/11 Truth (http://pilotsfor911truth.org).

160 Political Leaders for 9/11 Truth (http://pl911truth.com).

161 Religious Leaders for 9/11 Truth (http://rl911truth.org).

162 Veterans for 9/11 Truth (http://v911t.org).

163 Information about these and other architects who question the official story can be found under "Engineers and Architects" at Patriots Question 9/11 (www.patriotsquestion911.com/engineers.html#Search).

164 Information about these and other engineers who question the official story can be found under "Engineers and Architects" at Patriots Question 9/11 (www.patriotsquestion911.com/engineers.html#Search).

165 In 2006, Christison published an essay entitled "Stop Belittling the Theories About September 11," www.dissidentvoice.org, August 14, 2006 (www.dissi-

dentvoice.org/Aug06/Christison14.htm). In a letter to friends explaining why he wrote it, he said: "I spent the first four and a half years since September 11 utterly unwilling to consider seriously the conspiracy theories surrounding the attacks of that day. . . . [I]n the last half year and after considerable agony, I've changed my mind" ("Letter from Bill Christison to Friends," e-mail letter sent August 14, 2006).

166 Annie Machon, *Spies, Lies and Whistleblowers: MI5, MI6, and the Shayler Affair* (London: Book Guild Publishing, 2005).

167 Intelligence Officers for 9/11 Truth (http://IO911Truth.org).

168 Journalists and Other Media Professionals for 9/11 Truth (http://mediafor911truth.org).

169 Lawyers for 9/11 Truth (http://l911t.com).

170 Medical Professionals for 9/11 Truth (http://mp911truth.org).

171 Pilots for 9/11 Truth (http://pilotsfor911truth.org).

172 Political Leaders for 9/11 Truth (http://pl911truth.com).

173 "Conspiracy Theories: Causes and Cures," 210.

174 Religious Leaders for 9/11 Truth (http://rl911truth.org). An especially valuable feature of this site is its collection of 9/11-related articles written by members of the Christian, Jewish, and Muslim traditions.

175 Scientists for 9/11 Truth (http://sci911truth.org).

176 Veterans for 9/11 Truth (http://v911t.org).

177 Russell Hardin, "The Crippled Epistemology of Extremism," *Political Extremism and Rationality*, ed. Albert Breton, Gianluigi Galeotti, Pierre Salmon, and Ronald Wintrobe (Cambridge: Cambridge University Press, 2002), 3–22, at 15.

178 Bill Willers, "An Attack from Harvard Law on the Escalating 9/11 Truth Movement," OpEdNews, February 4, 2010 (www.opednews.com/articles/AN-ATTACK-FROM-HARVARD-LAW-by-Bill-Willers-100203-909.html).

179 Philip Shenon, *The Commission: The Uncensored History of the 9/11 Investigation* (New York: Twelve, 2008), 388–89.

180 Ibid., 317.

181 Ibid., 390.

182 Ibid., 321.

183 Griffin, *The 9/11 Commission Report: Omissions and Distortions*, 282, quoting Peter Lance, *Cover Up: What the Government is Still Hiding about the War on Terror* (New York: HarperCollins/ReganBooks, 2004), 139-40.

184 Ibid., citing Lance, *Cover-Up*, 215–20.

185 Ibid., 94–101.

186 Ernest May, "When Government Writes History: A Memoir of the 9/11

Commission," *New Republic*, May 23, 2005 (http://hnn.us/articles/11972.html). I cited this article in *Debunking 9/11 Debunking*, 108.

187 Thomas H. Kean and Lee H. Hamilton, with Benjamin Rhodes, *Without Precedent: The Inside Story of the 9/11 Commission* (New York: Alfred A. Knopf, 2006), 269–70.

188 Ibid., 33.

189 Ibid., 116.

190 *The 9/11 Commission Report: Final Report of the National Commission on Terrorist Attacks upon the United States*, authorized edition (New York: W. W. Norton, 2004), xv, xvi.

191 Kean and Hamilton, *Without Precedent*, 269–70 (emphasis added).

192 Ibid., 123.

193 Quoted in Griffin, *Debunking 9/11 Debunking*, 179.

194 "The Sept. 11 Records," *New York Times*, August 12, 2005 (http://graphics8.nytimes.com/packages/html/nyregion/20050812_WTC_GRAPH IC/met_WTC_histories_full_01.html). An explanatory note at the top says: "A rich vein of city records from Sept. 11, including more than 12,000 pages of oral histories rendered in the voices of 503 firefighters, paramedics, and emergency medical technicians, were made public on Aug. 12. The New York Times has published all of them."

195 NIST, *Final Report on the Collapse of the World Trade Center Towers*, September 2005 (http://wtc.nist.gov/NCSTAR1/PDF/NCSTAR%201.pdf), 163.

196 Griffin, *The New Pearl Harbor Revisited*, 45–48.

197 NIST, "Answers to Frequently Asked Questions," August 30, 2006 (http://wtc.nist.gov/pubs/factsheets/faqs_8_2006.htm), Question 12.

198 Jennifer Abel, "Theories of 9/11," *Hartford Advocate*, January 29, 2008 (www.hartfordadvocate.com/article.cfm?aid=5546).

199 "Conspiracy Theories: Causes and Cures," 206, 211, 210.

200 One apparent example is provided by Van Romero, who had become very successful at landing government contracts for his employer, the New Mexico Institute of Mining and Technology; see Griffin, *Debunking 9/11 Debunking*, 255.

201 See "Most Wanted Terrorists: Usama bin Laden," Federal Bureau of Investigation (www.fbi.gov/wanted/terrorists/terbinladen.htm), which says: "Usama Bin Laden is wanted in connection with the August 7, 1998, bombings of the United States Embassies in Dar es Salaam, Tanzania, and Nairobi, Kenya. These attacks killed over 200 people. In addition, Bin Laden is a suspect in other terrorist attacks throughout the world." (Haas learned about this omission from Paul Sheridan, who was evidently the first member of the 9/11 Truth Movement to notice it.)

202 Ed Haas, "FBI says, 'No Hard Evidence Connecting Bin Laden to 9/11'" Muckraker Report, June 6, 2006 (http://web.archive.org/web/

20060610053720/www.teamliberty.net/id267.html).

203 "State Department's Todd Leventhal Discusses Conspiracy Theories," Embassy of the United States, London, July 14, 2009 (www.america.gov/st/webchat-english/2009/July/20090714143549iaecnav0.4049581.html).

204 Dan Eggen, "Bin Laden, Most Wanted for Embassy Bombings?" *Washington Post*, August 28, 2006 (www.washingtonpost.com/wp-dyn/content/article/2006/08/27/AR2006082700687.html).

205 Ibid.

206 Haas, "FBI says, 'No Hard Evidence Connecting Bin Laden to 9/11.'"

207 Todd Leventhal, "Al Qaida Confirms It Carried Out the September 11 Attacks," America.gov, April 29, 2009 (www.america.gov/st/webchat-english/2009/April/20090501132747atlahtnevel4.168338e-02.html). Although nothing at this site identifies Leventhal as the author of this article, he identifies himself as its author in the previously cited interview, "State Department's Todd Leventhal Discusses Conspiracy Theories."

208 "Could the Bin Laden Video Be a Fake?" BBC News, December 14, 2001 (http://news.bbc.co.uk/2/hi/1711288.stm); "'Feeble' to Claim Bin Laden Tape Fake: Bush," CBC, December 14, 2001 (www.cbc.ca/world/story/2001/12/14/bush_osama011214.html); Steven Morris, "US Urged to Detail Origin of Tape," *Guardian*, December 15, 2001 (www.guardian.co.uk/world/2001/dec/15/september11.afghanistan).

209 Bruce Lawrence is the editor of *Messages to the World: The Statements of Osama bin Laden* (London and New York: Verso, 2005).

210 Lawrence made these statements on February 16, 2007, during a radio interview conducted by Kevin Barrett of the University of Wisconsin at Madison. It can be heard at Radio Du Jour (www.radiodujour.com/people/lawrence_bruce).

211 For quotations, see David Ray Griffin, *Osama bin Laden: Dead or Alive?* (Northampton: Olive Branch Press, 2009), 27–29.

212 Morris, "US Urged to Detail Origin of Tape."

213 Griffin, *Osama bin Laden,* 23.

214 Toby Harnden, "US Casts Doubt on Bin Laden's Latest Message," *Telegraph*, December 27, 2001 (www.telegraph.co.uk/news/worldnews/asia/afghanistan/1366508/US-casts-doubt-on-bin-Laden%27s-latest-message.html); "Dr. Sanjay Gupta: Bin Laden Would Need Help if on Dialysis," CNN, January 21, 2002 (www.cnn.com/2002/HEALTH/01/21/gupta.otsc/index.html).

215 To compare the face of the man on this video with that of images taken from undoubtedly authentic bin Laden videos, see "The Fake 2001 bin Laden Tape" WhatReallyHappened.com (http://whatreallyhappened.com/WRHARTICLES/osamatape.html). This article also provides a link to the video in question. For a comparison of the nose of the man on this video with the real

bin Laden's nose, see "Osama bin Laden Gets a Nose Job" (www.awitness.org/news/december_2001/osama_nose_job.html).

216 See "Transcript of Bin Laden Videotape," National Public Radio (www.npr.org/news/specials/response/investigation/011213.binladen.transcript.html).

217 Griffin, *Osama bin Laden,* 31–33.

218 Leventhal, "Al Qaida Confirms It Carried Out the September 11 Attacks."

219 Griffin, *Osama bin Laden,* 51–53.

220 Ibid., 49-51.

221 See Ibid., 50-51, and also Najwa bin Laden, Omar bin Laden, and Jean Sasson, *Growing Up Bin Laden: Osama's Wife and Son Take Us Inside Their Secret World* (New York: St. Martin's, 2009), Chapter 2, "Married Life," on which bin Laden's first wife says: "Many of the instructors [at Osama bin Laden's schools] were from England, so Osama was well spoken in that language" (19).

222 "Ex-CIA Operative Discusses 'The Devil We Know,'" Interview with Terry Gross on *Fresh Air*, WHYY, October 2, 2008 (www.npr.org/templates/story/story.php?storyId=95285396); Robert Baer, "When Will Obama Give Up the Bin Laden Ghost Hunt?" *Time*, November 18, 2008 (www.time.com/time/world/article/0,8599,1859354,00.html).

223 Angelo M. Codevilla, "Osama bin Elvis," *American Spectator*, March 2009 (http://spectator.org/archives/2009/03/13/osama-bin-elvis/print).

224 Leventhal, "Al Qaida Confirms It Carried Out the September 11 Attacks."

225 *The 9/11 Commission Report,* 146.

226 Thomas H. Kean and Lee H. Hamilton, with Benjamin Rhodes, *Without Precedent: The Inside Story of the 9/11 Commission* (New York: Alfred A. Knopf, 2006), 118, 122-24.

227 Ibid., 119.

228 Thomas H. Kean and Lee H. Hamilton, "Stonewalled by the C.I.A.," *New York Times*, op-ed page, January 2, 2008 (www.nytimes.com/2008/01/02/opinion/02kean.html?_r=1).

229 *The 9/11 Commission Report: Final Report of the National Commission on Terrorist Attacks upon the United States*, authorized edition (New York: W. W. Norton, 2004), 160.

230 Kevin Fagan, "Agents of Terror Leave Their Mark on Sin City," *San Francisco Chronicle*, October 4, 2001 (http://sfgate.com/cgi-bin/article.cgi?file=/chronicle/archive/2001/10/04/MN102970.DTL).

231 Ibid.; also David Wedge, "Terrorists Partied with Hooker at Hub-Area Hotel," *Boston Herald*, October 10, 2001 (http://web.archive.org/web/20011010224657/www.bostonherald.com/attack/investigation/ausprob10102001.htm).

232 "Terrorist Stag Parties," *Wall Street Journal*, October 10, 2001 (www.opinion-journal.com/best/?id=95001298).

233 All four passenger manifests, which were released September 17, 2001, can be found at http://web.archive.org/web/20010917033844/ www.cnn.com/ SPECIALS/2001/trade.center/victims/AA11.victims.html.

234 Thomas R. Olmsted, M.D. "Still No Arabs on Flight 77," Rense.com, June 23, 2003 (www.rense.com/general38/77.htm).

235 Richard A. Serrano, "Heroism, Fatalism Aboard Flight 93," *Los Angeles Times*, April 12, 2006 (http://rednecktexan.blogspot.com/2006/04/ heroism-fatalism-aboard-flight-93.html).

236 David Bamford, "Hijack 'Suspect' Alive in Morocco," BBC, September 22, 2001 (http://news.bbc.co.uk/1/hi/world/middle_east/1558669.stm).

237 "Panoply of the Absurd," *Der Spiegel*, September 8, 2003 (www.spiegel.de/international/spiegel/0,1518,265160,00.html); Steve Herrmann, "9/11 Conspiracy Theory," The Editors (blog), BBC, October 27, 2006 (www.bbc.co.uk/blogs/theeditors/2006/10/911_conspiracy_theory_1.html).

238 See Jay Kolar's "Afterword" to "What We Now Know about the Alleged 9-11 Hijackers," which is in the second (paperback) edition of Paul Zarembka, ed., *The Hidden History of 9-11-2001* (New York: Seven Stories Press, 2008).

239 Ibid.

240 David Maraniss, "September 11, 2001," *Washington Post*, September 16, 2001 (www.washingtonpost.com/ac2/wp-dyn/A38407-2001Sep15).

241 Charles Lane and John Mintz, "Bid to Thwart Hijackers May Have Led to Pa. Crash," *Washington Post*, September 13, 2001 (www.washingtonpost.com/ ac2/wp-dyn/A14344-2001Sep11).

242 Kerry Hall, "Flight Attendant Helped Fight Hijackers," *News & Record* (Greensboro, N.C.), September 21, 2001 (http://webcache.news-record.com/legacy/ photo/tradecenter/bradshaw21.htm).

243 FBI, "Interview with Deena Lynne Burnett (re: phone call from hijacked flight)," *9/11 Commission, FBI Source Documents, Chronological, September 11, 2001, Intelfiles.com*, March 14, 2008 (http://intelfiles.egoplex.com:80/2008/03/911-commission-fbi-source-documents.html).

244 See Greg Gordon, "Widow Tells of Poignant Last Calls," *Sacramento Bee*, September 11, 2002 (http://holtz.org/Library/Social%20Science/History/ Atomic%20Age/2000s/Sep11/Burnett%20widows%20story.htm), and Deena L. Burnett (with Anthony F. Giombetti), *Fighting Back: Living Beyond Ourselves* (Longwood, Florida: Advantage Inspirational Books, 2006), 61.

245 A. K. Dewdney, "The Cellphone and Airfone Calls from Flight UA93," Physics 911, 2004 (http://physics911.net/cellphoneflight93.htm). For discussion of this issue, see David Ray Griffin, *The New Pearl Harbor Revisited: 9/11, the Cover-Up, and the Exposé* (Northampton: Olive Branch Press, 2008), 112–14.

246 Tim O'Brien, "Wife of Solicitor General Alerted Him of Hijacking from Plane," CNN, September 12, 2001 (http://archives.cnn.com/2001/US/09/11/pentagon.olson).

247 9/11 Commission Staff Statement 16 (www.9-11commission.gov/staff_statements/staff_statement_16.pdf).

248 Shoestring, "The Flight 77 Murder Mystery: Who Really Killed Charles Burlingame?" Shoestring911, February 2, 2008 (http://shoestring911.blogspot.com/2008/02/flight-77-murder-mystery-who-really.html).

249 "Transcription of FBI Interview with Theodore Olson," September 11, 2001 (http://intelfiles.egoplex.com/2001-09-11-FBI-FD302-theodore-olsen.pdf).

250 Tim O'Brien, "Wife of Solicitor General Alerted Him of Hijacking from Plane," CNN, September 11, 2001, 2:06 AM (http://archives.cnn.com/2001/US/09/11/pentagon.olson); "America's New War: Recovering from Tragedy," *Larry King Live*, CNN, September 14, 2001 (http://edition.cnn.com/TRANSCRIPTS/0109/14/lkl.00.html).

251 *Hannity & Colmes*, Fox News, September 14, 2001; "Barbara K. Olson Memorial Lecture," November 16, 2001, (www.fed-soc.org/resources/id.63/default.asp); Toby Harnden, "She Asked Me How to Stop the Plane," *Daily Telegraph*, March 5, 2002 (http://s3.amazonaws.com/911timeline/2002/telegraph030502.html).

252 See the National Transportation Safety Board's flight path study for AA Flight 77, put out February 19, 2002 (www.gwu.edu/~nsarchiv/NSAEBB/NSAEBB196/doc02.pdf).

253 FBI, "T7 B12 Flight 93 Calls-General Fdr- 5-20-04 DOJ Briefing on Cell and Phone Calls From AA 77 408," May 20, 2004 (www.scribd.com/doc/18886083/T7-B12-Flight-93-Calls-General-Fdr-52004-DOJ-Briefing-on-Cell-and-Phone-Calls-From-AA-77-408).

254 See Griffin, *The New Pearl Harbor Revisited*, 60–61.

255 "Ashcroft Says More Attacks May Be Planned," CNN, September 18, 2001 (http://edition.cnn.com/2001/US/09/17/inv.investigation.terrorism/index.html); "Terrorist Hunt," ABC News, September 12, 2001 (http://911research.wtc7.net/cache/disinfo/deceptions/abc_hunt.html).

256 Anne Karpf, "Uncle Sam's Lucky Finds," *Guardian*, March 19, 2002 (www.guardian.co.uk/september11/story/0,11209,669961,00.html). Like some others, this article mistakenly said the passport belonged to Mohamed Atta.

257 Sheila MacVicar and Caroline Faraj, "September 11 Hijacker Questioned in January 2001," CNN, August 1, 2002 (http://archives.cnn.com/2002/US/08/01/cia.hijacker/index.html); 9/11 Commission Hearing, January 26, 2004 (www.9-11commission.gov/archive/hearing7/9-11Commission_Hearing_2004-01-26.htm).

258 See *The New Pearl Harbor Revisited*, Chap. 3.

259 Jere Longman, *Among the Heroes: United 93 and the Passengers and Crew Who*

Fought Back (New York: HarperCollins, 2002), 215.

260 In light of the absurdity of the claims about the passports of al-Suqami and Jarrah, we can safely assume that the ID cards of Majed Moqed, Nawaf al-Hazmi, and Salem al-Hazmi, said to have been discovered at the Pentagon crash site (see "9/11 and Terrorist Travel," 9/11 Commission Staff Report [www.9-11commission.gov/staff_statements/911_TerrTrav_Monograph.pdf], 27, 42), were also planted.

261 Lane and Mintz, "Bid to Thwart Hijackers May Have Led to Pa. Crash."

262 Quoted in Ross Coulthart, "Terrorists Target America," Ninemsn, September 2001 (http://web.archive.org/web/20060827010442/www.sunday.ninemsn.com.au/sunday/cover_stories/transcript_923.asp).

263 Jim Yardley, "A Trainee Noted for Incompetence," *New York Times*, May 4, 2002 (www.nytimes.com/2002/05/04/us/a-trainee-noted-for-incompetence.html).

264 *The 9/11 Commission Report*, 242.

265 Marc Fisher and Don Phillips, "On Flight 77: 'Our Plane Is Being Hijacked,'" *Washington Post*, September 12, 2001 (www.washingtonpost.com/ac2/wp-dyn?pagename=article&node=&contentId=A14365-2001Sep11).

266 E-mail from Ralph Omholt, October 27, 2006.

267 Griffin, *The New Pearl Harbor Revisited*, 76–77.

268 Dan Balz and Bob Woodward, "America's Chaotic Road to War: Tuesday, September 11," *Washington Post*, January 27, 2002 (www.washingtonpost.com/wp-dyn/content/article/2006/07/18/AR2006071801175.html). This article was the first in a six-part series, "Ten Days in September."

269 "9/11: Interviews by Peter Jennings," ABC News, 11 September 2002 (s3.amazonaws.com/911timeline/2002/abcnews091102.html).

270 Susan Taylor Martin, "Of Fact, Fiction: Bush on 9/11," *St. Petersburg Times*, July 4, 2004 (www.sptimes.com/2004/07/04/news_pf/ Worldandnation/Of_fact__fiction__Bus.shtml). Bush himself lingered in the classroom so long that a reporter who was normally supportive dubbed him the "Dawdler in Chief"—see Bill Sammon, *Fighting Back: The War on Terrorism from Inside the Bush White House* (Washington: Regnery, 2002), 90.

271 See Griffin, *The New Pearl Harbor Revisited*, 1–10, 81–91.

272 Charles Lewis, "What I Heard LAX Security Officials Say During the 9/11 Attacks," 911Truth.org, September 7, 2008 (www.911truth.org/article.php?story=2008071025531345). Lewis' statement included a report on a private conversation he had in 2006 with Captain LaPonda Fitchpatrick of the LAWAPD, who was head of Security in the Airport Operations Area. Having started to tell her that he thought the 9/11 attacks could not have succeeded without inside participation, "She replied that LAX security was well aware that 9/11 was an inside job" (n.4).

273 9/11 Commission Hearing, May 23, 2003 (www.9-11commission.gov/

archive/hearing2/9-11Commission_Hearing_2003-05-23.htm).

274 David Ray Griffin, *The Mysterious Collapse of World Trade Center 7: Why the Final Official Report about 9/11 Is Unscientific and False* (Northampton: Olive Branch, 2009), Appendix B (267–69).

275 NIST, "Answers to Frequently Asked Questions," August 30, 2006 (http://wtc.nist.gov/pubs/factsheets/faqs_8_2006.htm), Question 2; Zdenek Bazant and Yong Zhou, "Why Did the World Trade Center Collapse?—Simple Analysis," *Journal of Engineering Mechanics* 128/1 (January 2002): 2–6 (www-math.mit.edu/~bazant/WTC/WTC-asce.pdf).

276 Graeme MacQueen and Tony Szamboti, "The Missing Jolt: A Simple Refutation of the NIST-Bazant Collapse Hypothesis," *Journal of 9/11 Studies*, Vol. 24: January 2009 (www.journalof911studies.com/volume/2008/TheMissingJolt7.pdf): 1–27.

277 Gordon Ross, "Momentum Transfer Analysis of the Collapse of the Upper Storeys of WTC 1," *Journal of 9/11 Studies*, Vol. 1: June 2006 (www.journalof911studies.com/articles/Journal_5_PTransferRoss.pdf): 32–39, at 37.

278 See "911 Eyewitness: Huge Steel Sections Ejected More than 600 Feet" (http://video.google.com/videoplay?docid=1807467434260776490) and the photo at www.reservoir.com/extra/wtc/wtc-small.1057.jpg. The images are also contained in "9/11 Mysteries: Demolitions," Part 3 (www.youtube.com/watch?v=L1A2s QkuT94&feature=related). At 5:35 into this part, the narrator says: "Here, a 600,000 pound chunk of steel; twice the weight of a Boeing airliner, was flung 400 feet, wedging itself deep into 3 World Financial Center on Vesey St."

279 Stated at Architects and Engineers for 9/11 Truth (www.ae911truth.org/profile.php?uid=998819).

280 Obeid made this statement on a BBC program entitled "The Conspiracy Files: 9/11—The Third Tower," BBC News, July 6, 2008, available at 911Blogger (www.911blogger.com/node/16541) and at Google Videos (http://video.google.com/videoplay?docid=9072062020229593250&ei=wfSRS7axM J6uqQOW0aiSAg&q=BBC%27s+%22The+Third+Tower%22#).

281 NIST NCSTAR 1-9, *Structural Fire Response and Probable Collapse Sequence of World Trade Center Building 7*, Draft for Public Comment, August 2008, Vol. 2 (http://wtc.nist.gov/media/NIST_NCSTAR_1-9_vol2_for_public_comment.pdf), 595–96.

282 "WTC 7 Technical Briefing" (video), NIST, August 26, 2008, at 1:03. NIST has removed this video and the accompanying transcript from the internet. However, Nate Flach has made the video available at Vimeo (http://vimeo.com/11941571), and the transcript, entitled "NIST Technical Briefing on Its Final Draft Report on WTC 7 for Public Comment," is available at David Chandler's website (http://911speakout.org/NIST_Tech_Briefing_Transcript.pdf).

283 David Chandler, "WTC7 in Freefall—No Longer Controversial," September 4, 2008 (www.youtube.com/watch?v=gC44L0-2zL8), at 2:45.

284 NIST NCSTAR 1-9, *Structural Fire Response and Probable Collapse Sequence of*

World Trade Center Building 7, November 2008, Volume 2 (http://wtc.nist.gov/NCSTAR1/PDF/NCSTAR%201-9%20Vol%202.pdf): 607.

285 "Questions and Answers about the NIST WTC 7 Investigation," NIST, August 21, 2008, updated April 21, 2009). Although NIST has removed both versions of this document from its website, Jim Hoffman's website has preserved both the original (2008) version, which denied free fall (http://911research.wtc7.net/mirrors/nist/wtc_qa_082108.html) and the updated (2009) version, which admitted it (http://911research.wtc7.net/mirrors/nist/wtc_qa_042109.html).

286 See Griffin, *The Mysterious Collapse of World Trade Center 7*, 231, 236–37, 241.

287 Ibid., 231–41.

288 See note 282, above

289 Joan Killough-Miller, "The 'Deep Mystery' of Melted Steel," *WPI Transformations*, Spring 2002 (www.wpi.edu/News/Transformations/2002Spring/steel.html).

290 Jonathan Barnett, Ronald R. Biederman, and R. D. Sisson, Jr., "Limited Metallurgical Examination," FEMA, *World Trade Center Building Performance Study*, Appendix C (http://911research.wtc7.net/wtc/evidence/metallurgy/WTC_apndxC.htm).

291 James Glanz and Eric Lipton, "A Search for Clues in Towers' Collapse," *New York Times*, February 2, 2002 (http://query.nytimes.com/gst/fullpage.html?res=9C04E0DE153DF931A35751C0A9649C8B63).

292 Barnett, Biederman, and Sisson, "Limited Metallurgical Examination," C-13.

293 That the official account of 9/11 contains this implausible claim is emphasized in the title of an article review of my 2009 book, *The Mysterious Collapse of World Trade Center 7,* by National Medal of Science–winner Lynn Margulis, "Two Hit, Three Down—The Biggest Lie," *Rock Creek Free Press*, January 24, 2010 (http://rockcreekfreepress.tumblr.com/post/353434420/two-hit-three-down-the-biggest-lie).

294 RJ Lee Group, "WTC Dust Signature Study: Composition and Morphology," December 2003 (www.nyenvirolaw.org/WTC/130%20Liberty%20Street/Mike%20Davis%20LMDC%20130%20Liberty%20Documents/Signature%20of%20WTC%20dust/WTC%20Dust%20Signature.Composition%20and%20Morphology.Final.pdf). This was the first version of a report prepared by the RJ Lee Group to support the case of the Deutsche Bank, against its insurer, that its building across from the Twin Towers had been contaminated by dust from "the WTC event." For some reason, a second version, titled "WTC Dust Signature," was issued in May 2004 (www.nyenvirolaw.org/WTC/130%20Liberty%20Street/Mike%20Davis%20LMDC%20130%20Liberty%20Documents/Signature%20of%20WTC%20dust/WTCDustSignature_ExpertReport.051304.1646.mp.pdf). In this version, most of the findings pointing to extremely high temperatures were removed, but it still reported the existence of "[s]pherical iron . . . that result[s] from exposure to high temperature"—meaning a temperature high enough to melt iron.

295 The published report of the USGS study—"Particle Atlas of World Trade Center Dust," 2005, by Heather A. Lowers and Gregory P. Meeker (http://pubs.usgs.gov/of/2005/1165/508OF05-1165.html)—did not mention the molybdenum. It became publicly known only by means of a FOIA request for the USGS data issued by Steven Jones and his colleagues, as reported in Steven E. Jones et al., "Extremely High Temperatures during the World Trade Center Destruction," *Journal of 9/11 Studies*, January 2008 (http://journalof911studies.com/articles/WTCHighTemp2.pdf).

296 WebElements: The Periodic Table on the Web (www.webelements.com/molybdenum/physics.html).

297 For more examples and further discussion, see Jones et al., "Extremely High Temperatures during the World Trade Center Destruction."

298 Niels H. Harrit, Jeffrey Farrer, Steven E. Jones, Kevin R. Ryan, Frank M. Legge, Daniel Farnsworth, Gregg Roberts, James R. Gourley, and Bradley R. Larsen, "Active Thermitic Material Observed in Dust from the 9/11 World Trade Center Catastrophe," *The Open Chemical Physics Journal,* 2009/2: 7–31 (www.bentham-open.org/pages/gen.php?file=7TOCPJ.pdf&PHPSESSID =d26b94378192fbeaedf31221d2843089).

299 "Danish Scientist Niels Harrit, on Nanothermite in the WTC Dust (English Subtitles)," April 6, 2009 (www.youtube.com/watch?v=8_tf25lx_3o).

300 "The Myth of Implosion" (www.implosionworld.com/dyk2.html).

301 "Conspiracy Theories: Causes and Cures," 209.

302 The footnote cites Imre Lakatos, "Falsification and Methodology of Scientific Research Programmes," *Criticism and the Growth of Knowledge*, ed. Imre Lakatos and Alan Musgrave (Cambridge: Cambridge University Press, 1970), 91–196.

303 See Malcolm R. Forster, "Lakatos's Methodology of Scientific Research Programs," September 24, 1998 (http://philosophy.wisc.edu/Forster/220/notes_3.html), or "Imre Lakatos," Wikipedia (http://en.wikipedia.org/wiki/Imre_Lakatos), which says (at least as of July 24, 2010): "A *progressive research programme* [*sic*] is marked by its growth, along with the discovery of stunning novel facts, development of new experimental techniques, more precise predictions, etc. A *degenerating research program* is marked by lack of growth, or growth of the protective belt that does not lead to novel facts" (emphases in original).

304 Ken Thomas, "Feds Investigating Possible Terrorist-Attack Links in Florida," Associated Press, September 12, 2001 (http://web.archive.org/web/20030402060235/www.nctimes.net/news/2001/20010912/10103.html).

305 Barry Klein, Wes Allison, Kathryn Wexler, and Jeff Testerman, "FBI Seizes Records of Students at Flight Schools," *St. Petersburg Times*, September 13, 2001 (www.sptimes.com/News/091301/Worldandnation/FBI_seizes_records_of.shtml).

306 Dana Canedy with David E. Sanger, "After the Attacks: The Suspects; Hijacking Trail Leads FBI to Florida Flight School," *New York Times*, September 13, 2001 (http://query.nytimes.com/gst/fullpage.html?res=9805E6DC1038F930A2575AC0A96 79C8B63).

307 Neil Mackay, "The Roots of the Worst Terrorist Attack in History," *Sunday Herald* (Glasgow), September 16, 2001 (http://web.archive.org/web/20010924002816/www.sundayherald.com/18498).

308 Evan Thomas and Mark Hosenball, "Bush: 'We're at War," *Newsweek*, September 24, 2001 (www.propagandamatrix.com/pentagon_officials_safe.htm).

309 Ibid.

310 *The 9/11 Commission Report*, 160.

311 Joel Achenbach, "'You Never Imagine' A Hijacker Next Door," *Washington Post*, September 16, 2001 (www.washingtonpost.com/ac2/wp-dyn/A38026-2001Sep15?language=printer).

312 Peter Finn, "A Fanatic's Quiet Path to Terror," *Washington Post*, September 22, 2001 (www.washingtonpost.com/ac2/wp-dyn?pagename=article&node=&contentId=A6745-2001Sep21&notFound=true).

313 Carol J. Williams, John-Thor Dahlburg, and H.G. Reza, "Mainly, They Just Waited," *Los Angeles Times,* September 27, 2001 (http://web.archive.org/web/20010927120728/www.latimes.com/news/nationworld/world/la-092701atta.story).

314 Johanna McGeary and David Van Biema, "The New Breed of Terrorist," *Time*, September 24, 2001 (www.time.com/time/covers/1101010924/wplot.html).

315 John Cloud, "Atta's Odyssey," *Time*, September 30, 2001 (www.time.com/time/printout/0,8816,176917,00.html). The version with the cranberry-drinking Atta also made it to a program on Australian television, which said: "According to bar staff, Atta spends almost 4 hours at the pinball machine drinking cranberry juice, while Al-Shehhi drinks alcohol with an unidentified male companion" ("A Mission to Die For: Timeline," ABC TV [Australia], November 12, 2001 [www.abc.net.au/4corners/atta/default.htm]).

316 *The 9/11 Commission Report*, 253.

317 Achenbach, "'You Never Imagine' A Hijacker Next Door"; Michael Dorman, "Unraveling 9-11 was in the Bags," *Newsday*, April 17, 2006 (www.newsday.com/news/nationworld/nation/ny-uslugg274705186apr17,0,1419064,print.story).Brian Whitaker, "Chilling Document Hints at 'Armageddon,'" *Guardian*, October 1, 2001 (www.guardian.co.uk/world/2001/oct/01/worlddispatch.brianwhitaker); "Hijackers' Step-By-Ste;," CBS News, September 28, 2001 (www.cbsnews.com/stories/2001/09/28/archive/main312898.shtml).

318 *The 9/11 Commission Report*, Chap. 1, note 1.

319 "Two Brothers among Hijackers," CNN Report, September 13, 2001 (http://english.peopledaily.com.cn/200109/13/eng20010913_80131.html); "Hijack Suspect Detained, Cooperating with FBI," CNN, September 13, 2001 (http://transcripts.cnn.com/TRANSCRIPTS/0109/13/ltm.01.html).

320 "Portland Police Eye Local Ties," Associated Press, *Portsmouth Herald*, September 14, 2001 (http://archive.seacoastonline.com/

2001news/9_14maine2.htm).

321 Joel Achenbach, "'You Never Imagine' A Hijacker Next Door."

322 "The Night Before Terror," *Portland Press Herald*, October 5, 2001 (http://web.archive.org/web/20040404001010/www.portland.com/news/attack/011 005fbi.shtml).

323 Affidavit signed by FBI agent James K. Lechner, dated September 12, 2001; available at Four Corners: Investigative TV Journalism (www.abc.net.au/4corners/atta/resources/documents/fbiaffidavit3.htm).

324 To view them, see "Passenger Lists," 9-11 Research (http://911research.wtc7.net/planes/evidence/passengers.html). To read cleaned-up versions, see "The Passengers," 911myths.com (http://911myths.com/html/the_passengers.html).

325 For further evidence of their inauthenticity, see *The New Pearl Harbor Revisited*, 174–75.

326 These and other replacements are discussed in Jay Kolar, "What We Now Know about the Alleged 9-11 Hijackers," 12–17.

327 FBI, "Interview with Deena Lynne Burnett," *9/11 Commission, FBI Source Documents, Chronological, September 11, 2001*, Intelfiles.com, March 14, 2008 (http://intelfiles.egoplex.com:80/2008/03/911-commission-fbi-source-documents.html).

328 *The 9/11 Commission Report*, 11, 29.

329 Affidavit signed by FBI agent James K. Lechner, dated September 12, 2001. Woodward and Sweeney are not identified by name in the affidavit, which simply refers to the former as "an employee of American Airlines at Logan" and to the latter as "a flight attendant on AA11." But their names were revealed in an "investigative document compiled by the FBI" to which Eric Lichtblau referred in "Aboard Flight 11, a Chilling Voice," *Los Angeles Times*, September 20, 2001 (http://web.archive.org/web/20010929230742/http://latimes.com/news/nationworld/nation/la-092001hijack.story).

330 Jerry Harkavy, "Flight Affidavit: Flight Attendant Made Call to Report Hijacking," Associated Press, October 5, 2001 (http://multimedia.belointeractive.com/attack/investigation/1005hijackercar.html).

331 *The 9/11 Commission Report*, 453n32.

332 Gail Sheehy, "9/11 Tapes Reveal Ground Personnel Muffled Attacks," *New York Observer*, June 20, 2004 (www.observer.com/node/49415).

333 Lichtblau, "Aboard Flight 11, a Chilling Voice."

334 Although the FBI's new position was provided to the 9/11 Commission and reflected in its report, this report disguised the position so effectively, with the exception of the aforementioned endnote about Amy Sweeney's call, that few readers noticed that it did not affirm the occurrence of any high-altitude cell phone calls.

335 Greg Gordon, "Prosecutors Play Flight 93 Cockpit Recording," McClatchy Newspapers, KnoxNews.com, April 12, 2006 (http://web.archive.org/web/20071130032831/www.knoxsingles.com/shns/story.cfm?pk=MOUSSAOUI-04-12-06&cat=WW). The quoted statement is Gordon's paraphrase of the testimony of "a member of the FBI Joint Terrorism Task Force."

336 See United States v. Zacarias Moussaoui, Exhibit Number P200054.

337 *The 9/11 Commission Report*, 455n57.

338 United States v. Zacarias Moussaoui, Prosecution Trial Exhibit P200054 (www.vaed.uscourts.gov/notablecases/moussaoui/exhibits/prosecution/flights/P200 054.html). This document can be more easily viewed in "Detailed Account of Phone Calls from September 11th Flights" (http://911research.wtc7.net/planes/evidence/calldetail.html).

339 FBI, "Interview with Theodore Olsen [sic]," *9/11 Commission, FBI Source Documents, Chronological, September 11, 2001,* Intelfiles.com, March 14, 2008, (http://intelfiles.egoplex.com:80/2008/03/911-commission-fbi-source-documents.html).

340 "America's New War: Recovering from Tragedy," *Larry King Live*, CNN, September 14, 2001 (http://edition.cnn.com/TRANSCRIPTS/0109/14/lkl.00.html).

341 Statement by Susan Ginsburg, senior counsel to the 9/11 Commission, at the 9/11 Commission Hearing, January 26, 2004 (www.9-11commission.gov/archive/hearing7/9-11Commission_Hearing_2004-01-26.htm). The Commission's account reflected a CBS report that the passport had been found "minutes after" the attack, which was stated by the Associated Press, January 27, 2003.

342 *The 9/11 Commission Report*, 40 and 446n209.

343 Ibid., 40.

344 Gregor Holland, "The Mineta Testimony: 9/11 Commission Exposed," 911truthmovement.org, November 1, 2005 (www.911truthmovement.org/archives/2005/11/post.php).

345 *The 9/11 Commission Report*, 41.

346 Richard A. Clarke, *Against All Enemies: Inside America's War on Terror* (New York: Free Press, 2004), 8.

347 "9/11: Interviews by Peter Jennings," ABC News, September 11, 2002 (s3.amazonaws.com/911timeline/2002/abcnews091102.html).

348 "The Vice President Appears on Meet the Press with Tim Russert," MSNBC, September 16, 2001 (http://georgewbush-whitehouse.archives.gov/vicepresident/news-speeches/speeches/vp20010916.html). I have examined this interview at in "Tim Russert, Dick Cheney, and 9/11," Information Clearing House, June 17, 2008 (www.informationclearinghouse.info/ article20108.htm).

349 Thomas H. Kean and Lee H. Hamilton, with Benjamin Rhodes, *Without Precedent: The Inside Story of the 9/11 Commission* (New York: Alfred A. Knopf,

2006), 259.

350 Ibid.

351 Ibid., 86; see also 253.

352 "FAA Communications with NORAD on September 11, 2001: FAA Clarification Memo to 9/11 Independent Commission," May 22, 2003. Available in the transcript of the 9/11 Commission hearing of May 23, 2003 (www.9-11commission.gov/archive/hearing2/9-11Commission_Hearing_2003-05-23.htm), and at 911Truth.org (www.911truth.org/article.php?story=2004081200421797).

353 9/11 Commission, Public Hearing, May 23, 2003 (www.9-11commission.gov/archive/hearing2/9-11Commission_Hearing_2003-05-23.htm).

354 *The 9/11 Commission Report*, 34.

355 "The 9/11 Commission Report: A 571-Page Lie," 911Truth.org, May 22, 2005 (www.911truth.org/article.php?story=20050523112738404); *Global Outlook*, April 2006: 100–06.

356 David Dunbar and Brad Reagan, eds., *Debunking 9/11 Myths: Why Conspiracy Theories Can't Stand Up to the Facts* (New York: Hearst Books, 2006), 6.

357 Philip H. Melanson, *Secret Service: The Hidden History of an Enigmatic Agency* (New York: Carroll & Graf, 2002).

358 Melanson is quoted in Susan Taylor Martin, "Of Fact, Fiction: Bush on 9/11," *St. Petersburg Times*, July 4, 2004 (www.sptimes.com/2004/07/04/news_pf/Worldandnation/Of_fact__fiction__Bus.shtml).

359 "Conspiracy Theories: Causes and Cures," 220, 226.

360 Ibid., 207.

361 Ibid., 206, 207.

362 Ibid., 204.

363 Ibid., 211–12.

364 Ibid., 212.

365 Ibid., 211n38.

366 Ibid., 207.

367 Ibid., 226.

368 Ibid., 220.

369 Ian Urbina, "Gunman at Pentagon Linked to Anger Against U.S.," *New York Times*, March 5, 2010 (www.nytimes.com/2010/03/06/us/06gunman.html?th&emc=th).

370 "Conspiracy Theories: Causes and Cures," 220.

371 See, for example, Kevin Ryan, "High Velocity Bursts of Debris From Point-Like Sources in the WTC Towers," *Journal of 9/11 Studies*, June 13, 2007

(www.journalof911studies.com/volume/2007/Ryan_HVBD.pdf); Steven E. Jones et al., "Extremely High Temperatures during the World Trade Center Destruction," *Journal of 9/11 Studies*, January 2008 http://web.archive.org/web/20060705021502/www.teamliberty.net/id273.html ; Kevin R. Ryan, James R. Gourley, and Steven E. Jones, "Environmental Anomalies at the World Trade Center: Evidence for Energetic Materials," *The Environmentalist*, 29 (2009): 56–63; Niels H. Harrit, Jeffrey Farrer, Steven E. Jones, et al., "Active Thermitic Material Observed in Dust from the 9/11 World Trade Center Catastrophe," *The Open Chemical Physics Journal,* 2009, 2: 7–31 (www.bentham.org/open/ tocpj/openaccess2.htm).

372 "Conspiracy Theories: Causes and Cures," 226.

373 Ed Haas, "Government Spokesman Says, 'I don't Understand the Public's Fascination with World Trade Center Building Seven,'" Muckraker Report, March 21, 2006 (http://web.archive.org/web/20060705021502/www.teamliberty.net/id273.html).

374 Ed Haas, "Change in Venue or Date Will Not Alter Decision," Muckraker Report, July 3, 2006 (www.teamliberty.net/id273.html).

375 Kean and Hamilton, *Without Precedent*, 323.

376 Ed Haas, "*Popular Mechanics* Invited to the National 9/11 Debate," 911Blogger.com, August 24, 2006 (www.911blogger.com/node/2262).

377 Griffin, *The 9/11 Commission Report: Omissions and Distortions* (Northampton: Olive Branch, 2005).

378 Dr. Gideon Polya, "Iraqi Holocaust: 2.3 Million Iraqi Excess Deaths," March 21, 2009 (www.countercurrents.org/polya210309.htm); "January 2010—4.5 Million Dead in Afghan Holocaust, Afghan Genocide," January 2, 2010, Afghan Holocaust, Afghan Genocide (http://afghangenocide.blogspot.com).

379 Russell Hardin, "The Crippled Epistemology of Extremism," *Political Extremism and Rationality*, ed. Albert Breton, Gianluigi Galeotti, Pierre Salmon, and Ronald Wintrobe (Cambridge: Cambridge University Press, 2002), 3–22, at 4.

380 Gary Dorrien, *Imperial Designs: Neoconservatism and the New Pax Americana* (New York: Routledge, 2004), 45.

381 Charles Krauthammer, "The Unipolar Moment," *Foreign Affairs* 70, Winter 1990 (www.foreignaffairs.org/19910201faessay6067/charles-krauthammer/the-unipolar-moment.html).

382 Arnold Beichman, "How the Divide over Iraq Strategies Began," *Washington Times*, November 27, 2002 (www.dailytimes.com.pk/default.asp?page=story_28-11-2002_pg4_10); Albert Wohlstetter, "Help Iraqi Dissidents Oust Saddam," *Wall Street Journal*, August 25, 1992; Paul D. Wolfowitz and Zalmay M. Khalilzad, "Saddam Must Go," *Weekly Standard*, December 1997; William Kristol and Robert Kagan, "Bombing Iraq Isn't Enough," *New York Times*, January 30, 1998 (www.nytimes.com/1998/01/30/opinion/bombing-iraq-isn-t-enough.html?pagewanted=1).

383 Andrew J. Bacevich, *American Empire: The Realities and Consequences of U.S. Diplomacy* (Cambridge: Harvard University Press, 2002), 44; David Armstrong, "Dick Cheney's Song of America," *Harper's*, October 2002 (www.thirdworldtraveler.com/American_Empire/Cheney's_Song_America.html).

384 Project for the New American Century, *Rebuilding America's Defenses: Strategy, Forces and Resources for a New Century*, September 2000 (www.newamericancentury.org/RebuildingAmericasDefenses.pdf).

385 Ibid., 51.

386 Claes Ryn, "The Ideology of American Empire," in D. L. O'Huallachain and J. Forrest Sharpe, eds., *Neoconned Again: Hypocrisy, Lawlessness, and the Rape of Iraq* (Vienna, Va.: IHS Press, 2005), 63–79, at 65.

387 Stephen J. Sniegoski, "Neoconservatives, Israel, and 9/11: The Origins of the U.S. War on Iraq," in O'Huallachain and Sharpe, eds., *Neoconned Again*, 81–109, at 81–82.

388 Julio Godoy, "U.S. Taliban Policy Influenced by Oil," Inter Press Service, November 16, 2001 (www.globalresearch.ca/articles/GOD111A.html).

389 This was reported by Niaz Naik, the highly respected Pakistani representative at the meeting; see George Arney, "U.S. 'Planned Attack on Taleban,'" BBC News, September 18, 2001 (news.bbc.co.uk/2/hi/south_asia/1550366.stm). In a story by Jonathan Steele, et al., entitled "Threat of U.S. Strikes Passed to Taliban Weeks Before NY Attack," *Guardian,* September 22, 2001 (www.guardian.co.uk/world/2001/sep/22/afghanistan.september113), one of the American representatives was quoted as confirming that this discussion of military action did occur.

390 "White House Warns Taliban: 'We Will Defeat You,'" CNN.com, September 21, 2001 (http://archives.cnn.com/2001/WORLD/asiapcf/central/09/21/ret.afghan.taliban).

391 "Remarks by the Vice President to the Veterans of Foreign Wars 103rd National Convention," August 26, 2002 (http://georgewbush-whitehouse.archives.gov/news/releases/2002/08/20020826.html).

392 Stefan Halper and Jonathan Clarke, *America Alone: The Neo-Conservatives and the Global Order* (Cambridge: Cambridge University Press, 2004), 201, 214.

393 Hardin, "The Crippled Epistemology of Extremism," 18.

394 Ibid., 19.

395 Matthew Engel, "US Media Cowed by Patriotic Fever, says CBS Star," *Guardian*, May 17, 2002 (www.guardian.co.uk/media/2002/may/17/terrorismandthemedia.broadcasting).

396 Hardin, "The Crippled Epistemology of Extremism," 19.

397 Ibid., 12.

398 "Conspiracy Theories: Causes and Cures," 204, 226.

399 Ibid., 220.

400 Ibid., 206.

401 Ibid., 219.

402 Ibid., 206n17: "We bracket the interesting question whether, on consequential-ist grounds, it is ever appropriate to undermine true conspiracy theories."

403 Ibid., 221.

404 Ibid., 221.

405 Ibid., 222.

406 "Conspiracy Theories," Preliminary Draft, 19.

407 When Van Jones was forced to resign from the Obama administration because it was discovered that he had signed a petition calling for a new investigation of 9/11, in light of information suggesting that the attacks had been orchestrated or at least allowed by the Bush administration (Scott Wilson and Garance Franke-Ruta, "White House Adviser Van Jones Resigns Amid Controversy Over Past Activism," *Washington Post*, September 6, 2009 (http:// voices.washingtonpost.com/ 44/2009/09/06/van_jones_resigns.html), pundits from the left as well as the right took this revelation as sufficient reason for his dismissal. From the right, Charles Krauthammer said: "You can't sign a petition . . . charg[ing] that the Bush admin-istration deliberately allowed Sept. 11, 2001 — i.e., collaborated in the worst massacre ever perpetrated on American soil — and be permitted in polite society, let alone have a high-level job in the White House" (Krauthammer, "The Van Jones Matter," *Washington Post*, September 11, 2009 [www.washingtonpost.com/ wp-dyn/content/article/2009/09/10/ AR2009091003408.html?referrer=emailarti-cle]). From the left, David Corn wrote: "As far as I can tell, the only thing the so-called 9/11 Truth movement has accomplished is this: it's caused the Obama administration to lose its most prominent expert on green jobs" (Corn, "How 9/11 Conspiracy Poison Did in Van Jones," Politics Daily, September 7, 2009 (www.politicsdaily.com/ 2009/09/07/how-9-11-conspiracy-poison-did-in-van-jones).

408 "Conspiracy Theories: Causes and Cures," 221.

409 Ibid., 222.

410 Ibid., 222-23.

411 Ibid., 224.

412 Ibid.

413 Ibid., 218.

414 Laurie A. Manwell, "In Denial of Democracy: Social Psychological Implica-tions for Public Discourse on State Crimes Against Democracy Post-9/11," *American Behavioral Scientist* 53 (February 2010): 848-84 (http://abs.sagepub.com/ content/vol53/issue6), at 849.

415 Ibid., 863.

416 Ibid.

417 "Conspiracy Theories: Causes and Cures," 221.

418 Upton Sinclair, "*I, Candidate for Governor: And How I Got Licked* (1935; University of California Press, 1994), 109.

419 "Conspiracy Theories: Causes and Cures," 223.

420 Ibid.

421 Ibid., 223n84.

422 Christopher Bollyn, "9/11 and Chertoff: Cousin Wrote 9/11 Propaganda for PM," Rumor Mill News, March 4, 2005 (www.rumormillnews.com/cgi-bin/archive.cgi?read=66176).

423 Ibid.

424 James B. Meigs, "Afterword: The Conspiracy Industry," in David Dunbar and Brad Reagan, eds., *Debunking 9/11 Myths: Why Conspiracy Theories Can't Stand Up to the Facts* (New York: Hearst Books, 2006), 102–03.

425 "Conspiracy Theories," Preliminary Draft, 18.

426 Jennifer Harper, "Explosive News," Inside the Beltway, *Washington Times*, February 22, 2010 (www.washingtontimes.com/news/2010/feb/22/inside-the-beltway-70128635/?feat=home_columns).

427 Predictably, the *Washington Times* soon published an editorial to make clear that the paper did not endorse any conspiratorial nonsense. Besides having a belit-tling title, "Truthers Gone Wild," the editorial dismissed the members of the 9/11 Truth Movement as "odd ducks" wearing "tinfoil hats" who are "in the grip of the conspiratorial mindset" and are "desperate to be noticed" (even though the occa-sion for this editorial was a story about 1,000 architects and engineers, supported by scientists and firefighters, who are calling for a new investigation). Doing damage-control, the editorial made sure that readers understood that Jennifer Harper's article in no way constituted the paper's endorsement of the 9/11 Truth Movement, saying: "[T]his newspaper reports on many shocking things—car acci-dents, major fires, the Obama administration's economy-wrecking fiscal excesses—and in no case should these stories be read as endorsements." However, Harper's article was celebrated by the 9/11 Truth Movement not as an "endorse-ment" of its ideas but simply because it reported objectively on what was said at the press briefing by Richard Gage—as articles about press briefings normally do. It was this fair, neutral treatment that pleased the movement. With its editorial, however, the *Washington Times* seemed to be saying that it would not make that mistake again, as it rallied its readers to reaffirm the true faith, saying: "The 'Truther' label is ironic because this is a group of people who can't handle the truth. The Sept. 11 attacks on America were definitely a conspiracy, but one organized and executed by al-Qaeda." And in case readers did not make it that far down into the article, the editorial placed its reaffirmation of faith at the top, saying: "*The truth behind 9/11 is simple—jihadists did it.*" The editorial concluded with a new formulation of an old item in the creed, saying that the collapse of "the

World Trade Center towers . . . can easily be explained without reference to nano-thermite" ("Editorial: Truthers Gone Wild," *Washington Times*, March 1, 2010 [http://washingtontimes.com/news/2010/mar/01/truthers-gone-wild]).

428 Lance deHaven-Smith, "Beyond Conspiracy Theory: Patterns of High Crime in American Government," *American Behavioral Scientist* 53 (February 2010): 795-825 (http://abs.sagepub.com/content/vol53/issue6), at 796.

429 Matthew T. Witt and Alexander Kouzmin, "Sense Making Under 'Holographic' Conditions: Framing SCAD Research," *American Behavioral Scientist* 53 (February 2010): 783-94 (http://abs.sagepub.com/content/vol53/issue6), at 786, 789.

430 Matthew T. Witt, "Pretending Not to See or Hear, Refusing to Signify: The Farce and Tragedy of Geocentric Public Affairs Scholarship," *American Behavioral Scientist* 53 (February 2010): 921-39 (http://abs.sagepub.com/content/vol53/issue6), at 935.

431 Ibid., 932 (emphasis in original).

432 Ibid., 932–34.

433 A photograph of The Split can be seen on Dotzler's website (www.markdotzler.com/Mark_Dotzler/split.html).

434 "Conspiracy Theories: Causes and Cures," 207, 210, 223.

435 Ibid. 221.

436 Ibid., 207.

437 Ibid., 223.

438 Ibid., 224.

439 Ibid., 224.

440 Sidney E. Mead, "Church History Explained," *Church History*, 32/1 (March 1963), 17-31 (http://links.jstor.org/sici?sici=0009-6407(196303) 32%3A1%3C17%3ACHE%3E2.0.CO%3B2-C).

441 David Ray Griffin, *The Mysterious Collapse of World Trade Center 7: Why the Final Official Report about 9/11 Is Unscientific and False* (Northampton: Olive Branch Press, 2009), 231, 236–37, 239, 241.

442 Thanks to members of the 9/11 Truth Movement, however, we can still view the video (http://vimeo.com/11941571) and read the transcript (http://911speakout.org/NIST_Tech_Briefing_Transcript.pdf).

443 Jonathan Barnett, Ronald R. Biederman, and Richard D. Sisson, Jr., "Limited Metallurgical Examination," FEMA, *World Trade Center Building Performance Study*, May 2002, Appendix C (http://wtc.nist.gov/media/ AppendixC-fema403_apc.pdf).

444 Dr. Arden L. Bement, Jr., Testimony before the House Science Committee Hearing on "The Investigation of the World Trade Center Collapse," May 1, 2002 (http://911research.wtc7.net/cache/wtc/official/nist/bement.htm).

445 "Questions and Answers about the NIST WTC 7 Investigation," updated April 21, 2009 (see note 285, above).

446 NIST NCSTAR 1-9, *Structural Fire Response and Probable Collapse Sequence of World Trade Center Building 7*, Draft for Public Comment, August 2008, Vol. 2 (wtc.nist.gov/media/NIST_NCSTAR_1-9_vol2_for_public_comment.pdf), 462.

447 *Interim Report on WTC 7,* NIST, June 2004 (wtc.nist.gov/progress_report/june04/appendixl.pdf), L-6-7. For documentation and discussion of NIST's claim about the lack of girder shear studs, see Griffin, *The Mysterious Collapse,* 212–15.

448 *Interim Report on WTC 7:* L-26. This contradiction is pointed out in a video, "NIST Report on WTC7 Debunked and Exposed!" (www.youtube.com/watch?v=qFpbZ-aLDLY), at 0:45 to 1:57.

449 See Griffin, *The Mysterious Collapse*, 187–88.

450 Graeme MacQueen, "118 Witnesses: The Firefighters' Testimony to Explosions in the Twin Towers," *Journal of 9/11 Studies*, Vol. 2: August 2006 (www.journalof911studies.com/articles/Article_5_118Witnesses_WorldTradeCenter.pdf): 47–106.

451 NIST, "Answers to Frequently Asked Questions," 2006 (http://wtc.nist.gov/pubs/factsheets/faqs_8_2006.htm), Q. 2.

452 "Request for Correction Submitted to NIST," *Journal of 9/11 Studies*, Vol. 12: June 2007 (www.journalof911studies.com/ volume/200704/RFCtoNISTbyMcIlvaineDoyleJonesRyanGageSTJ.pdf), 23. This letter was signed by Bob McIlvaine, Bill Doyle, Steven Jones, Kevin Ryan, Richard Gage, and Scholars for 9/11 Truth and Justice.

453 NIST, "Letter of Response to Request," September 27, 2007; published in *Journal of 9/11 Studies*, Vol. 17: November 2007 (www.journalof911studies.com/volume/2007/NISTresponseToRequestForCorrectionGourleyEtal2.pdf).

454 Ruvolo is quoted in the DVD "Collateral Damages" (www.thebravest.com/merch/Videos/collateraldamagesdvd.htm). For just this segment plus discussion, see Steve Watson, "Firefighter Describes 'Molten Metal' at Ground Zero, Like a 'Foundry,'" Infowars.com, November 17, 2006 (www.infowars.com/articles/sept11/firefighter_describes_molten_metal_ground_zero_like_foundry.htm).

455 James Williams, "WTC a Structural Success," *SEAU News: The Newsletter of the Structural Engineers Association of Utah*, October 2001 (www.seau.org/SEAUNews-2001-10.pdf).

456 Quoted in Francesca Lyman, "Messages in the Dust: What Are the Lessons of the Environmental Health Response to the Terrorist Attacks of September 11?" National Environmental Health Association, September 2003 (www.neha.org/pdf/messages_in_the_dust.pdf).

457 "Mobilizing Public Health: Turning Terror's Tide with Science," *Magazine of Johns Hopkins Public Health,* Late Fall 2001 (www.jhsph.edu/Publications/

Special/Welch.htm).

458 "NIST Engineer, John Gross, Denies the Existance [*sic*] of Molten Steel" (http://video.google.com/videoplay?docid=-7180303712325092501&hl=en), at 1:10.

459 "Conspiracy Theories: Causes and Cures," 218 (italics in original).

460 Ibid.

461 Ibid.

462 Glenn Greenwald, "Obama Confidant's Spine-Chilling Proposal," Salon.com, January 15, 2010 (www.salon.com/news/opinion/glenn_greenwald/2010/01/15/sunstein); the statement about being barred is in Update III.

463 "Conspiracy Theories," Preliminary Draft, 20.

464 "Conspiracy Theories: Causes and Cures," 219.

465 Ibid., 225, 219.

466 Ibid., 224–26.

467 Ibid. 225.

468 Ibid., 225, emphasis added.

469 Ibid., 226.

470 Ibid.

471 Ibid., 225.

472 Ibid.

473 Ibid., 224.

474 "Public Relations and Propaganda: Restrictions on Executive Agency Activities," CRS Report for Congress, Congressional Research Service, Library of Congress, Updated March 21, 2005 (www.fas.org/sgp/crs/misc/RL32750.pdf). This document was cited in Diane Farsetta and Sheldon Rampton, "Pentagon Pundit Scandal Broke the Law," PR Watch.org, April 28, 2008 (www.prwatch.org/node/7261), which Greenwald quoted.

475 Joshua Bolton, director, Office of Management and Budget, "Use of Government Funds for Video News Releases," Memorandum for Heads of Departments and Agencies, March 11, 2005 (www.whitehouse.gov/omb/memoranda/fy2005/m05-10.pdf).

476 "Conspiracy Theories: Causes and Cures," 220.

477 Mark Crispin Miller, "Obama's Info Chief Advocates Disinformation and Domestic Covert Ops," OpEdNews, January 15, 2010 (www.opednews.com/articles/Obama-s-Info-Chief-advocat-by-Mark-Crispin-Mille-100115-63.html).

Index

AA11. *See* Flight 11.
AA77. *See* Flight 77.
Abel, Jennifer, 49
Abrams, Elliott, 100
Afghanistan war, 96, 99–100, 101, 103–04, 108, 184n378
Aimer, Captain Ross "Rusty," 37
Allende, Salvador, 15
American Behavioral Scientist, 121, 123
Amos, Tony, 73–75
Anderson, John Edward, 33
Andes, Roy, 36
Arbenz, Jacabo, 13
Architects and Engineers for 9/11 Truth, 32–33, 67, 119, 135
Aristide, Jean-Bertrand, 18
Arnold, Terrell E., 34
asbestos, at Ground Zero, 16
Atta, Mohamed: as alleged ringleader, 58; evidence against his being a devout Muslim, 73–75; incriminating evidence allegedly found in luggage of, 75–77
autopsy lists, no Arab names, 58, 128

Baer, Robert, 56
Balsamo, Rob, 37
Barnum, Daniel B., 32
Bearden, Milt, 62, 85
Bedell, John Patrick, 94
belief, sociology of, 166–67n128
Bement, Arden, 129
Ben-Veniste, Richard, 84
Bill of Rights (US), 142, 146
bin Laden, Osama, 21–22, 26, 52–56, 58, 84, 102, 127, 150, 171n201, 172–73n215, 173n221
Binalshibh, Ramzi, 56
Blair, Prime Minister Tony, 19
Bohrer, Richard, 82
Bohm, David, 30
Bollyn, Christopher, 116–17
Bolton, John, 100
Bowman, Lt. Col. Robert, 33, 113
Bradshaw, Dr. Mary Ellen, 36
Bradshaw, Sandra, 60

British Petroleum, 145
Brouillet, Carol, 92
Bukhari, Adnan, 76, 78
Bukhari, Ameer, 76, 78
Burger, Ronald, 131
Burlingame, Charles "Chic," 61
Burnett, Deena, 60, 78, 85
Burnett, Tom, 60, 85
Bush, President George H.W., 16–17,
Bush (–Cheney) Administration (Bush, President George W.), 3–4, 11, 17, 19–20, 21, 22, 26, 35, 42, 47, 55–56, 64, 85. 86, 87, 90–91, 99, 100–105, 108–109, 113–18,119, 127, 152–53

Carter, President Jimmy, 15
cell phone calls from airliners, 60–61, 78–80, 181–82n334
censorship, 133
Center for Process Studies (Claremont), 30
Chandler, David, 68–69, 92, 113, 129, 177n282
Cheney, Vice President Dick, 65–66, 81–82, 86, 100, 101, 119, 145
Chertoff, Ben, 116–18
Chertoff, Michael, 116–18
Chiesa, Giulietto, 35
Chossudovsky, Michel, 92
Christison, William, 34, 113
CIA, 13, 14–15, 20, 23, 34, 55–57, 62, 90, 119, 127, 143, 144, 161n63, 162nn65,67,72
Clarke, Richard, 82
Clinton Administration, 17
Cobb, Dr. John B., Jr., 30, 39
Codevilla, Angelo, 56
Cognitive infiltration, xii, 89, 132–146, 154–55; and "cognitive diversity," 134, 144–45, 154
COINTELPRO (FBI Counterintelligence Program), 14, 136–137; declared illegal, 137, 140, 153, 162n69
Congress, 120, 137, 141, 143, 166n116
Connell, Mike, 20

Obama, President Barack, vii, xii, 39, 40, 143, 186n406, 187n427
Obeid, Kamal, 67
October Surprise (1980), 15
Oles, Paul Stevenson, 32–33
Olmsted, Dr. Thomas, 58
Olson, Barbara, 59, 61, 80, 85
Olson, US Solicitor General Ted, 61, 80, 85
al-Omari, Abdullah, 76–77
Omholt, Ralph W., 38
open societies, 10–11, 13, 23, 111–14, 132–34
Operation Gladio, 13
Operation Mockingbird, 13
Operation Northwoods, 12, 13, 21, 149
Orwell, George, 122
Oswald, Lee Harvey, 166n116

Pahlavi, Mohammad Reza Shah, 13
Palin, Sarah, 123
Panama, 16
Papadopoulos, George, 15
Papandreou, George, 14–15
paranoia, 1
passports; at crash sites, 59, 62, 80–81, 176n260, 182n341
Patriots Question 9/11, 31, 169n163
Pentagon (building):
    claim that it was struck by al-Qaeda pilot Hani Hanjour, 63, 113;
    wedge 1 as target, 63–64;
    stand-down order, 65–66;
    time of strike, 81–83, 86;
    March 2010 shooting at Pentagon, 93–94;
    ID cards of hijackers allegedly found at crash site, 176n260
Pentagon (officials), 14, 42, 101, 143, 144
Pepper, William F., 23, 166n115
Perle, Richard, 101
Pigden, Charles, 1, 2, 3, 4–7, 22, 149, 160n34
Pilots for 9/11 Truth, 32, 37
Pinochet, General Augusto, 15
Pisano, Isabel, 35
plutocracy, America as, 145–46
Political Leaders for 9/11 Truth, 32, 38, 143

Pollman, Dr. Christopher, 36, 169–70n165
Polya, Dr. Gideon, 99
Popular Mechanics, 30, 84, 98, 116–18
Presidential Emergency Operations Center (PEOC), 65, 81–82, 86
US press as free, 3, 10–11, 13, 18–21, 22, 23, 24, 104, 111–13, 118, 161n63
process philosophy, 30
"progressive research program," 72, 179n303
Project Censored, 20
Project for the New American Century (PNAC), 101, 185n384
Project MKULTRA, 12, 21, 127, 149
propaganda, government, viii, 13, 137–38

al-Qaeda, 11, 26, 28, 33, 45–50, 52–53, 56–58, 62–64, 70–71, 76, 85, 91, 102, 108, 113, 127, 128, 141, 148, 150, 152, 187

Rather, Dan, 103
Ray, James Earl, 24
Ray, Col. Ronald D., 42
Razer, Lt. Col. Guy S., 42
Reagan, Brad, 98
Reagan, President Ronald, 15, 35
Reeves, Gene, 39
Religious Leaders for 9/11 Truth, 32, 39, 170n174
Rice, Condoleezza, 82
RJ Lee Group, 70, 178n294
Robertson, Leslie, 131
Rodriguez, William, 48
Romero, Van, 170n200
Roosevelt, President Franklin D., 90
Ross, Gordon, 66
Rumsfeld, Donald, 63, 101, 145
Ruvolo, Philip, 131, 189n454
Russell, Bertrand, 29
Russert, Tim, 82
Ryan, Kevin, 92, 113, 179n298, 184n371, 189n452

al-Sabah, Nayirah, 16
Sabow, Col. James E., 94

Sandinista government, Nicaragua, 15
Scholars for 9/11 Truth and Justice,
    189n452
Scientists for 9/11 Truth, 40
Scott, Peter Dale, 92, 112
Secret Service, 64, 85, 86
shear studs, 130
Al-Shehhi, Marwan, 74–75, 180n315
al-Shehri, Wail, 77
al-Shehri, Waleed, 59, 77, 128
Shenon, Philip, 44, 45, 47
Sheridan, Paul, 170n201
Shukums Bar, 73
Shinn, Roger, 160n31
Sinclair, Upton, 115
Skousen, Joel M., 38
Southern Christian Leadership
    Conference, 14
stand-down order, 64, 66
State Crimes Against Democracy
    (SCADs), 121, 123
State Department (US), 34, 52, 58, 143,
    172n207
steel, melted and sulfidized, 69–70
Stossel, John, viii
Strauss, Leo, x, 4
Sturm, Douglas, 39
Suharto, General, 14
Sunder, Shyam, 68–69, 113, 129
Sunstein, Cass R., vii; summary of his
    contradictions, 147–156
al-Suqami, Satam, 62, 80–81, 176n260
Sweeney, Amy, 78, 181n334
Swiss-cheese steel, 69, 129–30
Szamboti, Tony, 113

Taliban, 101, 102, 185n389
terrorism, ix, 12, 19, 26
thermite, 49, 70
Thorpe, William, 30
Tomb, Rex, 52–54
Tower, North, 49, 62, 65, 66, 80
Towers, Twin, 48, 55, 66–71, 86, 113, 120;
    reported explosions in, 121, 130–31;
    horizontal ejections from, 121,
        176n278
truth, definition of, 8–9, 161n56

United 93. *See* Flight 93.

Ventura, Governor Jesse, 38
Vermeule, Adrian, vii
Veterans for 9/11 Truth, 32, 41
Vietnam war, 96, 108
von Bülow, Dr. Andreas, 38

Waddington, C. H., 30
Warren Commission Report, 166n116
Washington Times, 119–21, 123
Watergate, 11, 12, 13, 21, 122, 127, 149
weapons of mass destruction, 19, 20, 90,
    92, 93, 102, 127
Webb, Gary, 15
Wecht, Dr. Cyril H., viii, 166n116
Weston, Burns, 36
White House, 65, 84, 85, 103, 141, 168n134
Whitehead, Alfred North, 29, 30, 39,
    168n134
Willers, Bill, viii, 44
Williams, Armstrong, 138
Williams, Bryan (NBC News), 123
Wittenberg, Russ, 113
Wohlstetter, Albert, 101
Wolfowitz, Paul, 101
Woodward, Michael, 78
Worcester Polytechnic Institute (WPI),
    69, 129
World Trade Center, 25, 112, 119, 121–
    22, 126;
    dust, 17, 40, 62, 70, 120–21, 128–29,
        140, 163–64n84, 178nn294–95,
        178n298, 184n371, 189n456
Wright, Sewall, 30
WTC 7: also called Salomon Brothers
    (and Salomon Smith Barney)
    building, 32, 48–49, 113, 120–21;
    collapse features of, 66–71;
    in free fall, 68–69, 129, 178n285;
    Swiss-cheese steel recovered from,
        69, 129–30;
    alleged raging fires in, 130
Wyatt, Nancy, 78–79
Wyndham, Dr. John D., 40

Zelikow, Philip, 44–47, 98, 112, 113
Zwicker, Barrie, 35